WHAT HAPPENED TO MICKEY?

WHAT HAPPENED TO MICKEY?

THE LIFE AND DEATH OF DONALD "MICKEY" MCDONALD, PUBLIC ENEMY NO. 1

by Peter McSherry

DUNDURN
TORONTO

Editor: Allister Thompson
Design: Jesse Hooper
Printer: Webcom

Library and Archives Canada Cataloguing in Publication

McSherry, Peter
    What happened to Mickey? : the life and death of Donald "Mickey" McDonald, public enemy no. 1 / by Peter McSherry.

Includes bibliographical references and index.
Issued also in electronic format.
ISBN 978-1-4597-0738-2

    1. McDonald, Mickey. 2. Gangsters--Ontario--Toronto--Biography. 3. Escaped prisoners--Ontario--Biography. 4. Trials (Murder)--Ontario--Toronto. 5. Bank robberies--Ontario. I. Title.

HV6439.C32T67 2013   364.1092   C2012-904617-5

1 2 3 4 5   17 16 15 14 13

We acknowledge the support of the **Canada Council for the Arts** and the **Ontario Arts Council** for our publishing program. We also acknowledge the financial support of the **Government of Canada** through the **Canada Book Fund** and **Livres Canada Books**, and the **Government of Ontario** through the **Ontario Book Publishing Tax Credit** and the **Ontario Media Development Corporation**.

Care has been taken to trace the ownership of copyright material used in this book. The author and the publisher welcome any information enabling them to rectify any references or credits in subsequent editions.

J. Kirk Howard, President

Printed and bound in Canada.

VISIT US AT
Dundurn.com | Definingcanada.ca | @dundurnpress | Facebook.com/dundurnpress

Dundurn	Gazelle Book Services Limited	Dundurn
3 Church Street, Suite 500	White Cross Mills	2250 Military Road
Toronto, Ontario, Canada	High Town, Lancaster, England	Tonawanda, NY
M5E 1M2	L41 4XS	U.S.A. 14150

This book is in memoriam of six friends who helped me a lot in life:

Rick Fielding, Denyse Guite, Bertram J. Hawkins,
Donald Ardene Heeney, Horst Reim, and Barbara Sears.

Contents

A WORD ABOUT NAMES

THE SUBJECT OF THIS book was born Donald John MacDonald, but started calling himself Donald McDonald in his teens, then Michael McDonald in his twenties. After a time he was known as "Mickey." He married as Donald John MacDonald and was charged with murder and some later offences under that name. His two wives used the name "MacDonald," never "McDonald," even when they lived with him while he was "McDonald." His criminal brothers, Alex and Edwin, always used their proper name, "MacDonald," but, inevitably, were sometimes referred to as "McDonald" in the press, as Mickey too most often was. Other misspellings of Mickey's surname — Macdonald, M'Donald — inevitably appeared as well. In this work, I have referred to him as "Mickey McDonald" except when he was otherwise under indictment as MacDonald or there was some other specific reason to do otherwise.

Similarly, there appears in Part II of this book a character who was born Nicholas Minnelli and later came to spell his name "Minelli." He was in Kingston Penitentiary as "Minnille" and his name sometimes appeared as that in the press. In this book he is "Minelli" except where it is otherwise warranted.

Four of the names used in this work are pseudonyms. Their use in the text was part of the cost of getting information that would otherwise not have been available. Jenny Law, who was a major source for my first book, *The Big Red Fox: The Incredible Story of Norman "Red" Ryan, Canada's Most Notorious Criminal*, had things to say about Mickey, too, and though she has long since passed away, I have continued our pact regarding the protection of her real identity.

The name of Roy "Binky" Clarke, who was undoubtedly the most valuable and enduring source in this work, is also a pseudonym. He passed away in 2011 after being a constant source of information, a close advisor, and a personal friend for 33 years.

Of those I approached who were associates of Mickey few would talk at all, and none of the MacDonald family, understandably, was interested in participating. Ulysses Lauzon, one of Mickey's partners in the Kingston Penitentiary escape of August 1947, had previously robbed banks with a youth who I have given the name "Joe Poireau." Joe, who has long-since rehabilitated himself, spoke with me forthrightly but wanted his family protected with a pseudonym — and, tacitly, that included the name of his sister, Elaine, who was involved in the story as well.

BOOK I

Gangland Toronto, 1939: The Days of Mickey and Kitty Cat McDonald

CHAPTER ONE

The Murder of Jimmy Windsor
(Saturday, January 7, 1939)

THE MURDER OF JIMMY Windsor, bookmaker and racketeer, on Saturday, January 7, 1939, frightened the City of Toronto as few other murders have ever done.

So far as the Toronto Police knew, Windsor was merely one of the city's estimated 1,500 bookmakers, bigger than most, smaller than some. By reputation, in a dozen years of operation, he had not once been convicted of registering and recording bets. In August 1938, the police had raided Windsor's home at 247 Briar Hill Avenue in North Toronto, but they found no evidence of anything illegal. According to Inspector of Detectives John Chisholm, James Windsor did not have a police record.

Windsor worked his handbook business from the White Spot Restaurant at 530 Yonge Street, a block south of Wellesley Street West.[1] He took few wagers directly and only accepted bets on horse races. He insulated himself by using runners who worked on commission to pick up bets at factories, barber shops, and cigar stores, where most of his "action" was actually placed. Six days a week, he would meet some or all of his commission men, usually at the White Spot, usually in the late morning. Information and money were guardedly exchanged over coffee or a light meal. If such a meeting lasted three quarters of an hour, it was a lot. This was in 1936, 1937, and 1938.

He was a dapper little man, jaunty of step, always well-turned out in a tailored suit and well-polished shoes. To a lot of people, he was "Mister Windsor." Sure, he was friendly enough; he would toss off a "Hi, how are you?" to almost anybody who spoke to him, but that was usually the end of it, unless, of course, there was some business to conduct. He seemed, though, to badly want people to know he was doing well — or so some who knew him said, then and later. There was all the jewellery that he wore — a gold diamond-studded wristwatch, a diamond tie-pin, and a gold ring with a large diamond centrepiece. At times, he was indiscreet enough to flash a fat roll of bills in public. He seemed not to see the hungry eyes of some of his casual watchers or, if he did see, didn't mind dangling his own success, real and imagined, before them.[2] This, in a Yonge Street walk-in-and-eat-for-15 cents restaurant, at the tail end of the Great Depression, when unemployment was everywhere, when wages were nothing, and relief was a bag of rolled oats and a few tins of whatever was cheap.

Saturday, January 7, 1939, was the last day of James Windsor's 46 years of life. Before noon, he drove his 1937 Chrysler Imperial downtown from his North Toronto home and parked not far from the White Spot. Then, together with Lorraine Bromell, his 19-year-old live-in girlfriend, Windsor went in to collect from "Mr. Phillips" and one or two of his other bet runners. The restaurant clientele surely noticed, as before, Lorraine's attractiveness, the manner in which she wore fine clothes, the jewellery she was dripping, and must have concluded, as at other times, that "Mr. Windsor" was a man of accomplishment.

In another compartment of his life, the bookie owned the Windsor Bar-B-Q, a barbecue-dance hall that his adult son, Jack, operated on Yonge Street north of Sheppard Avenue, in the suburban Village of Lansing.[3] This business, which opened in 1936, had acquired an unsavoury reputation due to noise and fighting around it late at night. After the tap rooms in the city closed at midnight, big cars full of men, including many Italians, often showed up there in search of whatever was on offer. On the recommendation of North York Chief Constable Roy Riseborough, the North York Township Council had recently "blue lawed" Windsor's business.[4] Thus, an 11:45 p.m. closing on Saturday nights, and a 12:45 a.m. closing during the week, were now being rigidly enforced. The slot machines that Windsor previously had there had already been forced out. All of which meant the Windsor Bar-B-Q was leaking money badly.

This last day, Windsor made an afternoon call at the home of Morgan Baker, member of the provincial legislature for North York, in the Town of Stouffville. He went there asking for Mr. Baker's help in getting a wine and beer license for the barbecue-dance hall. For a full hour, between 3 and 4 p.m., Windsor appealed to Baker, calmly, coolly, affably, while Lorraine sat alone, outside, in the Chrysler Imperial on a frosty January afternoon. He got nowhere. Baker spoke of the bookie's "downtown business," which he maintained was much-talked-about in Lansing, and said that North York already had too many licensed establishments. He advised Windsor to take the matter up with the liquor board himself.

Windsor's last stop of the day was the barbecue. Whatever else he went there for, he took a few minutes to sing songs with his son, Jack, and two employees. "A regular barbershop quartet," one of the participants later said.

At 7:20 p.m., James Windsor was comfortably seated at the kitchen table of his North Toronto home, in company with his two married half-sisters, Evelyn McDermott and Edith Warner; his young brothers-in-law, John V. "Jack" McDermott and Edward Warner; and Lorraine Bromell. The household was just finishing its evening meal when a loud knock came at the front door. Evelyn McDermott, nearest the hallway, was holding Edith Warner's four-month-old daughter on her lap. She passed the child to her mother and went to answer the knock.

"Is Jimmy in?" a medium-sized man in a dark, close-fitting over-coat and a grey fedora hat asked when the front door to James Windsor's home was opened.

Unsuspectingly, Mrs. McDermott admitted the man to the hall and was surprised when he was followed into the house by two others, one tall, one short, holding handkerchiefs up to their faces. The lead man, she was shocked to observe, carried a large black revolver in his right hand. He immediately began asking questions in a low, clipped voice: Where was Jimmy Windsor? Who else was in the house? Was there anybody upstairs?

When satisfied that all in the house, especially Windsor, were in the kitchen, the man turned Mrs. McDermott around, put his right hand, which held the handgun, onto the now terrified woman's shoulder, and shoved her along the hallway to the back of the house. He was by then holding a white handkerchief over the lower half of his face with his left hand.

The sudden burst of armed intruders into the kitchen caused all regular conversation to instantly come to a fearful halt. Pushing Evelyn McDermott aside, the lead man stalked briskly to the head of the table, pointed his big black revolver at James Windsor and coldly demanded, "Come on outside, Jimmy. Come out to the car."

The bookmaker stared and said nothing.

The man repeated his instruction in a sharper tone. "Come on out to the car, Windsor," he again threatened, flourishing the dark weapon in his right hand.

Windsor still did not speak. Lorraine Bromell would later say he seemed "stunned" by what was happening. To some others, he appeared to be assessing the situation. The previous evening he had discussed a recent rash of "shakedowns" of bookmakers in the city with Jack McDermott, who was 20 years his junior and much less streetwise. Possibly Windsor considered, as others would later, that the invaders were a gang of extortionists looking for "protection money" from a racketeer who could not easily go to the police. Jack McDermott was afterwards certain that "Mr. Windsor" would never sit still for anything of the sort.

"What's this all about?" Windsor finally asked, calmly.

Looming over the bookie, the gunman said, "Come on, open up the box." This was said only once. Then the same man, who was visibly growing angrier with each failed demand, instructed Windsor even more sharply, "Come out to the car."

Then he put his hand, forcibly, on Windsor's shoulder.

At this, James Windsor slowly started to rise from his chair. As he did so, he made the mistake of saying in a changed tone, "All right, you don't have to get tough about it."

The gunman did not hear this as compliance, as did some others in the room. Instead, as it seemed, he interpreted Windsor's changed posture and the tone of the words he spoke as a threat to resist.

"All right, God damn you," the man swore loudly, "Maybe this will bring you" — and he meanly fired the big black gun point blank at James Windsor's guts. The shot made only a weak sound that was later described as both a "pop" and a "plop." The bullet penetrated Windsor's trousers below the third button of the fly.

It was right then, immediately after shooting Windsor in the groin, that the killer, according to the later testimony of all five eye-witnesses, took the handkerchief away from his face for a brief moment. Some said he put it in his left-side coat pocket.

Hit in the abdomen by a .455-calibre bullet that coursed downward into his left leg, severing his femoral artery, the bookmaker — according to later medical testimony — was doomed to bleed to death the moment he was shot. Still, he rose to his feet and staggered up against the kitchen stove where, with one blood-covered hand raised in the air, he weakly bleated, "Get me a doctor, quick."

His two brothers-in-law at the kitchen table had jumped to their feet when the gunman fired. The women were screaming. Evelyn McDermott frantically pleaded, "Call a doctor. Don't let him die."

The sound of the hall telephone's cord being ripped from the wall was an unseen member of the gang's response to that plea.

Ever since the intruders first entered the kitchen, a second gunman, taller than the first, masked, wearing a peaked cap pulled down low over his forehead, had been wordlessly pointing a rusty-looking revolver at those at the table. This man was later variously described as having "lovely blue eyes," "pretty blue eyes and nice eyebrows," and "piercing blue eyes."

"Keep quiet or you'll get the same," this pretty-eyed gunman now menaced the household.

Within seconds of being shot, Windsor, stricken as he was, was shoved towards the hall by the killer, who was being helped by a short, dark-complexioned man, who had flashed in from the hallway. This short man, barely noticed by most of the witnesses before this, dragged the bookie as the killer pushed him. The dying man took only three or four steps before he collapsed heavily in the hallway, just beyond the kitchen, his head hitting the cellar door with a thud.

There, on the floor, Jimmy Windsor was stripped of his jewellery and his pockets were gone through for what money he had. The man who shot him, not having gotten what he came for, began slapping and kicking Windsor while swearingly demanding not "the box," but "the bag." Windsor was past answering. The beating continued, the bookie being kicked repeatedly by the angry man who had pulled the trigger.

At real risk to herself, Lorraine Bromell bravely got up from the table and tried to stop the beating by getting the intruders what they wanted. When she couldn't produce anything more, she too was kicked by the berserk killer, who at the same time ordered her back into the kitchen.

The short man in the hall was heard urging the others, "Come on, let's go. Let's get out of here."

But the ugly scene went on and on — an estimated four to seven minutes from the first knock — before the killer in the hall called to the man in the kitchen, "Come on, Jim. We're done here."

There remained only the tall man with the "piercing blue eyes," who then spoke for only the second time. "All right, upstairs," he ordered forcefully, compelling the frightened family members, one by one, at gunpoint, to step over James Windsor's body in the hall, then to go up the staircase to the second floor of the house. They did as they were told without looking back at the second gunman, whose footsteps followed them partway up the stairs, then waited there until they were out of sight.

In a few seconds, those on the second floor heard the sound of a car starting fast away from Briar Hill Avenue. When it died away, Jack McDermott called downstairs to make certain none of the gang still remained in the house. There was no answer. McDermott then telephoned the police on the upstairs extension.

Detective-Sergeant Harry Glasscock and Detective William Coleman, patrolling nearby in a cruiser, were literally at the door "in less than two minutes." Their own call for detective assistance went over the police radio at 7:33 p.m.[5] Already the two detectives had bent over the dying man asking again and again, "Who did this to you, Mr. Windsor? Who did this to you?" Windsor's only response was to mouth the word "doctor" two or three times. He lived a few minutes more, then gave a big sigh and passed away.[6]

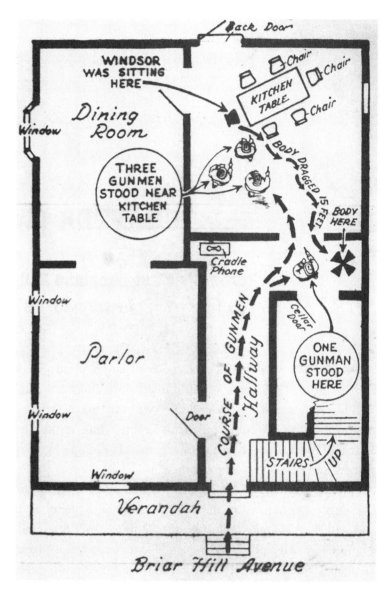

A diagram of one of the most frightening murders in all of Toronto's history appeared in the *Evening Telegram* of January 9, 1939. The drawing was captioned: "Invading his home at 247 Briar Hill Avenue Saturday night, one of four gunmen shot and killed James Windsor, operator of a North Yonge Street barbecue stand and dance hall. He was slain as he rose from a table in the kitchen to greet his 'callers.'" Five adult members of Windsor's family witnessed the killing. (*The Evening Telegram*)

CHAPTER TWO

Toronto's First Gangland Killing
(January 7–February 23, 1939)

LESS THAN AN HOUR after it happened, news of James Windsor's death was on the radio. There was only minimal information. Prior to the mid-1930s, radio stations in Toronto did not have much news — and not until World War II did change really come. Thus, at the time of the Briar Hill Avenue shooting, real news was still thought to be in the newspapers and people looked for it there.

On Monday, January 9, the Windsor Murder, as the incident would soon be most often termed in the press, was the blackline of all three Toronto dailies, the *Globe and Mail*, the *Toronto Daily Star*, and the *Evening Telegram*. All represented the crime to their readers as "Toronto's first Gangland killing," and all linked the murder to previously-reported violence and "gang warfare" between cliques of criminals in the Jarvis and Dundas streets area, which had been a serious concern in the city for several months.[1] Another theory held that "Italian gangsters" — extortionists, perhaps local, perhaps from Hamilton, Detroit, or Buffalo — were the culprits behind the killing. The banner headline on the morning *Globe*, first paper on the street on Monday, January 9, blared: MURDER CLIMAXES GANG WAR; TWO HELD. Underneath, the lead story reflected the fear and the confused understanding that the killing engendered in the city. The main thread running through the lead stories of the *Globe* and *The Star* was that Windsor had been killed because he had refused to pay "protection money" to a gang that was intent on bleeding him. *The Star*'s account conjured up the worst of the horror in its first gripping sentence: "A gangland execution squad killed James Windsor in his Briar Hill Avenue home Saturday night before the eyes of his family." *The Star* claimed that 32 Toronto bookmakers were known to have been victimized during the previous month. The *Telegram*, which did not specifically refer to the "protection racket," told its readers that the murder was "obviously a case of gangland vengeance ... the first of its type that has ever occurred in Toronto ... the most cold-blooded in the history of Toronto ... the culmination of a long series of battles between Toronto gangs." The papers printed pictures of Windsor, of his home, of the Windsor Bar-B-Q, of Lorraine Bromell, and of the eyewitnesses and others hiding their faces as they went in or out of police headquarters. There were diagrams of the inside of Windsor's home — the murder scene. Photos of alleged suspects, Frank "Dago Kelly" Pallante and Albert "Patsy" Adams, both of whom the Toronto Police had seen fit to detain as vagrants, the catch-all holding charge of the day, were also published.

In 1939, Toronto was still "The Queen City," "The City of Churches," "Toronto the Good," where, it was said, "On Sundays you could shoot a cannon ball down Yonge Street and not hit anybody, or anything, at all."[2] The city was still then an unsophisticated, Wasp-ish Triple-A town, well-known for insular thinking and narrowness of outlook. A heavy-handed police force — backed by the city burghers, a conservative judiciary, most of the churches, a mostly conservative press, and such still-powerful national lobbies as the Lord's Day Alliance and the Women's Christian Temperance Union — enforced a plethora of civic by-laws that strictly monitored public morality and behaviour. In limited areas, though, the then so-called "consensual vices" — bookmaking, bootlegging, and prostitution — were usually allowed to exist, so long as they did not lead to bigger problems or there were no complaints that were persistent or could not otherwise be smoothed over. These so-called "victimless crimes" were thought by some to be more easily regulated that way and the police often got valuable information from those who were involved in them. Beyond that, the Toronto Police "gave all the trouble they could" to the city's real criminal element, such as it was. The Vagrancy Act, patterned on an 1824 British statute in use against prostitutes and other "loose, idle or disorderly person(s) or vagrant(s) ... found wandering abroad and not giving a good account of themselves..." was a usable tool readily employed against those suspected of serious crimes as well as those who did not show respect for the police.[3]

"With the Vag Act, you could keep them in jail for at least a week," remembered Art Keay, a plainclothesman of that era in downtown No. 2 Division. In 1978, Mr. Keay spoke, too, of a police method that was then more often resorted to than in a later time: "Do you know what "tried summarily" meant? You gave them a good going over. The police were more physical in those days because there was never any such thing as a civil action against a policeman. You never heard of it. People had a lot more respect for the uniform in those days...."[4]

The upside of all of this was that, in a city of 650,000 — with several hundred thousand more in adjoining townships and villages — there was not a lot of crime.[5] In fact, there had been only one murder in the City of Toronto in each of the three previous lean years, 1936, 1937, and 1938.

In such a danger-free community, the fear engendered by "the Windsor Murder" was pervasive. The extraordinary brutality of the killing and the fact the perpetrators had boldly invaded a home in one of a safe city's safest sections served to raise public anxiety and concern to a level rarely, if ever, known before. Initially, eyewitnesses to the murder had given investigating officers to understand that the perpetrators appeared to be Italians. Their descriptions in the press reflected this fact. In conservative, law-abiding Toronto, this conjured up a style of crime that the local citizenry was already quite fearful of: "American-style organized crime," which was then largely a press euphemism for what was perceived to be Mafia-style organized crime. "Al Capone shooting people to death in front of the Rosedale United Church on Glen Road on every other weekday," was how Maurice LaTour, an old safecracker, laughingly exaggerated this fear in an interview in 1979.[6] Since the early 1920s, in the days of the Ontario Temperance Act (OTA), this anxiety had grown into a not-so-far-off palpable reality. Rocco Perri of Hamilton, once self-styled as the "King of the Bootleggers," was thought to hold sway by violence, and the threat of violence, only 40 miles distant via the Lakeshore Highway.

Within a few hours of the murder, Attorney General Gordon Conant, Toronto Mayor Ralph Day, Chief Constable D.C. Draper, and the Toronto Board of Police Commissioners, all issued statements designed to assure the worried public that organized crime would not be tolerated within any of their jurisdictions or areas of authority. On Monday, January 9, the Province of Ontario posted a $1,000 reward for information leading to the arrest and conviction of the perpetrators. The City of Toronto and the Board of Police Commissioners both announced $500 rewards, bringing the total on offer to $2,000. This was money meant to get police informants talking. A police circular dated Tuesday, January 10, published descriptions of four perpetrators, two of whom, including the shooter's description, carried the phrase "looked like an Italian." The medium-sized killer, supposedly Italian-looking, was said to have "a dark, sallow complexion," a regular nose that was "fairly wide at the nostrils," and teeth that were "decayed and wide-apart."[7]

The Windsor Murder had immediate effects on the street. Bookmakers, and to a lesser extent bootleggers, became more conservative in how, and with whom, they did business. Many suspended operations entirely. The Toronto Police, called on the carpet in an editorial in the *Evening Telegram* titled "Apparent Laxity of Police Must Be Explained," were asked to give reasons why such social evils as bookmaking and bootlegging were permitted to exist in Toronto at all.[8] The public response of the police was to increase the frequency and the publicity surrounding the activities of the hard-hitting raiding squad that targeted such racketeers, which had been in place since May 1938 — this, now on the apparent reasoning that, if no one was making money by taking bets or selling illicit liquor, no one else would likely try to extort them or kill them. Reporters followed the Gang-Busting Squad as they beat down the doors of bookmakers and booze-can operators with axes and battering rams.

At 247 Briar Hill Avenue, James Windsor's body lay in an open satin-lined casket in a flower-filled front room for two and a half days. Uniformed police stood guard at the front of the house, as detectives mingled with those inside. At 9 a.m., Wednesday, January 11, a requiem mass was sung for the bookmaker at St. Monica's Roman Catholic Church on Broadway Avenue. The church was full with mourners, plain-clothesmen, and those of the curious who could not be kept out. About 75 people followed a funeral car to the graveside interment in Mount Hope Cemetery, where women covered their faces with black veils and men turned up their collars, so as not to show up in any pictures in the daily press or in some scandal paper like *The Tattler*.[9] Speculation that the funeral might turn into a rowdy circus, as had that of Rocco Perri's murdered wife, Bessie, in August 1930, when thousands of unruly "morbids" and gawkers pushed and shoved the mourners, even almost knocking the weeping husband into the grave, proved unfounded.[10] News accounts of the Windsor funeral concentrated on the quiet fear that hung over the event and the fact, considered mildly scandalous by some, that James Windsor was interred in a burial plot with a woman who was not his legally-married wife.

The Windsor news story was Page One in all three dailies for a week and appeared semi-regularly after that till February 23, 1939, when the Toronto Police arrested two brothers for the murder. After that the focus became the alleged murderers, not the murder or its solution. Windsor's life was picked over thoroughly, beginning with his childhood in a hard-scrabble section of Parkdale. He had worked as a bartender in the Ocean House at Sunnyside before the Ontario Temperance Act came on in 1916, affording him the opportunity to make a lot more money selling liquor illegally than ever he had made doing so within the law.[11] By 1923, Windsor was worth enough to put a down payment on the Briar Hill Avenue house. He was by then long-since split from his wife and four children, and was living with Lavina "Violet" Frawley, the lady in the grave, who had predeceased him by a year and a week. When Ontario Temperance ended in 1927, Windsor adapted and set up his bookmaking business. A story that he was worth $100,000 before the Stock Market Crash of 1929 was likely a pressman's exaggeration. It seems impossible to credit stories such as the one that named Windsor as an associate of William "The Butcher" Leuchter, a Rocco Perri acolyte who was blown up in a car full of alcohol near Ann

Arbor, Michigan, on November 30, 1938. More likely Jimmy Windsor's long-before OTA career was that of a "one bottle man" who had quietly delivered liquor throughout Parkdale in an old car — and merely made an independent, if mildly illegal, living.

In the first week's news there were several alternate theories as to why the bookie died. To some, including two of the eyewitnesses to the killing, the killer's level of anger seemed to suggest a personal hatred of Windsor himself — revenge for some previous wrong or slight. There was a pressman's yarn that said Windsor died for switching allegiance from one American gang to another, that three killers from Buffalo, in company with a Toronto "fingerman," had done the murder. Then there were "the bag" stories — that "the bag" the killer was after was a small cloth pouch in which Windsor carried diamonds and other jewels in a hidden pocket in his trousers, and also the more likely tale that "the bag" was merely a bag-like, box-shaped carrying device in which Bar-B-Q receipts were taken home, a practice Windsor had discontinued months before. Inevitably, there was the suggestion that the bookie had brought about his own death by welching on a bet. Which his friends and professional acquaintances said he would never do. The most obvious thought, that Windsor was merely the victim of a robbery, got little mention, as the murderers hadn't bothered to snatch jewellery that was very apparently worn by the three women in the house.

Eventually the public got tired of the murder story, as the public always does. There wasn't much more to report or to invent. There were other stories that unsettled readers more, especially having to do with the impending war in Europe. Still, when 47 days after the event, the Toronto Police charged Donald "Mickey" MacDonald, a well-known local thief, and his teenaged brother, Alex, with the murder, Toronto breathed a small sigh of relief. Things would be that much safer on Glen Road, in Toronto the Good, for a little while longer.

CHAPTER THREE

Mickey at the Corner
(1907–1938)

IN MAY 1939, AS part of the Windsor Murder investigation, Detective-Sergeant Alex McCathie summed up the man thought to be James Windsor's actual killer in a report to Chief Inspector John Chisholm:

> Donald (Mickey) McDonald has been known to me for a number of years, and during that time has always been engaged in criminal activities. On his own admission, these activities have covered the past fifteen years.... His known associates are practically all criminals and prostitutes, and to my knowledge he has never been engaged in any legitimate employment.[1]

Prior to the winter of 1938–1939, Mickey McDonald was seen by the Toronto Police as a small-time criminal of a type that was apt to become dangerous. As Toronto detectives knew him, Mickey was not a particularly clever thief. He drank too much, he talked too much, and, especially when drunk, was given to outbursts of erratic violence. By February 23, 1939, the day of his arrest for murder, Mickey had spent nearly seven of the preceding 15 years behind bars and he was then under sentence of another two years. Worse, from the police point of view, he had recently been arrested in possession of a revolver, with the apparent intention of using it to commit a crime.

In appearance, the adult Donald McDonald was medium-sized, fair-skinned, dark-haired, and clear of hazel eye. He dressed well and was almost always neat and trim. His left cheek wore a small, not unattractive mole. People noticed his normally pleasant demeanour, his usual politeness, and his outgoing manner. In the Toronto underworld of the day, such as it was, Mickey was thought to be both good-looking and dapper. Many women were charmed by him, to the extent that it was claimed he had numerous affairs and assignations. Detective-Sergeant John Nimmo, who became his eventual nemesis, at least twice testified to Mickey's sense of humour when under the influence of alcohol. "He is very funny," Nimmo observed in court. "In fact, better than going to a show."[2]

He was born Donald John MacDonald on April 11, 1907, in Scotland, likely in the Highland city of Inverness, from where his parents, Alexander Robertson MacDonald and Margaret Renfrew MacDonald, originated. In March 1911, Donald's father, looking for a better life for his family, came to Canada, alone, on board the 10,000-ton steamer *Megantic*, Liverpool to Halifax, as a "British Settler Third Class" — in ship's steerage — with the equivalent of $88 Canadian on his person. MacDonald's ticket into Canada was that he was prepared to work for a specified time as "a farm servant" in the Toronto area. By the summer of 1914, Alexander, his wife Margaret, known as "Maggie," and their several youngsters, including "Donnie," were settled together in a house at 7 Bird Avenue, near Dufferin Street and St. Clair Avenue, in Toronto's west end.[3] The MacDonalds would eventually issue 10 children over a 24-year period, 9 of whom — 6 girls and 3 boys — lived to adulthood. Donald was the oldest boy.

After 1916, Alexander MacDonald laboured 25 years, shoeing delivery-wagon horses for the Canada Bread Company and, according to himself in May 1939, never missed a day's work. Nor did he ever miss Sunday worship. He was a stern, square, God-fearing Scot and an active member of the Church of God, a conservative evangelical congregation then much given to tract distribution and street-corner preaching. According to a story, Mickey's father, whose fixed sense of right and wrong was easily brought forth, was himself a street-corner preacher.

Donald attended Hughes and Earlscourt schools and got an elementary education in normal fashion. Even then, people noticed his politeness and outgoing personality. But by the time he reached the age of eleven, something had started to go wrong. The boy was stealing. His Juvenile Court record shows that he was convicted of six offences in the five years before he reached the age of sixteen. Theft, trespassing, shopbreaking and theft, disorderly conduct, and theft again were the charges. The worst happened in August 1919, when, aged 12, "Donnie" — his mother's name for him — was put on probation and his father had to make restitution to a shopkeeper whose store was broken into. Otherwise, there were warnings, $2 fines, and another probation.

Age 14 and no longer in school, Donald reached a point in life where he was quite normally expected to work and bring home his wages. According to what he later told a counsellor in reformatory, he began work by labouring six months at the Dominion Shipbuilding Yards, where he was paid $14.40 a week. After that, he was a bellboy on a passenger ship that ran between Toronto and Prescott, Ontario, in the Thousand Islands. At other times, so he said, he was the driver of a Canada Bread Company truck and a chauffeur.

About this time, Donnie decided he would rather be "Donald McDonald" than "Donald MacDonald" and, later, he would consistently misrepresent that he was born in Canada, not Scotland. His religion, likely never practised, had become "Presbyterian," his mother's church, not the Church of God, to which he had been taken as a boy. His father's thick Scottish brogue he probably did not like either. Years later, he said that he left home at sixteen.

In September 1925 came the first of Donald's many appearances in Toronto Police Court. Aged 18, he had stolen the motorcar of a Lansdowne Avenue doctor, crashed it into another vehicle, then attacked the other driver. Magistrate J. Edmund Jones convicted him of auto theft and aggravated assault, and awarded a sentence of two years less a day, to be served on remand.[4] Donnie could not manage this leniency. A few days later, he and another troubled youth grabbed $15 from the cash-box of Josephine Columbo's Davenport Road candy store and escaped in a waiting car. Detective Fred Skinner of the Ossington Avenue Station pulled the pair out of their beds in the early hours of the morning and charged them with robbery with violence. In court, however, likely after some parental begging, the two were allowed to plead guilty to simple theft. This time, though, when Magistrate Jones passed sentence of two years-less-a-day, Donald had to "do the time." Many years later, Detective Skinner remembered Mickey as being both likeable and polite. "He often met me on the street. He would always stop to talk to me. He always called me 'Mr. Skinner,'" recalled the detective.[5]

Donnie became Guelph Reformatory's #37514 on October 6, 1925. He did not then, or later, serve time well. His Guelph medical sheet runs several pages and has to do with mostly trivial medical matters — colds, headaches, constipation. Likely the tensions of life "inside" caused him anxiety. He was a worrier who eventually developed a gastric ulcer, which had to be treated in Guelph and later in Kingston Penitentiary. He made a good impression where it mattered, though, and was released "on permit," on September 27, 1926, to go to work. Six months later, on March 18, 1927, The Office of the Commissioner for the Extra Mural Employment of Sentenced Persons, at 40 Richmond Street West, Toronto, notified the Superintendent of Guelph Reformatory that Donald McDonald had "disappeared" and was therefore "unlawfully at large from your institution."[6]

Why would such as Mickey want to work for wages when there was "easy money" — big money — to be made selling illicit liquor?

Mickey had escaped to Detroit, Michigan, where, according to the street story, he became for a time a distributor of good Canadian whisky on behalf of a Windsor racketeer named Raymond "Dolly" Quinton. This was the heyday of the Volstead Act — American Prohibition — when, even though the Province of Ontario was itself "dry" by reason of the Ontario Temperance Act, the federal government permitted the manufacture and sale of liquor "for export," ostensibly only to countries where liquor consumption was legal. Along the Detroit River, on the Windsor side, every day congeries of rumrunners in boats both big and small, many of them rowboats, would pull up to any of a dozen or more government docks, sign a B-13 form — a declaration that they were buying liquor to take to "Cuba" or some other country where the consumption of alcohol was legal — then they would sell the liquor wherever they cared to. The usual destination from Windsor was, of course, Detroit, where good Canadian whisky was in high demand, but much whisky and other liquor was simply U-turned back into Ontario to be bootlegged throughout the province.

Mickey's career in alcohol distribution could not have lasted long before he was pushed out of the game by the Detroit Police or, more likely, by competitors who were too tough to give an argument. But he adapted. In July 1930, at Detroit, as "Michael McDonald," he was sentenced to from 9 months to 10 years for "indecent liberties," a charge that he himself later variously described as having to do with his living with an underage girl, and as having to do with the making of pornographic pictures. He served the minimum 9 months in Michigan State Prison at Jackson, Michigan, then was released on April 10, 1931, the day before his twenty-fourth birthday.

Mickey learned much in the Michigan lockup, and, it seems, by the time of his release had chosen crime as his career. Now calling himself "Michael McDonald" — hence the nickname "Mickey" — he returned to Toronto and headed straight for Jarvis and Dundas streets, a location that, by this time, was becoming known as a gathering spot for bootleggers, prostitutes, drug dealers, assorted criminals, and all of their hangers-on and fellow travellers. "The Corner" was what those "in the know," including the police, had begun calling the intersection. On the street, the term would hold up as such for the next 30 or 35 years.

Mickey was soon tied into a loosely-associated gang of shopbreakers who lived an expensive criminal lifestyle. They did "kickins" by night, spent their afternoons at racetracks, were often at bootlegging establishments, and often philandered among prostitutes. The gang's usual target was women's clothing stores, which yielded items that could be easily disposed of for cash.

On August 5, 1931, as "Michael McDonald," Mickey appeared with two others before Magistrate Robert J. Browne charged with the theft of 130 ladies dresses from the store of L.A. Finch at 483 Bloor Street West. Associates Louis Gallow and Jimmy Douglas were convicted and sent "down East" for three years each, but the magistrate threw out the case against Mickey. Two nights later, Mickey celebrated by making a drunken show of refusing P.C. Fred Falconer's suggestion that he "move along" from the corner of Church and Dundas streets. He was charged with "obstruct police." That cost $50 and court costs on pain of 30 days in the Langstaff Jail Farm.

Then came the night in a Sherbourne Street booze can when Mickey McDonald, for no reason that made any sense, smashed a banjo over the head of a prostitute who was known on the streets as "The Old Gray Mare." She was the wife of William "Big Bill" Cook, a pimp, drug dealer, and gunman, who was also the former doorman of the Chicory Inn, a roadhouse on the Lakeshore Highway in Clarkson. It was at the Chicory Inn that Bill Cook had famously shot Oscar Campbell, a thug at least as dangerous as himself who had previously bested Cook in a street fight by whacking him over the head with a hammer. A few months before the banjo incident, Cook was acquitted of shooting Campbell with intent to maim.

Big Bill caught up with Mickey inside Trotter's Lunch, a Dundas Street East restaurant-cum-dive, at 4 a.m., Sunday, October 13. There followed a comic-opera attempt at murder, in which Mickey found the courage to physically attack Cook, who was 30 or more pounds heavier than he was, while Bill fired a gun at Mickey before he got the gun out of his own pocket and, so, shot himself in the leg. Cook was then beaten and kicked by Mickey and others among Trotter's swanky clientele, one of whom grabbed Cook's gun and left with it. In a state of high excitement, Mickey then clobbered the restaurant manager over the head with the receiver of his kitchen phone, when the man, somewhat ridiculously, tried to establish order in his place of business.

The next afternoon, at the Lakeshore Racetrack, Mickey met Detective Frank Crowe and, in a jocular conversation between "friendly enemies," made the mistake of having too much to say about what had happened at Trotter's. He would not afterward sign a statement naming Cook and wound up being charged with assault occasioning actual bodily harm on the restauranteur. Worse, he was bound over as a material witness against Big Bill, who was claiming to the police that he had been mysteriously shot on Sherbourne Street by a stranger. Cook's coat, which had a bullet hole through the pocket, told the true story, while Mickey — who chose to maintain his reputation as "good people" — perjured himself, very obviously, in the interest of Bill Cook, a man he hated and who hated him. On December 17, 1931, again as "Michael McDonald," Mickey pleaded guilty to aggravated assault before a County Court judge and was meted out a sentence of two years in prison. Twenty-nine days later, before Justice Hugh Edward Rose in the Supreme Court of Ontario, he pleaded guilty to perjury and was handed three years concurrent with the first sentence. Mickey smiled and wore an air of nonchalance at both proceedings.

As inmate #2479, McDonald spent his first 10 months in Kingston Penitentiary working in the canvas shop ("the mailbags") where he toiled at the manufacture and repair of Canadian Postal Department mailbags. These were the last days of the Silent System and of a rigid set of prison rules and regulations put in place decades before. The Kingston riot of

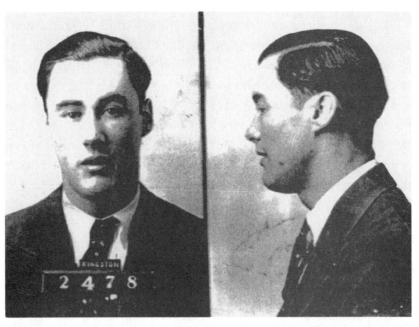

"Mickey" McDonald as photographed upon his first admission to Kingston Penitentiary on January 16, 1932. (Library and Archives Canada)

October 17, 1932, was the convicts' idea of their first move in a process of change. At 3 p.m., about 450 of the institution's 700 inmates walked away from their work and barricaded themselves in the Shop Dome before being overcome by guards with guns and herded back to their cells. Mickey McDonald was one of 32 later charged and tried before a County Court judge. Two guards and a shop instructor testified to having observed Mickey taking an active role in the riot, one saying that Mickey appeared to be giving orders in the Dome. Thus, on August 5, 1933, after a lengthy trial, again as "Michael McDonald," Mickey was convicted of riotous destruction of property and sentenced to 6 months in reformatory, to be served after the completion of his Kingston sentence.

During the 33 months he was in "the Big House," Mickey's weight dropped from 161 to 138 pounds. A medical examination in September 1934 concluded, "This man is principally run down from a lack of exercise in the open air."[7] A psychologist's assessment stated, "At the present time he is quite embittered towards the penal system and feels that he

William "Big Bill" Cook, pimp, drug dealer, gunman, and the man who tried to shoot "Mickey" McDonald in Trotter's Lunch in the early morning of October 13, 1931. (Library and Archives Canada)

was harshly treated. His father is regularly employed and has promised to obtain steady work for Michael when he is discharged from custody."[8] As always, Mickey's parents were worried and trying to help. Their letters to the right authorities got the result that Mickey was allowed to serve his six-month sentence in the Mimico Reformatory rather than in Guelph. But 13 days after Mickey entered Mimico, a jailhouse "rat" named him as being involved in sending out letters by the "underground method." Superintendent J.R. Elliott interviewed Mickey and, the same day, reported to Deputy Provincial Secretary C.F. Neelands:

> I had hardly spoke to him when he flew into a rage in a threatening manner, calling me a Son-of-a B, Bastard etc., completely losing his head. He is a bad character....
>
> He is now in the cells.
>
> I will see him again in the morning, and if his attitude is not changed I will recommend the strap and possible removal to another institution.[9]

Given time to think, Mickey became cutely submissive. The cost of his tantrum was a charge of "Insolence to the Superintendent," which lengthened his stay in Mimico by 26 days. He was released February 1, 1935.

He was soon back at The Corner, again mixing with others like himself who imagined the "easy money" of a life of crime, and the uncertain existence that came with it, were to be preferred to a life of honest labour. Twice in 1935 he was before the courts charged with offences related to shopbreaking. In May 1935, together with Jack Cosgrave and another man, Mickey was stopped in a rented truck in possession of a jimmy and several types of keys. The three were charged with "possession of housebreaking instruments." The case got to court but all were acquitted. In September, Mickey and Leo Gauthier, a long-time associate, were arrested after a pursuit by car from the scene of a break-in at Hooper's Drug Store at 391 Jarvis Street. They got off, perhaps because the taxi driver who fingered them to the police found reason to water down his story in court.

These days Mickey at times went about with a fat roll of bills in his pocket, which he soon frittered away on gambling and alcohol. He was often broke and asking for a loan. Then he was apt to turn into a mere street-corner clip-artist, rolling drunks or steering marks to rigged card games — any mean little "score" for a desperate buck.[10] The Toronto Police saw him as one of their "usual suspects" and would routinely pick him up and question him in connection with shop break-ins, house burglaries, and at least one armed robbery. In normal circumstances, Mickey's disposition was sunny and pleasing, but, when down-on-his-luck and drunk, which he now often was, he was known to get nasty, to pick fights, to take his inner anger out on almost anyone who was handy at the moment. Years later, Jenny Law, a prostitute of the 1930s, remembered Mickey as good-looking, well-dressed, well-groomed "trouble." He was, she said, barred from a lot of the tap rooms and bootlegging "joints" in the vicinity of The Corner. "He would go to a bootlegger's, get drunk, and start a fight, so he wouldn't have to pay," Jenny remembered in a tone of wonderment.[11]

The MacDonald family, now renting a house at 3 Poplar Plains Road in central Toronto, saw Mickey as it suited him, although, as his mother later said, he made a practice of calling her on the phone every day.[12] When he did come home, he often brought one or more of his risky "friends." His parents' need to continue loving their wayward son allowed people with corrosive ideas, Mickey especially, to have exposure to their younger boys, Alex and Edwin. It was a mistake that would have serious consequences. Maggie MacDonald would live to see the day when all three of her sons were in federal prisons at the same time. Detective-Sergeant Alex McCathie, at least twice a visitor to the MacDonald home in 1935, went there on October 26 and, afterwards, reported:

> .... armed with a search warrant and in company with other officers, I had occasion to search the home of the McDonald (sic) family. Upon entering the premises I was assured by Mrs. McDonald that none of the goods outlined in the search warrant were concealed in the premises, but on executing the warrant articles stolen from two shops which had been broken and entered in Toronto, and a store which had been broken and

entered in Preston, Ontario, were found in practically every room in the house. Members of the family were found to be wearing stolen clothing, which they admitted had been brought to their home by John Cosgrave, a dangerous shopbreaker, an associate of Donald (Mickey) McDonald....

A further search was made of the premises occupied by one of the McDonald daughters, who was married, and further stolen articles found in her possession....

Previous to this I had contact with the McDonald family as a result of locating a stolen car in their garage...[13]

No one at the house knew anything about the car, and none of the MacDonalds were arrested as receivers of stolen goods by reason of the fact that Maggie MacDonald and two of her minor children appeared as Crown witnesses against Jack Cosgrave at his trial in Preston.

On December 15, 1935, Donald John MacDonald, aged 28, legally married Margaret Holland, a strikingly beautiful 19-year-old girl. In the following months, Margaret — usually as "Mary Wilson" — was charged twice with keeping a disorderly house (a euphemism of the law for keeping a house of prostitution), charged once with vagrancy, and once with public drunkenness. "Kitty Cat," as Margaret became known on the streets, had a Depression-era job as a prostitute, while Mickey, having borrowed $200 from a bookmaker named Cecil Clancy, tried briefly to make a living as a bookie himself.[14] He soon gave that up and went back to being a thief. A comment on the marriage might be that Kitty tried to commit suicide in October 1936. Maggie MacDonald promised in Toronto Police Court that she would look after her daughter-in-law. "She had some trouble," Maggie told Magistrate Cowan. According to a story, the trouble was Mickey, who hadn't quit his philandering ways.

Early on the morning of December 3, 1936, Mickey and Kitty, likely both drunk, were perambulating along Queen Street East near Carlaw Avenue when Kitty chanced to admire some apparel in the window of Pearl Trimball's Riverdale Ladies Wear. Mickey impetuously decided to

Mickey McDonald and wife, Margaret "Kitty Cat" MacDonald (she was always MacDonald), circa 1935–37. This photograph appeared in the late edition of the *Telegram* of February 24, 1939, the day after Mickey and his brother Alex were charged with the murder of Jimmy Windsor. (York University Libraries, Clara Thomas Archives and Special Collections, *Toronto Telegram* fonds, ASC07405)

show Kitty how easy a "kickin" really was. The police of the nearby Pape Avenue Station arrived in short order, to find the thief still in the store, with 14 overcoats and 3 dresses piled up by a door.[15] Charged with shop-breaking and let out on a $10,000 bond, Mickey promptly absconded bail. He made for Windsor, Ontario, and his friends of the 1920s. There, on January 30, 1937, Mickey, Dolly Quinton, and another man were drinking beer in the tap room of the British-American Hotel with their coats on hangers behind them when someone noticed a revolver showing from a pocket of one of the coats. Windsor detectives soon after arrested all three suspects, since all denied owning the guilty coat. Mickey, who gave the name John Ross of 121 Main Street, Moose Jaw, Saskatchewan, later flew into an angry "you-don't-have-to-do-this-to-me" rage at one of the arresting officers and, as part of this, volunteered that the gun-heavy coat was his. The detective's account of this before Magistrate D.M. Brodie in Windsor Police Court got Mickey a conviction for possession of a revolver without a permit — and a sentence of two years in Kingston. Plainly, as the magistrate said in court, Mickey's having had too much to say was the reason for his conviction.

Mickey entering Kingston on April 3, 1937. (Library and Archives Canada)

Back in Toronto, on March 24, 1937, a County Court jury found Mickey guilty of the December 3 shopbreaking, after which Judge James Parker kindly awarded him two years, concurrent with the Windsor sentence. Judge Parker was impressed with Mickey's fine manners in court and with the fact that, afterwards, he insisted on shaking hands with each member of the jury.

CHAPTER FOUR

Kitty Cat in Gangland
(October 1938–January 1939)

IF THE CORNER WAS a street term for an intersection, the label "Gangland" for the larger area surrounding Jarvis and Dundas streets was a newspaper phenomenon. The name began in the wake of the vicious beating of a young policeman named Harold Genno on the night of May 8, 1938. That happened in an alley off St. Patrick Street, west of University Avenue, but, fueled by many further incidents, the designation "Gangland" soon moved eastwards to the environs of The Corner.[1] Nearby, there were a dozen small-to-medium-sized hotels within a few hundred yards of each other and, after 1934, when Ontario legalized the practice, they were all serving full-strength "beer by the glass" — a concentration that tended to draw those who were "looking for something" as well as others who, in one way or another, were out to make money out of what they were "looking for." The term "Gangland" would be in the daily press for a season or two and, after that, lived on in the pages of Toronto's old tabloid papers, *Hush, Flash, Tab, Justice Weekly*, and some others, till the last of their days in the 1970s.[2] In the beginnings of this, Mickey McDonald, and especially Kitty Cat, played significant roles.

In the early fall of 1938, increased violence among a half dozen small bootlegging operations in the Jarvis-Dundas-Church streets area was mostly directed against the best-organized and least-violent faction. This was headed by William "Lefty" Thomas, a street-corner newsdealer, who was also a bail bondsman, a bookmaker, and the money man behind bootlegging and beer-running operations run by agents of his in and around the Gangland area. At the same time, Thomas was a particular target of a violent street predator who was simply looking to "jack up" — extort — anyone, anyway he could. Bookmakers, bootleggers, and non-violent thieves were easy "marks" for Johnny "The Bug" Brown, a volatile ex-convict with a long record involving armed robbery, gun violence, and psychiatric assessment. Brown, who was born Ivan Stefanyk in Hamilton, Ontario, "hit up" Lefty and his crew several times before this became known outside Lefty's circle of associates. Like Jimmy Windsor, as racketeers them-selves, Thomas and his people could not be seen to give information against Brown, and they were not formidable enough to deal with him themselves. Inevitably, they guardedly talked to detectives. They wanted The Bug off their backs but feared to be part of any obvious effort to put him away.

While Mickey was "away at school," Margaret "Kitty Cat" MacDonald (she was always "MacDonald") got herself involved in all of this when she began co-habitating with Charlie Dorland, then Lefty Thomas's fair-haired boy and principal lieutenant. In early October 1938, Charlie and Kitty moved into Apartment 2 at 539 Church Street. The place was elabo-rately furnished with money put up by Lefty, seemingly with the idea of combining two kinds of good time on the premises.

For ex-convict John Cullinan, who operated a bare-bones blind pig at 568 Church Street, the proximity of this new and better place would have been upsetting, even if, on the evening of October 4, 1938, Kitty and friend, Norma "The Blonde" Taylor, had not gone to Cullinan's place to gloat. Soon Edward Near, a buddy of Dorland's, took a tele-phone message at 539 Church. "If you don't come and get Norma and Margaret, I'll kill them," Cullinan told Near. Together with Norm Cook, who did late-night beer deliveries for Dorland, Near did as asked.

In the wee hours of October 5, Charlie Dorland got a phone call that told him he had to go out. Then, soon after, Cullinan's lady friend, Millie Dinwoodie, knocked at the back door of Apartment 2 at 539 Church. Kitty, who later said she "thought it was a friendly visit," admitted Millie, who was followed in by Cullinan, Johnny "The Bug" Brown, Joseph Constantino, Verne Epter, and three other men. Most of the eight intruders were connected with one of three nearby bootlegging factions, or in the cases of Brown and his partner, Constantino, with the ongoing extortion and robbery of selected bootleggers and bookmakers. All but two of the eight had served time in prison or reformatory.

Cullinan began by ripping Kitty's telephone off the wall, then announced there was "going to be a fight between Millie and Norma." Brown pulled a gun to enforce matters. The fight wasn't much of a contest. Millie, a big powerful girl, dragged The Blonde off a couch by the hair and throttled her. Then Cullinan and Epter both took a turn. Kitty and a woman named Rita McIntosh were also beaten up. The apartment's new furniture and fixtures were completely wrecked at a cost of more than $200. Norma Taylor had her diamond ring and $18 stolen. A few days later, Margaret "Kitty Cat" MacDonald brazenly told the tale at a preliminary hearing in Toronto Police Court — which threatened to put all of her eight early-morning "visitors" in the penitentiary. As was reported, Kitty, wearing a stylish fur jacket, told Magistrate Robert J. Browne, "They smashed all the lights and threw the lamps on the floor. The place was in darkness. My clothes were ripped off my back." What she described was termed "a miniature riot."[3]

The incident itself was a front page story in the *Globe and Mail* of Thursday, October 6. The story played upon the same public fears as the Windsor Murder would three months later: violence, robbery, extortion, all of which happened inside a private residence, into which unwanted armed intruders forced entry. After this time, terms like "Gangland," "Gangwar," and "shakedown" appeared regularly in the Toronto press for months. The disquieted public was assured by Mayor Ralph Day and other members of the Toronto Police Commission that the situation would be cleaned up. Inspector Charles Scott of No. 2 Station at Dundas and Bay streets, said the same. "Gang warfare will not be tolerated by the police," Inspector Scott promised. "An attempt will be made to prevent the different Jarvis and Dundas street gangs from taking the law into their own hands."[4]

Mickey McDonald, after 20 months in Kingston Penitentiary, came home on November 7, 1938, and stepped into the middle of what for any of his kind would have been a trying situation. An acquaintance was living with his wife; Johnny Brown, one of his more violent jailhouse "friends," had recently punched his wife in the face; and his wife, who liked living dangerously, was now trying to help the police put several of his "friends" — Brown in particular — away for significant lengths of time.

Late on the night of Saturday, November 12, Johnny the Bug and Joe Constantino went to Alexander MacDonald's home on Poplar Plains Road with a bottle of liquor. Mickey went out to Brown's car and shared the bottle with them. The three smoothed matters over between themselves. Kitty, already reclaimed from Dorland, was convinced by Mickey that her best course was to get on side with "Brownie," Joe, and himself, who had just then made a plan to "take off" another of Lefty Thomas's bootlegging establishments. Straight away, "The Cat" switched sides and drove the three in Brown's car to the vicinity of 463A Church Street, where Mickey acted the part of the Trojan Horse. James Elder,

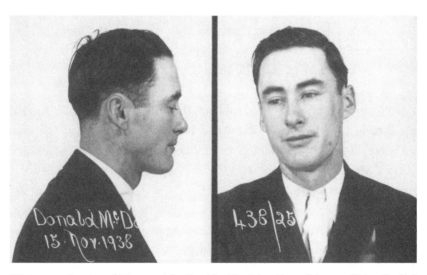

Mickey on the day of his arrest for the blackjack beating of James Elder, "Lefty" Thomas's Church Street bootlegger. (Archives of Ontario, file 4-32 #409)

45

the keeper of the house, would not have opened the door to Brown or Constantino. When the three barged in, others on the premises fled. Elder put up a fight and was blackjacked into submission. The raiders escaped with a small amount of cash, seven bottles of whisky, a bottle of gin, forty-eight quarts of beer, and a man's overcoat. Thus, Mickey McDonald was out of prison all of six days before he committed the offence that would send him back again.

It was, of course, another Page One headline, since seemingly the law had lost its force in a central section of the city. The *Globe's* story of Tuesday, November 15, 1938, was headed "Gang War Flare-Up Puts Two More In Jail." Kitty's participation in this violent event was the lead:

> Blonde Margaret (Kitty) MacDonald, one of the central figures in the recent outbreak of warfare between rival bootlegging gangs in Toronto, was arrested with her husband last night on a charge of robbery with violence.
>
> A man known to police as a member of a bootlegging gang was badly beaten by three men who broke into an apartment Sunday ...
>
> Under arrest are Mrs. MacDonald and her husband, Mickey. The woman, known in the Church-Dundas-Jarvis district as Kitty, was the tenant of the apartment which was wrecked several weeks ago and furnished the spark which started the blaze of violence.[5]

Within a few hours of the robbery, the Toronto Police had rounded up Brown, Constantino, Mickey, and Kitty, but had to let all of them go when, at the last moment, James Elder quaked at preferring charges. After a Monday conference with Crown Attorney James W. McFadden, however, Detective-Sergeant John Hicks and Detective John Nimmo arrested all four again and charged them all with robbery with violence.

The trials of those connected to the major "Gangland incidents" of October 5 and November 13 did not get to court until January 1939. During the 51 days after November 20, 1938, including the night of James Windsor's murder, Mickey McDonald was out of jail on $2,000 bail. During some of this time, he stayed with Kitty in a second-floor flat at 233 Broadview Avenue, where the couple did a lot of socializing with others of similar interests. It seemed convenient that Leo Gauthier, one of Mickey's long-time partners-in-crime, was released from "the pen" on November 22. Leo was soon paired off with Marjorie Constable, a friend of Kitty's who then "worked the street" in the vicinity of The Corner. A short time after their first meeting, Leo and Marje moved into an apartment at Sherbourne and Dundas streets. In the first forty-eight hours of 1939, the two couples rang in the New Year by bunking in together in a single room in the seedy Frontenac Arms Hotel at 306 Jarvis Street.

Three days after the Windsor Murder, on the morning of Tuesday, January 10, 1939, Mickey surrendered to face the music over the beating of James Elder. His trial, and the much-publicized trials of the others charged in connection with the same event, took place before County Court Judge James Parker and a jury that same afternoon. Elder and two others belonging to Lefty Thomas's outfit had been charged as material witnesses and, so, as an alternative to going to jail themselves, were made to tell of what they saw, heard, and suffered at 463A Church Street in the early morning of November 13, 1938. For the defence, Brown and Mickey went into the box and told lying stories. Constantino and Kitty did not testify. The jury took four and a half hours to settle on guilty verdicts for Mickey, Brown, and Constantino. Kitty was found not guilty.[6]

"I am quite in accord with your verdict," Judge Parker told the jury. "The evidence disclosed these men went to Elder's place for a certain purpose and they carried out that purpose with violence."[7]

The judge then remanded the three for sentence. Six detectives escorted the convicted men through the corridors of City Hall and, afterwards, to the Don Jail. The *Globe and Mail* of January 11 told its readers, "In gathering up the three, the police made their first arrests in the series of gang raids and shakedowns that have kept the Toronto underworld seething for several months past."

A few days later, the eight invaders of Kitty's apartment went before Judge Ian Macdonell and a County Court jury. They were all charged with robbery with violence, assault occasioning actual bodily harm on a female, burglary, and wilful damage to property. Their three-day trial

WHAT HAPPENED TO MICKEY?

ended in the conviction of Brown, Cullinan, Constantino, Verne Epter, and Millie Dinwoodie on one or more of the charges. Kitty, who switched sides again, seemed to glory in her role as star witness against the lot and, as ever, took obvious delight in showing herself off in beautiful clothes. The October 5 Gangland incident, her previous flamboyant appearance in Toronto Police Court, and this County Court trial were the first widely-reported "events" in Kitty's establishing her almost 30-year reputation as Toronto's most scandalous woman. In the 1930s, few women in Toronto would go into open court and boldly tell that they were living with a man other than their husband, to whom they had returned upon his release from prison, and no daily newspaper used the word "prostitute." Instead, the press employed phrases like *"The woman, known in the Church-Dundas-Jarvis district as Kitty..."* which said the same thing in a code acceptable to the straight-laced citizens of Toronto the Good. Like the term "Gangland," Mickey's wife's reputation, fueled by many future arrests and misadventures, would live almost as long as the scandal sheets. The connotations of the names "Kitty Cat" and "Gangland" would be virtually inseparable. In fact, one was a habitual frequenter of the other — and much of Toronto knew it.

January 27, 1939, was the day of final reckoning for all convicted of the two high-profile Gangland crimes. In Judge Parker's court, Mickey's father, in his thick Scottish brogue, made an "eloquent plea" for "my son, Donald, known as 'Mickey,'" his errant *boy* of almost 32 years of age. Mr. MacDonald told a version of what had happened following Mickey's return from prison:

> ...After a few days the telephone began to ring. His old companions found he was home. He tried to dodge them, and time after time we denied his presence in the house. Drink is his downfall. Whatever he did that night, it was not by deliberate choice. I do not ask anything for this boy other than the clemency of the court.[8]

Judge Parker sentenced "Michael McDonald," John Brown, and Joseph Constantino to two years each in Kingston Penitentiary.

Then it was Judge Ian Macdonell's turn on the Bench.

"Gang warfare, such as was never thought possible in Toronto, must end," Judge Macdonell told the five who stood convicted before him. "I am afraid you must be made an example of. It is my painful duty to inflict severe sentences on you."[9] Brown was then awarded five years consecutive to the two years he was given a few minutes before, and Constantino two years consecutive with his previous two. Cullinan, considered the ringleader on October 5, got five years. Verne Epter, once known as the undisputed head of the "Jarvis Street Gang," was given four years. Millie Dinwoodie was let off with a suspended sentence. That day's *Toronto Star* wore the banner: 5 OF GANG SENT TO 'PEN,' 7 YEARS FOR ONE.

The Star's Page One lead-all story was titled "Pleading Father Hears Son Sent to Penitentiary." Because of Alexander MacDonald's pathetic appeal in court, the story concentrated largely on Mickey, who got only two of the 22 years handed down. Mug shots of the five who were "going inside" appeared together in the *Star* and the *Telegram*, on Page Two of both papers.

Johnny "The Bug" Brown, the man with the gun in the Toronto Gangwar of 1938. (Library and Archives Canada)

Mickey's two-year sentence was by this time the least of his worries. Already he had reason to believe that he would be charged with the murder of James Albert Windsor. His days as a criminal of minor importance were over.

CHAPTER FIVE

The Line-up of Sunday, January 22
(January 22, 1939)

MICKEY MCDONALD FIRST KNEW he had real reason to worry about being charged with the murder of James Windsor on Sunday afternoon, January 22, five days before he was sentenced by Judge Parker to two years in the Elder case. Early that afternoon, together with several other Don Jail inmates, Mickey was suddenly and unexpectedly vanned to Toronto police headquarters to be in an identification line-up that was to be paraded before the five eyewitnesses to the Windsor Murder.

This was a procedure Mickey knew well.

Those to be displayed, whether they were brought to the line-up theatre from the jail, from one of the police stations, or from the detective room at headquarters itself, were taken there by a route that insured they would not encounter any of the witnesses in advance of the "show up" and thereby contaminate their evidence in any subsequent prosecution. Mickey and others from the jail were brought into the building by way of the underground garage, then taken up to the fifth floor in the back-corridor freight elevator.

The line-up room was a long narrow rectangle with a raised platform along the entire length of one wall. A thin wire mesh separated the men on the platform from those who were there to view them, and an array of lights created the effect that the witnesses could see the men in the line-up, but they themselves could only be seen as shadows by those on the other side of the mesh curtain.

When all was in readiness, Mickey and thirteen others were marched through a door onto the platform and told to spread themselves out facing the mesh. Sergeant of Detectives Herbert McCready, in charge of the line-up, called each witness into the room, one at a time, by knocking on a door at the opposite end of the identification room to which those on display had entered. Each time, before he did so, the men on the platform were allowed to re-arrange themselves in any order that suited them. Then, as each witness came in, McCready gave them the same instruction: *There are some men lined up here. Look them over carefully and individually, and if there is anyone there who you have seen on any occasion, let me know.* After viewing the line-up, each witness left by a door at the opposite end of the room to the door they came in.

Unknown to the police, the five eyewitnesses to Windsor's death had made a secret agreement among themselves not to identify anyone in the line-up room as instructed by detectives both before and during the viewing. The five were then living under 24-hour-a-day police protection at 247 Briar Hill Avenue, and this would be so until mid-April, 1939, when the house was put up for sale and the entire household, tired of threatening letters and all manner of bothersome strangers at their door, moved. After that, there would be six months more of the same close security at an undisclosed location. All of the eyewitnesses, including Lorraine Bromell, who stayed with the family until the entire ordeal was over, lived in deathly fear that, having seen the face of the angry killer who shot James Windsor, the killer, or killers, or their associates, might return and murder them to prevent their testifying. The agreement was made after Jack McDermott saw, or thought he saw, a man who was in an earlier line-up walking on College Street. Later, in court, the admission of this understanding would serve to weaken the witness value of all five of their positive identifications of the gunman all would identify as James Windsor's actual killer, and of the blue-eyed man who held those at the dinner table at bay.

Jack McDermott, the first to answer Herbert McCready's knock, said and did nothing to unnerve Mickey McDonald or anyone else in the identification parade. Later, McDermott would testify that he spotted Mickey as the actual killer of James Windsor the moment he entered the room and, upon a close inspection of the others on the platform, recognized "the man with the yellow gloves" as the blue-eyed gunman. Before leaving the building, McDermott went into Inspector of Detectives John Chisholm's office and, in the presence of Chief Constable D.C. Draper and Inspector Pat Hogan, notified Chisholm that Donald "Mickey" McDonald was the gunman who shot Windsor and "the man with the yellow gloves" was his accomplice.[1]

The next eyewitness to enter the identification room surely gave Mickey immediate and serious reason to worry. Later, in court, Edith Warner would testify that, upon first spotting a side view of Mickey's face, she loudly blurted out, "There is the profile of the man that did the killing."[2]

At this remark, or something like it, Mickey stooped down low on the platform, tried to look under the mesh curtain, and aggressively demanded to know, "Is that me?"

"Yes, that's you. Now straighten up," Herbert McCready snapped back sharply.

Edith Warner was too frightened to say anything more.

She would later tell in court, more than once, that she had recognized both Mickey and "the tall man with the yellow gloves" as two of the men who had invaded the Briar Hill Avenue house. She would also testify that she made a positive identification of Mickey McDonald as her brother's killer in the line-up room. But the written record of the line-up did not show that. Mrs. Warner was recorded as having said that Mickey's profile was "*like* the profile of the man I saw at 247 Briar Hill Avenue."[3]

Evelyn McDermott, who had gotten the best look at the killer's unmasked face when she answered the knock at the front door, asked Mickey, alone among the fourteen men on the platform, to step forward and smile. She was, of course, looking for the gunman's supposedly "decayed and wide-apart" teeth, which she would later testify she had described to the police as being merely "black-looking."[4] Mickey did as asked and Mrs. McDermott said nothing else — in the identification room or after she passed through it. She would later testify that she told her husband at home that she thought she saw two of the gunmen in the line-up parade — the shooter and "the man that held us back."[5]

Edward Warner went through the room, as he would later testify, noticing Mickey and the second gunman in the same way as all of the others. He too kept to the compact and said nothing until he was back at 247 Briar Hill Avenue.

The last to be called into the identification room was Lorraine Bromell. She did less than Edith Warner or Evelyn McDermott to worry Mickey but more than the two men. As she later testified, one at a time, she asked Mickey, Mickey's long-time associate Louis Gallow, and "the man with the yellow gloves," to step forward and show their teeth in a smile. Lorraine would remember that when she asked "the man who did the shooting" to show his teeth, he "stood forward and made some funny little cracks, and made funny faces and said, 'I am not the man you want.'"[6] The other two men only did as requested, quietly and without attracting unnecessary attention to themselves. Lorraine afterwards identified Mickey and "the man with the yellow gloves," but not the short, dark-complexioned Louis Gallow, as being two of those who were in the Briar Hill Avenue house. When asked later in court, 'Why not Gallow, too?' she answered that she was not sure of him; the others she was sure of.[7]

Thus, none of the five eyewitnesses made an identification of anyone in the line-up parade in the manner that Herbert McCready had instructed them to do. Instead, after collecting all of the positive identifications at the Briar Hill Avenue house, and after the eyewitnesses very likely had discussed the matter among themselves, Jack McDermott telephoned Inspector Chisholm and notified him that all were in agreement that Mickey was the killer and "the man with the yellow gloves" was his armed accomplice.[8]

When questioned later in court about whether anything extraordinary had happened at the line-up on January 22, Mickey said: "One lady asked me to smile, and I smiled. I cracked a joke with her, and says, 'If you dance, I will smile.' And she says, 'No, that is not the man.'"[9] Mickey would also testify that another woman asked two others and himself to step forward and show their teeth.

In the written record of Edith Warner's answer to Sergeant McCready's question, "Where did you see this man before?" the witness was recorded as having said, "His profile is *like* the man I saw at 247 Briar Hill Avenue. I am only going by the profile, because it was only the profile that I saw." About this, at his later trial for murder, Mickey McDonald would testify that he did not remember hearing those words at all — in effect, that they were a police fabrication, in which Edith Warner had participated.[10]

* * *

In a perverse sense, confinement was good for Mickey. It got him away from liquor and sobered him up, which had the effect of perking up his criminal instincts. Jail got his defensive network functioning. Some of those he met up with on the fifth floor before the line-up — men brought there from elsewhere than the Don Jail — surely caused the inner alarm to go off inside his criminal mind. It was not anxiety that he could express, since those in the line-up were instructed not to talk to each other and, more so, because any accusation in public would serve to label Mickey as guilty himself. More than that, though, his then already burgeoning suspicion might be wrong and, if voiced, whether right or wrong, would likely trigger another kind of major problem. Any criminal who names another as an informer better be ready to fight, or even kill, over it. It's a dangerous accusation to make because it's a dangerous thing to be accused of. Mickey, rightly, kept his suspicions to himself.

So far as Mickey was concerned, the most worrisome presence in the line-up was that of Jack Shea, a criminal "friend" and ally who had been wanted for a bank robbery at Port Credit since December 9, 1938. After hiding out in Toronto for six weeks, Shea was arrested on the morning of Saturday, January 21, the day before this line-up. Mickey and the police both knew Shea as many kinds of criminal, including as a smooth and clever con artist. At Port Credit, Shea had moved up to bank robbery with Leo Gauthier, and "the man with the yellow gloves," and, as a three-time loser, if convicted, was now likely looking at a sentence of 10 to 15 years in "the Big House." This being a weekend, most likely Mickey came to the line-up not knowing Shea had been arrested while, at the same time, wondering why he, himself, was now suddenly a suspect in the Windsor Murder. Shea's unexpected presence surely supplied a possible, or probable, answer. Mickey's big worry about Shea was not only that he now found himself in a line-up of murder suspects right after Shea's being freshly caught, but that Shea had likely been arrested in an apartment that Mickey had vis-ited several times in the 12 days prior to his giving himself up on the James Elder robbery-with-violence charge. In fact, as both he and Shea would later agree, Mickey had gone to Shea's apartment on the night of the Windsor Murder. And that would be, as Mickey would have surely considered it might be, the biggest part of the rub.

If Shea had turned "rat," Mickey knew, he would have had to cough up something big to get consideration for himself on the charge he was now facing. James Windsor's murderers would do nicely. Had Shea talked to the police about him? And, if so, what would, or could, he have told them? What would, or could, Shea have been able to concoct, if he did not actually know anything solid? Or if Shea was a part of the Windsor Murder himself? Depending on the truth of the matter, some or all of these questions were all over Mickey's mind a few seconds after he spotted Jack Shea's presence. Not maybe. Not perhaps. Take it to the bank. Shea would have known, or should have known, what Mickey was thinking — but, like Mickey, he was best off to say nothing and await developments. The situation was like a boxing match where neither com-petitor ought to lead for fear of a devastating counterpunch.

The criminal world is a world of paranoia. Mickey knew this, too. Jack Shea's reputation in that world was as solid as his own. Shea was widely thought to be "good people," "solid," "a stand-up guy." Mickey must surely have hoped and considered, as well, that all of these sudden suspicions were only his own paranoid criminal mind acting upon imaginary fears. It had happened before that he had doubted a trusted associate, only to be proven wrong. It is a part of criminal life.

Depending on what Shea really did know, Mickey was surely more than mildly alarmed at Shea's presence there that afternoon. Edith Warner's seeming identification of his profile could only have com-pounded his concern.

Another upsetting presence was that of Louis Gallow, born Luigi Gallo, a short, dark thief of Italian extraction who well fit the description of the man who came in from the hallway and dragged Jimmy Windsor to the spot on the hall floor where he died. Though not under arrest at the moment, Gallow was, in fact, now suspected by the police of being that man. Older than the others, Louis had a criminal record rife with crimes of theft and violence dating back to 1914, and he was known by the police to be a long-time criminal associate of Mickey's. If Gallow and Mickey were both real parts of the gang that killed Windsor, and Shea knew this, all of what Mickey was thinking about Shea's presence in the line-up was grossly magnified by Gallow being there, too. Gallow, himself, if he was truly part of the gang that killed Windsor, and if he had reason to think or know that Shea knew this, would have been worried by Shea being there too.

And, so, it was with "the man with the yellow gloves," whose presence would have disturbed Mickey in the same way as would have Gallow's — and for family reasons as well. "The man with the yellow gloves" was Mickey's 19-year-old brother, Alex, who had taken Mickey's place in the robbery of the Bank of Commerce in Port Credit, since Mickey was indisposed at the time. Alex and Leo Gauthier were already charged with that robbery, and both were out on $7,500 bail on the night of the Windsor Murder, and at the moment, too. At 9 a.m. that Sunday morning, 15 days after Windsor's death, a dozen detectives, armed with a warrant, had appeared at the Poplar Plains Road house and, as Alexander MacDonald Sr. later said, "without knocking or stopping at the door went from the top to the bottom of the house, and searched it all."[11] They found nothing. Alex was pulled out of bed and taken to headquarters for questioning, and to be paraded in this line-up. Later that afternoon, Herbert McCready misled Alex by telling him, "You haven't been identified, so you can go."

Leo Gauthier was there on Sunday, January 22, too. He and Jack Shea were also being looked at by two victims of the $100 robbery of the Dominion Shoe Repair, at 467 Queen Street East, Toronto, which happened four days before, on the early evening of Wednesday, January 18. The Toronto Police had obtained three search warrants that morning and made simultaneous raids on the living quarters, not only of Alex MacDonald, but of Gauthier and Gallow as well. One consequence was that Mickey was not the only rounder in the identification parade who was worried about Jack Shea. Alex, Gallow, and Gauthier were all thinking similarly, Leo with somewhat less to lose than the others.

CHAPTER SIX

Jack Shea and the Port Credit Bank Robbery
(December 9, 1938–January 21, 1939)

ON FRIDAY, DECEMBER 9, 1938, a month before the Windsor Murder, Jack Shea, as he would later testify, was one of three gunmen who robbed the Canadian Bank of Commerce in the Village of Port Credit, 12 miles west of Toronto, of $2,732.48. This violent crime, which for nearly a year afterwards was routinely referred to in the Toronto-area press as "the Port Credit bank robbery," was absolutely essential to the charge of murder in the death of James Albert Windsor being preferred against Mickey McDonald and his brother, Alex MacDonald, and, similarly, essential to the eventual disposition of that charge against Mickey. For nearly a year, the two prosecutions — the murder and the bank robbery — were anything but mutually exclusive in the eyes of the Attorney General of Ontario, the Crown Attorneys of York and Peel Counties, the Ontario Provincial Police, the Toronto Police, the Port Credit Police, the attorneys for all of the defendants in the two criminal cases, the defendants themselves, the Toronto and area press, and the interested public.

The son of a Montreal policeman and a well-spoken former student at McGill University, John Roderick Shea was a strange duck to be mixed up with the likes of Mickey McDonald and Leo Gauthier. At different times, Shea claimed to be a chartered accountant and a stock broker who had been worth $90,000 before the Crash of 1929 — and he was believed by some to be both. An OPP wanted circular, dated December 31, 1938, described John Roderick Shea, aged 36, as a man of slim build, about 6 feet tall, weighing 165 pounds, having a thin face, a dark complexion, blue eyes, and "a very pleasant and talkative manner." He was also said to be a thief who "drinks, bets horses, and is a ladies man."[1]

In 1930, Jack Shea was convicted of forgery, and uttering and false pretenses at Winnipeg, Manitoba, and sentenced to two years in Stony Mountain Penitentiary. Four years later, in February 1934, Shea was one of a gang of shopbreakers who made off with 160 parcels of silk, valued at $10,000, the property of the Canadian Celanese Company, at 106 Spadina Avenue, Toronto. The thieves broke through a brick wall at night and loaded the silk onto a rented livery truck. On his way to Montreal with the stolen goods, Shea skidded the truck into a ditch on an icy Highway 2, near Cardinal, Ontario, and was arrested later in Toronto.

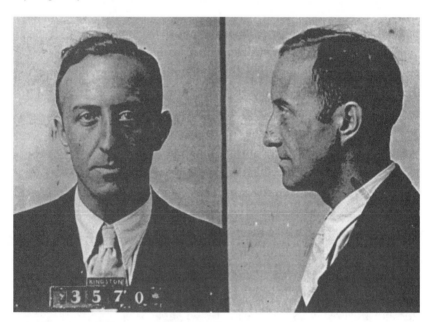

John R. "Jack" Shea, as he looked on October 13, 1934. One of the Port Credit bank robbers of December 9, 1938, Shea would testify against his partners in that crime as well as against Mickey and Alex MacDonald for the murder of Jimmy Windsor. (Library and Archives Canada)

The others involved were not caught and were never certainly identified.[2] On September 29, 1934, a jury convicted Shea of shopbreaking and, three days later, he was sentenced by a County Court judge to five years in Kingston Penitentiary. While awaiting his day in court, Shea cunningly broke out of the Don Jail and was chased through the Don Flats, and along a residential street east of the Don Valley.[3] He was found hiding in the yard of Withrow Public School. His twenty minutes of freedom cost a year in the lockup, concurrent with the shopbreaking sentence.

Any competent bank robber knows that the robbery is the easy part and the getaway is the hard part. The Port Credit robbers botched the robbery, almost committing murder, and planned their getaway so poorly that, 90 minutes after the stickup, Shea was certain to be going back to prison as a consequence. Another of the three talked about the robbery — and to the wrong person. Inexperience, financial desperation, alcohol, and stupidity foiled them, though Jack Shea and Alex MacDonald were certainly bright men, and Shea and Gauthier were experienced criminals.

In the days before the robbery took place, Mickey and Leo Gauthier were both seen in and around Shea's rooming house at 48 Twenty-Ninth Street in the Village of Long Branch, and in the beverage room of a nearby hotel, where the three were sufficiently apparent that a sharp-witted bookmaker, who operated from there, was later able to finger them as the bank robbers to the police. Shea, Mickey, and Gauthier were supposed to work "the score," but Mickey went on a drinking spree instead. Teenaged Alex MacDonald, who barely knew the other ex-convicts, went to a beer parlour with them and asked in on "the job." After four months of operating Pop's Lunch, a Parkdale food counter and delivery service that his father had bought for him, Alex was tired of working for a living. He wanted to go out to British Columbia and figured "easy money" was the way to get there. Alex had already served a reformatory term for possession of burglary tools and another for riotous destruction of property while an inmate of the Guelph Reformatory.

About 11:40 a.m. that bleak Friday, the three robbers, all wearing coveralls, peaked caps, and cotton gloves, strutted into the Port Credit Bank of Commerce and pulled revolvers.

"All right, this is a holdup. Get down on the floor, all of you," Gauthier barked.

Accountant Ray Bryant, furthest from the door, did not properly hear the instruction and made an unlucky move to fetch a book from his desk.

One of the robbers promptly shot him.

Hit in the right arm above the elbow, the accountant did not immediately fall, but blood was soon gushing through a quarter-sized hole in his arm, colouring his suit coat red.

"Stop shooting," Jack Shea shouted, in fear of worse, his face visibly creased with anger and frustration.

After this, the gunmen — all unmasked — settled in to work and, using all manner of threats and foul language, forced four staff and one lady customer, who came in after the robbery was in progress, to lie facedown on the floor. Then Shea athletically jumped the bank's counter and ransacked the teller's cage, stuffing bills and change into the deep pockets of his coveralls.

One of the thieves spotted a man outside in a truck, who seemed too interested in what was going on inside, so after Gauthier refused to do it, Shea went out and brought the watcher into the bank at gunpoint. He was forced to lie face-down on the floor with the others by a gunman with "a snarly voice" — Gauthier — who threatened to kill him if he did not do as he was told.

Then the bandits turned their attention to the vault.

"Open that safe in a hurry or I'll put a bullet through your head," one of the robbers now menaced the wounded accountant.

Bryant, seeping blood, got up from the floor and did his best to meet the demand. He worked the half of the combination he knew with trembling fingers before managing to get it across to the robber who had a gun in his ribs — Shea — that the other half was known only by Norman Thacker, the bank's teller. Thacker was brought to the vault in the same manner and made to open its door.

Meantime, in the customer area, Leo Gauthier — "the short man" — ushered two more patrons into the bank and, on pain of instant death, got them to lie down, faces to the floor. Alex watched the bank's front entrance.

In a minute or two, Jack Shea had gathered up what money he found in the vault, not knowing there was $4,000 in a drawer he might have opened, but didn't. The three thieves then left the bank in what seemed no particular hurry.

Outside, there were by then 30 or 40 people on the street, all or most of whom had already gathered that a robbery had taken place inside the Bank of Commerce.

The robbers briskly crossed the Lakeshore Road and went down a side street where, incredibly, they got into a pea-green light delivery truck with the words "Rogers-Deforest-Crosley-Majestic Radio" written on its side, and with two large loudspeakers on its top. A citizen took the license plate number of this preposterous getaway vehicle, which, it was shortly learned, was registered to Damon Stannah, the proprietor of Stannah's Radio Store in Long Branch.

The police soon found out from Stannah that the usual driver of the truck was "J. Roddy Shea," a salesman, radio repairman, and deliveryman, whom Stannah had hired earlier that year and whose pleasing manner and all-around ability he was quite impressed with. Stannah had considered making Shea the manager of the store but hesitated because three appliances Shea had sold had been paid for with worthless cheques totalling $450. He did not know that Shea had been released from Kingston Penitentiary on February 14, 1938, or that he was a convicted confidence man, cheque passer, shopbreaker, and jailbreaker. Nor did he know that Shea had been selling other radios and refrigerators for cash, then creating bogus paperwork that said the goods would be paid for "on time." The truth was that Shea's legitimate talents could not keep pace with his liking for fine whisky, fast women, and slow horses. The reason he had organized the bank robbery was that his scheme at the store was collapsing. It had reached the point where impending sales of electric goods for cash could not make all of the bogus time payments. He needed more money than he was earning and stealing at Stannah's store — and he had to have it right away or he would be found out.

The green truck went west on the Lakeshore Highway, then north on Mississauga Road, where it was seen travelling at high speed. Somehow the robbers cut back east into the west end of Toronto, where most of the artifacts and clothing used in "the job" were dumped in an industrial lot in south Parkdale. After a fast split of the swag, Shea's accomplices were dropped off not far from there and found their own ways home.

Shea, still driving Stannah's truck, then went 4 or 5 miles west to 48 Twenty-Ninth Street, Long Branch, the rooming house where he lived. There he learned the police had already been looking for him. He knew then that the truck had been "made" — identified — and it would not be long before the police would be back knowing enough to suspect him of being much more than the victim of the theft of a vehicle. Shea quickly packed a bag and prevailed upon a casual friend to drive him into Toronto. Later that day he answered a classified ad for a rented room at 72 Gloucester Street, close by the city's downtown. About 3 p.m., the police found Stannah's truck on Twenty-Ninth Street. They had missed catching Jack Shea by an hour or more.

But far worse had already happened.

About 2:30 p.m., less than three hours after the robbery, a well-practised police informant had telephoned Constable Alex S. Wilson, at Ontario Provincial Police (OPP) headquarters at Queen's Park, Toronto, claiming to know the identities of the three Port Credit bank robbers. Jack Shea and the MacDonalds perhaps never knew that the initial stool pigeon in the chain of events that would follow was Marjorie Constable, Leo Gauthier's girlfriend of less than three weeks, whom OPP Inspector George MacKay years later would describe as "a good-looking woman from the Bruce Peninsula who slept with the crooks then gave information to the police about them."[4] Gauthier, "the short man" at Port Credit, who, as Shea would later say, was quite drunk after the robbery, was untoward enough to have allowed his prostitute-girlfriend in on what ought to have been a professional secret. The eventual cost to Leo would be a 10-year sentence behind the grey limestone walls of Kingston Penitentiary. He was lucky that was all it was.

A half hour after the phone call, Wilson brought Miss Constable to Chief Inspector A.B. Boyd's office, where she named Jack Shea, Leo Gauthier, and Alex MacDonald, as the three Port Credit robbers, and Alex as the quick-shooting gunman who wounded the accountant. Shea would later testify in a Brampton courtroom that Gauthier, not Alex, shot Bryant. The accountant did not know who shot him.

Notified by Shea that too much was already known at Long Branch, Gauthier vacated Marje Constable's apartment in favour of an apartment on Lippincott Street. That meant the police, who obtained warrants for the arrest of the three perpetrators that same evening, could only immediately lay their hands on Alex, who resided at his parents' home on Poplar Plains Road. They chose to wait on Alex's arrest until Marje reconnected with Gauthier again.

A week later, Miss Constable — hungry for the Canadian Bankers' Association's long-standing reward of up to $5,000 for information leading to the arrest and conviction of any person or persons responsible for the robbery of any bank in Canada — again contacted P.C. Wilson, this time with information concerning Leo Gauthier's whereabouts. At 7:20 that evening, by pre-arrangement with Marje, a combined squad of OPP and Toronto detectives arrested Gauthier at a table in May's Restaurant

Arrested for the Port Credit bank robbery on the information of his girlfriend, Marjorie Constable, Leo Gauthier would be convicted and sentenced to 10 years in Kingston. (Library and Archives Canada)

at 404 College Street, where Leo had unsuspectingly kept a dinner date with his devious lady friend. At the same time, a similarly-constructed squad of police, including Port Credit Chief Telfer Wilson, arrested Alex MacDonald at his parents' home.

The two robbery suspects were taken to the detective offices at Toronto police headquarters, searched, separately interrogated, and placed in a line-up, where both were viewed by five eyewitnesses to the Port Credit bank robbery. The identification parade produced one positive identification of Alex MacDonald as having been seen walking outside the bank on December 9, and one tentative identification of Leo Gauthier as one of the men inside the bank. Peel County Crown Attorney A.G. Davis later characterized the identification evidence against the robbers as "weak." Still, the two were charged with the crime. On December 22, a Brampton police magistrate remanded them and set bail at $7,500 for both. Alex made bail the next day. Gauthier got out on December 29.

Alex MacDonald, Mickey's 19-year-old brother, took his older brother's place in the Port Credit bank robbery. He would be charged with that crime and with the murder of Jimmy Windsor as well. (Library and Archives)

* * *

On the afternoon of December 30, 1938, at Gauthier's request, Mickey McDonald met Jack Shea by appointment in a west end tavern. For three weeks, Shea had been laying low in the Gloucester Street room and, alternately, in a furnished apartment on Westmount Avenue, near Dufferin Street and St. Clair Avenue West. As a trusted ally, Mickey was asked to help Shea move to a more convenient location and, afterwards, to run errands for Shea, who, for obvious reasons, did not wish to walk the streets more than he had to. About 6:30 p.m., the pair answered a newspaper ad for a two-room furnished apartment over a grocery store at 209A Ossington Avenue. Shea introduced himself to Mrs. Caldare, the landlady, as "Dave Turner." He said he was a railway inspector who was at times required to go out at night but rarely in the daytime. Mickey was introduced as "Clarke McCabe," a friend. The rent was $6.25 a week.

Later, Mickey's and Shea's remembrances of what happened in the 12 days between Shea's rental of the apartment and January 10, 1939, when Mickey was required to give himself up to face the charge of robbery with violence, would diverge sharply. There was agreement about the events of December 30, and agreement that, beginning late on the night of Tuesday, January 3, they both joined with Leo Gauthier on a train trip to Ottawa, where whatever they went there for turned into a drunken revel with two women who Mickey and Shea picked up in a Hull nightclub. Later, Jack Shea would testify that the real purpose of the Ottawa trip was to rob a bank and that Mickey badly needed $50 as an advance for his lawyer, Frank Regan, who had threatened not to be in court on January 10 unless the money was paid. Though they didn't use the word, Mickey and Gauthier essentially told in court that the true purpose of the Ottawa misadventure was "tourism." No bank was robbed, and Gauthier had to wire his father for enough money to get the entire group back to Toronto. They went and came back in less than three days, arriving home on the morning of Friday, January 6, poorer than before they went. Supposedly, Mickey still needed the all-important $50. The Windsor Murder happened 30 hours later.

Clearly, from what Shea and Mickey were afterwards able to agree on, Mickey was extraordinarily indiscreet with regard to Shea's secret whereabouts. He brought several drinking friends to the apartment, none of whom, from a criminal perspective, ought to have been taken there. Gauthier was one thing, but, in the week between January 3 and January 10, Mickey also took to 209A Ossington Avenue Cecil "Doc" Clancy, a middle-aged bookmaker, who was a long-time boozing companion of his own; Teddy Wells, a twice-convicted safecracker who often tippled with Mickey and Clancy; and Joe Smith, an alcoholic gofer, who liked to hang around with criminals. To all of these, Mickey introduced Shea as "Dave Turner." Clancy, for certain, knew better, as he had had prior contact with Jack Shea that Mickey did not know about, and he knew Shea was wanted for bank robbery. Mickey later testified that Shea took him into the apartment's back room and asked, "Why did you bring that drunk here? He might talk." Mickey said, though he couldn't hear it, Clancy had Shea's concern figured out, but, for obvious reasons, said nothing. According to Mickey, though both were by then badly befogged by drink, he and Clancy left shortly after for The Corner by taxi.[5]

On the morning of Friday, January 6, Mickey and Gauthier met Marjorie Constable not far from her stroll. All three went to 225 Sherbourne Street, near Dundas, where Leo and Marje rented another apartment. By the next evening, Marje had three broken ribs, such that Leo had to take her to the Toronto General Hospital, from where he managed to make three verifiable telephone calls roughly coincident with the time of the deadly incident at 247 Briar Hill Avenue. The telephone calls were Leo's very-convenient alibi.

Whatever the story was at the time, it seems likely that Leo had Marje figured out and gave her a beating. Then, by design, he gave the appearance of forgiving her or of pretending to believe that he was wrong. The romance was on again. A criminal acquaintance of Mickey's, interviewed years later, got it right when he said, "Leo would have suppressed her guilt for the sake of his own good health."[6] The same, obviously, could be said for Marje. In their league, staying together, notwithstanding their mutual grievances, made sense. They both had to keep on breathing.

Yet Leo was the alcoholic flannel mouth that he was and, so, inevitably, Miss Constable made her third contact with P.C. Alex Wilson, by telephone, on the evening of Friday, January 20. By then Marje knew the address of Jack Shea's hideout, that two revolvers were stashed in a buffet in the apartment and, supposedly, that Shea, Gauthier, and Alex MacDonald were planning to pull off another "score" over that weekend. P.C. Wilson immediately gave the information to the Toronto Police, who raided Shea's apartment at 9 o'clock the following morning. A five-man squad of detectives, led by Detective-Sergeant John Hicks, managed to catch Shea sound asleep in bed and arrested him without incident. The early edition of that Saturday afternoon's *Evening Telegram* flashed the banner: ARREST MAN FOR PORT CREDIT BANK HOLDUP. The officers had found two fully-loaded revolvers, a .32- and a .38-calibre, in the buffet. The police did not then, or ever, find the weapon that killed James Windsor — said by an expert witness at trial to have most likely been a Webley .455-calibre revolver.[7]

P.C. Wilson's memorandum of these events, addressed to Chief Inspector Boyd and clock-dated Saturday, January 21, 10:30 a.m., ended with a pregnant sentence: "There is some suggestion that Shea may have been mixed up in the Windsor Murder of the 7th."[8]

Now where might P.C. Wilson have got an idea like that? And who might have had her eyes on the $2,000 reward for the murderers of James Windsor?

CHAPTER SEVEN

Jack Shea's Tale
(January 21, 1939, and after)

BECAUSE THE EYEWITNESSES TO the murder of James Windsor had indicated some of the killers, including the actual shooter, were Italians, Detective-Sergeants William McAllister and Frank Crowe, who were initially in charge of the investigation, naturally focused on suspects of Italian origin.[1] They soon learned that, in the months before his death, Windsor had been having worrisome trouble with a gang of 8 or 10 Italian men, some as old as 37, who were frequenters of the Windsor Bar-B-Q on North Yonge Street. The elite of this crowd were known criminals, who possessed records for such offences as possession of heroin for the purpose of trafficking, armed robbery, and theft. After his son's funeral, Albert Windsor of 453 McNab Street North, Hamilton, had a lot to say about this same faction, who he thought to be the murderers of his son:

> ... This bunch that started to hang around there got the idea they were running the place. If someone did something they didn't like, they would gang him. They just seemed to move in on Jimmy. They were making

his place a headquarters and because they said they
were keeping order they wanted money.[2]

"Jimmy was worried about it," Jack Windsor, the victim's stepbrother
agreed — and he said, too, that Jimmy had concern over what would
happen to him if he tried to get rid of them. He tried, instead, to manage
them with make-believe friendliness and small favours and preferments.
"They kept after him for money all the time," said Jack Windsor.[3]

On December 29, 1938, Frank Pallante, a part of this risky crowd,
had been one of three who went to 247 Briar Hill Avenue and solic-
ited Windsor for a contribution to Johnny "The Bug" Brown's "Defence
Fund." As a bookmaker himself, Windsor had little sympathy for those
who were known to extort bookies, but what could he do? This gang
from the barbecue were casual associates of Brown, a known gunman
for whom no less a figure than Rocco Perri had once posted $3,000 bail.
Windsor handed over only $10 for The Bug's fund — and the solicitors
of the cause were later said to be unhappy with that. Their supposed
buddy, who decorated himself in diamonds, gave them, instead of the
fat contribution they expected, handbills that advertised the New Year's
party at the Windsor Bar-B-Q.

A problem for the detectives following this line of investigation was
that the Windsor household unanimously absolved these suspects of
being the perpetrators of the crime. None of the gang from the Bar-B-Q
were among the killers, they all said, both before and after viewing them
in a line-up.

At the same time, the publication of Frank Pallante's name as
having been picked up the day after Windsor's death brought a small
flood of whispered information from bookies and gamblers in west
end Toronto. Most or all of these were saying that the same four men
were actively extorting bookmakers and gaming operators in that part
of the city. On February 17, 1939, Louis Spizziri, Louis Spadafina,
Armando Cosen, and Frank Pallante — all frequenters of the Windsor
Bar-B-Q — appeared at a preliminary hearing in a packed Toronto
Police Court charged with "demand money with menaces" — extortion.[4] Cornelius Sheehan, a longtime dice- and card-game operator,

testified against the four under the pseudonym "Mr. X," and they were all sent to trial. But on their subsequent day in County Court, June 13, 1939, Judge Daniel O'Connell declared the evidence against the four accused to be "most unsatisfactory" and acquitted them all without requiring a defence. In the interim Donald and Alex MacDonald had been charged with, and tried for, the murder of James Windsor — which meant the $2,000 reward for the murderers was no longer on offer. That had helped end whatever impulse there was among the west end gambling set to testify against the four extortion suspects, either as murderers or as extortionists.

The important effect of this first suspicion of the killers as being Italians was that it provided the defence in the murder trial with its necessary alternate theory of the murder. The eyewitnesses had at first described the murderers as dark-complexioned Italians, not pale-skinned Scots. Then the same five witnesses had switched to fingering the MacDonald brothers, Mickey and Alex. Why? the defence would want to know. How was it reasonably possible for them to make such a mistake in their initial identifications, then afterwards switch to being so definite about an apparently contradictory truth?

Jack Shea's arrest on Saturday, January 21, had changed the focus of the murder investigation. Long before being caught, Shea had surely made up his mind that he had to cut "a deal" to sell Mickey, and the others he was criminally involved with, both for the Windsor Murder and the Port Credit bank robbery. As a three-time loser, Shea was facing too many years "inside" for the bank heist and the shooting of the bank's accountant and, as he would later testify, he feared being implicated in the murder by reason of Mickey's loose mouth. He saw a way out for himself at what was meant to be great cost to Mickey, Alex, Louis Gallow and, to a lesser extent, Leo Gauthier.

An OPP report, clock-dated 4:30 p.m. on the day of Shea's arrest, states, "After questioning by Insp. Lougheed, Shea made a statement admitting his part in the bank robbery." Lougheed's own report, for whatever reason, is not available.[5]

On the evening of the same day, January 21, Shea requested an interview with Detective-Sergeant John Hicks and Detective John Nimmo, two of those who had arrested him that morning. Upon their arrival at the Claremont Street Station, where Shea was then being held, as Alex McCathie's later case synopsis states:

> ... Shea immediately informed them that the two revolvers which had been found in his room were two of the three revolvers that were used in the murder of James Windsor, and that the actual murderer of James Windsor was Donald (Mickey) McDonald, and that his companions in the crime were his brother, Alex McDonald (sic) and Louis Gallow....[6]

What Shea wanted, as future events would indicate, was "a wash" — total immunity — on both the Port Credit bank robbery charge and any charges against himself that might arise out of the murder of Windsor. In return, he would explain to the police how and why the murder happened, name others who had information that would help convict the men involved, and he would testify against those he named as the murderers as well as his accomplices in the Port Credit bank holdup. Such an agreement would, of course, never be made public, or even its existence acknowledged, by the authorities — but that is what it came to be, if, indeed, it was not exactly the proposition Shea put to the police on the evening of Saturday, January 21, 1939.

Fifty years later, Gwyn "Jocko" Thomas, *The Daily Star's* junior police reporter at the time, recounted a mildly different version of what he was then told of Shea's bargain with those in authority:

> A senior detective had told me that Mickey's brother, Alex MacDonald, and a man named John Shea had been charged with bank robbery ... Shea had then approached the police and offered to tell them what had happened to Jimmy Windsor if the robbery charge was dropped. A deal was made, and Shea told how he, Mickey, Alex and a Louis Gallo (sic) had gone to Windsor's house to rob him. Only Alex and Mickey, who was very drunk,

were armed, and Mickey shot Windsor for speaking to
him sarcastically.[7]

If the murder happened as understood by Gwyn Thomas, Shea
needed more than a bank robbery charge dropped: he needed the authorities to somehow overlook his participation in the murder. If he really
went to Windsor's home with the other three, Shea had formed a common
intention with them to commit a felony and, under Section 69-2 of *The
Criminal Code of Canada*, was as guilty of murder as the actual killer and,
thus, stood to be hanged, as did all of the others involved.[8]

Shea did not have to be as clever as he was to know how badly the
Toronto Police needed to clear up the Windsor case and, as a bright,
experienced criminal, he ought to have known that he needed a lawyer
to protect his interests in the deal he was trying to make. He may have
understood too that, ultimately, the only person who could say Yes or
No to such an arrangement was Gordon Conant, the attorney general
of Ontario. Later, when he was several times queried about a deal with
Shea, Conant answered by refusing to comment on the case at all. Cecil
L. Snyder, the special prosecutor who would press the murder indictment against the MacDonalds, when asked, always flatly denied any such
agreement existed. Any admission of "a deal" would, of course, serve to
greatly weaken Shea's value as a witness. Thus, if Shea was at Windsor's
house at the time of the murder, it was imperative for Shea to deny that he
was there and it was similarly imperative for Shea to deny there was any
agreement that would allow him to go free in return for his testimony.

Shea likely understood this before he spoke to the police. He had,
or would soon have, a believable story to tell in the witness box and, if
it was true that he was, in fact, at the Briar Hill house at the time of the
murder, then the story he would tell in court, which did not acknowledge his presence there, was simply a pretextual story that nicely tied
the MacDonalds to the murder and, at the same time, gave an account
of how he knew they were responsible for the crime. Shea's version of
their guilt, true or not, did not disqualify him as a usable witness and it
in no way risked any subsequent prosecution of himself for the murder.
Very importantly, too, Shea supplied a motive for Mickey's part in the

crime. The killing of Jimmy Windsor, as Shea divulged it to the police, was nothing more complicated than a botched armed robbery. Mickey's impelling motive was the $50 he badly needed as an advance for his lawyer, Frank Regan, who, so Mickey had supposedly been told, would not have been in court for him on January 10, on the charge of robbery with violence on James Elder, Lefty Thomas's Church Street bootlegger.

On the afternoon of Monday, January 23, Shea was removed to the Peel County Jail at Brampton, where he was set up for most of the ensuing 10 months as the Windsor case's eponymous stool pigeon. Detectives went there to question him many times. He gave them a lengthy statement, signed and later back-dated to January 23, 1939, in which the critical part of his tale had the MacDonald brothers coming back to his Ossington Avenue apartment soon after the murder, whereupon, almost as he came through the door, Mickey blurted out the startling admission, "I have just killed a man," without ever saying the victim's name. There followed, as Shea would later testify several times, an oddly foolish argument between Mickey and Alex, in which the MacDonalds unnecessarily shared a lot of dangerous information with Shea and with Cecil Clancy, who Shea informed the police was present at the time and, though very drunk, had also heard, and understood, Mickey's confession of murder. Shea would tell this story, real or imagined, in public for the first time, in Toronto Police Court on March 10, 1939, the first day of a preliminary hearing that would be "the longest in the history of the court."[9]

Shea's credibility, the Crown and the detectives knew, would be a major issue at the subsequent murder trial. The investigators had to scrupulously check his story in great detail, to make certain it was substantially true and would hold up in court. Shea had an extensive criminal record and, most importantly, he was facing serious charges in connection with the Port Credit bank robbery and, possibly in connection with the Dominion Shoe Repair robbery in Toronto. He had not been tried or sentenced on either charge — and, because of this, had an obvious self-interested motive to seek favour with the Crown by way of his testimony in the Windsor case. The Crown knew that a jury would be asked to consider whether Jack Shea was purposely lying Mickey and Alex into a hangman's noose in order to get consideration for himself in connection with the robbery charges, and, further, as would also be more than suggested at trial, in order to get free of the consequences of his own likely involvement in the murder. Shea would deny all of this, of course, and, when his time came to tell his tale in court, he would perform nearly as well as any well-practised con artist might have.

One has to wonder about Shea's story. That a career criminal, even a witless one, would make such an unnecessary admission, virtually as a form of gossip, to another — especially to another whom he knew was wanted on a major "beef" — seems almost to exceed the known limits of criminal stupidity. What could have been Mickey's purpose in sharing such information except to put a noose around his own neck and that of his teenaged brother? Certainly, Mickey was an erratic and talkative professional thief at times — but could he have been this unwise? Did this really happen? Jack Shea said it did and, eventually, Cecil Clancy, who supposedly had only listened and tried not to appear to hear, said so too. As a police document attests, when, 26 days after the murder and 12 days after Shea "rolled over" on Mickey and the others, detectives, in need of corroboration of Shea's story, first questioned Clancy, they found the bookmaker in a state of great fear over what he later testified he had overheard. With real reason, Clancy, who was certainly criminal-minded enough to understand the danger, was said by the police to be palpably afraid that Alex MacDonald, who was then at large on bail, might take "serious steps" to insure his silence forever.[10] It seems odd that Shea and Clancy — who barely knew each other — decided to take a car trip to Clancy's cousin's Read, Ontario, farm, two days after the murder, ostensibly "to get off the liquor," and that this happened immediately after an arranged meeting with Mickey at the Duke of York Tavern in the east end of Toronto. If nothing extraordinary had taken place, would it not have been unusual, or at least odd timing, for these two virtual strangers to go off together in such a fashion?[11]

CHAPTER EIGHT

Toronto's First Gangland Murderer
(January 22, 1939–March 15, 1939)

AFTER HIS CONVICTION FOR robbery with violence, Mickey signed the waiver that relinquished his right of appeal then waited to be removed to Kingston Penitentiary. Day after day, he sat playing bridge in the corridor outside his cell in the Don Jail, but nothing happened. Cullinan, Constantino, and Epter all went. Johnny Brown, who stayed, faced further charges in Toronto and Hamilton, including armed robbery, shopbreaking, and escape custody. After the line-up of January 22, Mickey began to hear stories that the police were grilling criminal associates about the Windsor Murder — and questions with his name on them were coming up at the back end of these conversations. Mickey knew what this meant. He was the real suspect and there was "a squawker" — and he already thought he knew who this must be.[1] How many other friends and criminal allies had been frightened or bribed into turning stool pigeon? he surely asked himself. The police then began grilling Mickey himself — all day, every day, for two weeks, as his mother later complained in the press.[2] True to his own persecution complex, Mickey started making noise in the jail that the police were going to charge him with the murder — shouting that it was all a "frame-up" by the cops.

On February 23, 1939, more than a month after Jack Shea had sold his criminal friends to the police, Sergeant of Detectives Herbert McCready, now with Detective-Sergeant Alex McCathie in charge of the Windsor investigation, formally charged Donald and Alex MacDonald with the murder. Louis Gallow was not charged, since he had not been identified by any of the five eyewitnesses at the line-up and, otherwise, there was only Jack Shea's hearsay story of Gallow's supposed involvement in the killing.

Alex MacDonald, aged 19, on his way to City Hall and Toronto Police Court on February 24, 1939. (York University Libraries, Clara Thomas Archives and Special Collections, *Toronto Telegram* fonds, ASCO7404

That evening Alexander MacDonald Sr., near his end as a working blacksmith and less than four years from the last breath of a hard life, was brought to No. 12 Station at Yonge Street and Montgomery Avenue on Herbert McCready's order. Old MacDonald broke down weeping at the situation he was faced with. McCready wanted him to prevail upon his son, Alex, to tell "the truth" about what happened on the night of the murder against the advice of his lawyer, Isadore Levinter, who had advised Alex to say nothing.[3]

The next morning, Friday, February 24, 1939, The *Globe and Mail*, first Toronto paper on the street, wore the streamer: TWO BROTHERS HELD IN BOOKIE'S SLAYING. The heading over the lead story was "Mickey McDonald Named By Police as 'Trigger Man.'" Later in the day, the *Daily Star* and the *Evening Telegram* had the arrest of the brothers as their black-lines, but their front-page stories led off with news of a disturbance Mickey had created that morning in Toronto Police Court. So it was that Donald "Mickey" McDonald, alcoholic, recidivist criminal and well-known frequenter of The Corner, came to be what Toronto and a good part of the rest of Canada then thought to be "Toronto's first Gangland murderer." That perception would last even after Jack Shea first told his story on the witness stand, whereupon Mickey might have become in the public eye only a dangerous armed robber who had tried to work "a score" that he was too drunk or too incompetent to handle.

After this, there followed nine months of prominently-displayed news stories, unremittingly full of the Windsor Murder and of the names of Alexander and Margaret MacDonald's sons, Donald especially.[4] This was so even as World War II impended, even as King George VI and his Queen Elizabeth visited Toronto, in what was part of reigning British Royalty's first-ever sojourn in Canada, and even after Toronto had adapted to living with the war in Europe on a daily basis. During this time, beginning with his arrest for murder on February 23, 1939, Mickey — dirty little Mickey from The Corner — became nothing less than one of Canada's best-known contemporary crime figures. His reputation as such would hold up for almost 20 years.

Every seat in Toronto City Hall's "A" Police Court was filled at 11 a.m., Friday, March 10, when His Worship Robert J. Browne, a grim-faced former policeman, went to the Bench. An air of quiet expectancy hung over the packed courtroom. Inevitably, as on other days of the four-day hearing, this near silence was broken by the sound of clanking steel from down below, a sound that grew louder as Mickey and Alex, in leg irons and handcuffs, were brought upstairs from the basement cells and into the courtroom. With the chained-up brothers came a flock of hovering sheriff's officers, detectives, and uniformed policemen, to augment those of the same who were already in the room. This too would be part of the ritual each day of the hearing. Outside in the hall thronged many dozens of thrill-seeking gawkers who had failed to get into the courtroom. These had to be content with passing glimpses of the accused men, who were now, of course, made most noteworthy by their being in grave danger of being hanged.

Mickey was represented by Frank Regan, the professional thief's deeply-committed friend. Mr. Regan was an advocate who believed, to the core of his being, that every person — a penniless, recidivist criminal, no matter — was entitled to a fair hearing. A lawyer of not inconsiderable ability, Regan resided for years in lawyerly penury at the Royal Cecil Hotel — Toronto's notorious "Bucket of Blood" — on the northwest corner of The Corner.[5] A lifelong bachelor and a devout Roman Catholic, he literally chose to live among the kind he represented — and he often did not get paid. In July 1933, he put in 17 days for Mickey McDonald at his Kingston trial for riotous destruction of property and, as he later said, never saw a penny for his work or his expenses. Jack Shea, in September 1934, at the end of his trial for shopbreaking, made a flowery speech wherein he eschewed crime forever and gratefully thanked "Mr. Regan" for defending him for nothing. By late 1938, Regan was telling the likes of Mickey and Johnny "The Bug" Brown that he wanted money "up front," or he would not be there. But he was always there, because in his quirky mind the judicial process was so badly stacked against his kind of client that, as Mickey had boldly shouted out at his arraignment, "There is no justice! We can't get justice here!"[6]

In law and order circles, Frank Regan was the perceived author of the Albert Dorland Affair, one of the worst scandals in Toronto Police history — a scandal that ended the career of Inspector of Detectives Alex

J. Murray. In the minds of some, the accusation "frame-up" hung over Regan like a dead baby, his famous advocacy of the cause of Dorland being what friends and foes alike saw as his defining effort. The issue was whether or not Dorland had been entrapped by a police informer into an armed robbery so that he could be, and was, shipped off to Kingston for 5 years. Armed with an affidavit signed by William Toohey, Dorland's former partner-in-crime and the alleged police agent, Regan remade Dorland, a gunman and career criminal, into "Canada's most famous wronged man."[7] A subsequent judicial inquiry saw the Toronto Police made out to be untruthful — "liars," in Gwyn Thomas's phrase — after which, if not before, the police and much of the judiciary saw Regan as an outright cop-hating "troublemaker."

Moreover, judges disliked Mr. Regan's courtroom style, a lengthening element to any court proceeding he was involved in. He would expend enormous amounts of a court's time, often in order to score niggling points of minor significance. Left alone, he would go back over the same ground again and again. In cross-examination, instead of asking questions of witnesses, he often gave lengthy speeches with a question at the end — in effect, giving evidence himself. He was forever jumping to his feet in court with yet another unlooked-for objection or motion. At times, he would phrase questions in an outrageous manner, or he would roar at witnesses as a form of emphasis, or he would too aggressively accuse witnesses of despicable motives, or of making things up, or of having poor morals. At times, he would create, or try to create, issues that were outside the scope of the matter at hand. Yet, a contemporary estimate of Frank Regan in a courtroom gave him credit for "an enormous capacity for assimilation of detail, a marvellous memory, as well as dogged persistence, and an utter indifference to the attitude of those about him."[8] All of this was fair enough, but none of it helped to actuate the process or did anything to endear Mickey's legal representative to the judges and magistrates before whom he appeared.

Alex MacDonald's attorney was much less painful. Isadore Levinter was a prominent civil litigator whose only career foray into criminal law would be his defence of Alex for murder. Possessed of a sharp mind and a good knowledge of the law, Mr. Levinter's involvement had come as a result of a friend's recommendation of a "nice young man" who, as the proprietor of Pop's Lunch, delivered food to his Parkdale business.

Three of the four days of the preliminary, seated in the same seats each day, were four of the brothers' main supporters: Mickey's attractive and unfailingly well-turned-out wife, Margaret; Florence MacDonald, pretty, dark-eyed, sixteen-year-old sister of the brothers, who, like Kitty, usually wore a fur jacket in court; Brigadier Elias Owen of the Salvation Army; and, if anyone would believe it, Marjorie Constable, described in the press as "a friend of the family." Alexander MacDonald Sr., who was needed at his work, was in court some days and not others. Kitty was most often noticed by *The Daily Star*, which, on March 10, typically reported, "Her smart ensemble, pert hat and blonde hair, made her the target of all eyes."

"Call John R. Shea," the court crier cried.

A kind of faint smile played on Mickey's mouth as his former friend and associate-in-crime, whom the press termed "a surprise witness," was sworn. Neither Mickey or Alex would make any complaint or sound while Shea's story unfolded over two hours or more.

Shea gave his evidence, in response to the questions of York County Crown Attorney James McFadden. He told of his criminal past, of his being charged with the Port Credit bank robbery, and of Mickey's going with him to rent the Ossington Avenue apartment on December 30. He said that the next evening, New Year's Eve, 1938, Mickey brought two revolvers — a .45- and a .38-calibre — to be stored in his dining-room buffet for use in a previously-discussed bank robbery at Ottawa. He told of Mickey drunkenly loading both of the guns in his front room on the afternoon of Tuesday, January 3, in the sight of Leo Gauthier, Joe Smith, and himself, and of the concern this caused among those who were there, Gauthier in particular. Which, as Shea related, meant nothing to Mickey, who persisted in loading the revolvers anyway. He also described the futile trip to Ottawa to rob a bank that began late that same night.[9]

Then Shea's testimony got to the evening of James Windsor's murder. He said that, about 6 p.m. on the night of Saturday, January 7, the two MacDonalds unexpectedly arrived at 209A Ossington with a very drunk

Cecil Clancy and, soon after, Mickey and Alex — both armed — went out "to do a job," leaving the little bookie behind at the apartment. The courtroom hushed when Shea got to Mickey's 8 p.m. return and his alleged immediate confession coming in the door: "I have just killed a man," which was the start of an alleged dispute with Alex, who thought Mickey had only shot "the mark" in the leg. Shea testified that he asked Mickey why he shot the man. Mickey's reply, Shea said, was, "I had to do it. He got tough with me and I had to let him have it."[10]

In the prisoner's box, it was then that a little smile came back on Mickey's mouth, but he said nothing.

Cross-examining Shea, Frank Regan asked, "Is it true you have made a deal with the police in reference to the sentence you may get on a Port Credit robbery?"

Shea's answer was "No."

"So you are coming out as a noble citizen to tell what you know. Will you be tried on the Port Credit charge?" asked Regan in a voice that was laden with sarcasm.

"Absolutely," Shea replied with seeming sincerity.[11]

Four other witnesses, including Cecil Clancy, whose evidence was meant as corroboration of the most important part of Shea's story, testified that day, but the headlines were all about Jack Shea's testimony and especially Mickey's alleged confession of guilt. The *Daily Star* and the *Evening Telegram* wore Page One streamers directly quoting Mickey's supposed admission. As pictured in the *Star*, "Shea was well-dressed and when he spoke he did so with emphasis. His cheeks quivered and his face turned red when he mentioned the return of the MacDonald brothers to his apartment."[12]

The hearing continued during the first three days of the following week. These were the same days that the world found out with certainty that the word of Adolph Hitler was worth nothing. The fascist dictator, who had guaranteed the borders of the remnant of Czechoslovakia that was not ceded to Germany by the Munich Agreement of September 29, 1938, grabbed again — taking for Nazi Germany the remainder of the Czech nation, the limits of which he had sworn at Munich to respect forever. Neville Chamberlain's policy of appeasement was, during these few days, shown to be the weak-kneed fraud that it was. The war that had been looming at least since March 1936, when Hitler's Germany re-occupied the demilitarized Rhineland, seemed by the end of the MacDonalds' preliminary hearing to be inevitable. Hitler was already talking about helping himself to a chunk of Poland, the so-called Danzig Corridor to the Baltic Sea, which separated Germany from German-administered East Prussia.

The eyewitness testimony of John V. McDermott began the new week of Monday, March 13. He told the story of the brutal murder of James Windsor, graphically, step-by-step, in chronological order. Mickey and Alex, both chewing gum with vigour, looked at the witness and, as at other times, smiled at each other, as if to show their lack of concern. At his story's end, Jack McDermott pointed accusingly at Mickey and emphatically charged, "*He* was the gunman."[13] A few seconds of silence followed, during which Mickey stared coldly at his accuser.

After McDermott's testimony, Magistrate Browne announced, "I have heard sufficient evidence to commit the accused for trial."[14]

This got both Isadore Levinter and Frank Regan to their feet in protest.

The purpose of the preliminary hearing, of course, was to determine whether or not there was a strong enough case against the MacDonalds to send them to trial. This meant, in the matter at issue, that the Crown had to disclose enough of its evidence before an inferior-court judge or magistrate for that trier of the facts to determine that there was, in substance, a case that might reasonably result in a conviction. Both the Crown and the defence lawyers surely recognized beforehand that committal of the MacDonalds for trial was a virtual certainty. In such circumstances, in a day when nothing like full disclosure of the evidence was required, for the lawyers representing the brothers the preliminary hearing was very much an opportunity to discover as much as possible of the Crown's case — and, further, to discover anything else that the Crown might not want the defence to know. Thus, Frank Regan and Isadore Levinter necessarily saw the preliminary hearing as an opportunity to "go fishing" — and, so, they demanded that it continue.

And that, for two more days, was what Magistrate Browne grudgingly allowed to happen. The lawyers for the MacDonalds then called a parade of witnesses who at the impending trial were most likely to testify for the Crown, if they were going testify at all. These included the other four eyewitnesses to the murder and a long line of policemen. The hearing finished at seven minutes after noon, Wednesday, March 15, abruptly, on a farcical note, after a detective of the police identification bureau failed to appear as expected by Mr. Levinter. The reason the detective was not there, smirked James McFadden, was that his subpoena had been wrongly dated for March 12, 1940. The court spectators couldn't help but laugh. Then Levinter attempted to call another detective, who wasn't there either. His subpoena had been wrongly dated, too.

"That settles it then. I have no witnesses before me," announced Magistrate Browne. "The accused are committed for trial." Then, amidst much lawyerly protest, His Worship straight away got up and disappeared through a door behind the bench.[15]

CHAPTER NINE

With Convincing Sincerity and Evident Forthrightness
(March 20, 1939–May 18, 1939)

ON MARCH 20, ATTORNEY General Gordon Conant asked Cecil L. Snyder, the senior counsel in his department, to personally handle the prosecution of the MacDonald brothers for the murder of James Windsor. This was significant. Cecil Snyder, as remembered by Gwyn Thomas, was "the most successful Crown prosecutor in the history of Ontario." By the time of his retirement from criminal law in 1947, in 38 murder trials, said Mr. Thomas, Cecil Snyder had failed to get a conviction only once.[1] At the time of the trial of the MacDonalds, he was as yet unbeaten. Notably, he had previously helped at least two of Frank Regan's former clients to the gallows.[2]

As both the MacDonalds were "entirely without funds," the Department of the Attorney General effected its then standard procedure in capital cases. The defendants were allowed to choose their own representation and the department paid their lawyers, Frank Regan and Isadore Levinter, $50 a day for their time in court, not to exceed $400 each. All of their costs came out of that. It would seem to have been a system that generally made for murder trials that were not overly long.

Isadore Levinter would have liked to have obtained a severance of Alex's trial from Mickey's, freeing Alex from the taint of his brother's criminal reputation, but this was not possible. As well, Mr. Levinter apparently had to make the brothers' parents understand the danger in trying to provide separate alibis for both Donnie and Alex, as Maggie MacDonald had indicated family members would do at the time of her sons' arrests.[3] This might have gotten Alex unnecessarily hanged. On the witness stand at the impending trial, Mickey's mother would say not a word about Donnie being on the telephone with his father at the time of the murder, as she had previously maintained he was, and a sad-faced Alexander MacDonald Sr., unasked, very pointedly stated, "I have no alibi for my son Donald."[4]

Then there was the problem of Mickey's wife.

Kitty was as unreasonably stubborn as anyone could be, she had little sense of consequences, and she just had to have as much attention as there was to be had. After the brothers were arrested, the family, instructed by their lawyers to say nothing to the press, had to shut Kitty up at 3 Poplar Plains Road to stop her talking. Then she took to shouting at the reporters from a third-floor window. If not right then, then eventually, she wanted to be part of Mickey's alibi, to testify they were together at The Corner at the time of the murder.[5] The lawyers would have none of it. If Kitty had been allowed to go into the box, the Crown would have had the right to cross-examine her on her police record — and that would have meant the jury would have repeatedly heard the word "prostitute" applied to Mickey's wife. The result would have been that Mickey would have been seen as a pimp, or as something very like a pimp, which would have greatly promoted the hanging of Mickey and Alex both. As it was, the jury likely had rumour of this anyway, but they did not have to consider it as established fact or as part of the evidence put before them.

The trial of Donald and Alexander MacDonald for the murder of James Windsor was heard before Justice George Franklin McFarland and an Ontario Supreme Court jury, at Toronto City Hall, Courtroom No. 3, commencing at 11 a.m., Monday, May 1, 1939. Public interest in the trial would be strong throughout, even with its last day being coincident with the first-ever visit of a reigning British monarch to Toronto, when more than a million people lined the streets of "the Queen City" to welcome King George VI and Queen Elizabeth, the Queen Consort. The courtroom was packed to capacity each day, as it was at the preliminary hearing, and the corridors of City Hall teemed with the idle curious, who only hoped to get in to see the spectacle. Conditions in the room during the trial would be, in the word of Justice McFarland, "atrocious." The windows could not be opened due to the iron-wheeled racket of passing streetcars on Queen Street, which made testimony unhearable. There were several days of unseasonably hot and humid weather. Two jurors fainted in the jury box, one being tended to by the pathologist who was on the witness stand at the time.

Mickey, as always neat and trim, wore a smile at the outset of what would later be described as "the longest murder trial and the speediest verdict in the court records of the province."[6] To observers, Alex seemed generally much more reserved. The brothers' attitude of indifference, at times displayed to Magistrate Browne, was now less to be seen and soon would disappear entirely.

In his Opening Address to the Jury, Cecil Snyder told his listeners that the motive for the murder was robbery, made necessary by Mickey's desperate need for $50 to pay Frank Regan to represent him on the robbery with violence charge he faced on January 10. The Crown's case, Mr. Snyder said, would be made up of two parts: what went on before the night of the murder of James Windsor, and what went on on the night of the murder. None of the first part, as presented, was evidence against Alex, who did not come under the Crown's purview until the actual day of the crime. The jury was forbidden to be told what they perhaps knew anyway: that Alex had been charged with the Port Credit bank robbery and the shooting of the bank's accountant.

John R. Shea, allegedly wearing a shirt and tie that belonged to Mickey, walked confidently to the witness stand before mid-afternoon on the second day of the trial. His testimony, the wellspring of the Crown's case, with cross-examinations by Frank Regan and Isadore Levinter, would not end till late on the afternoon of the following day. Shea's time on the stand would account for 10 percent of the recorded testimony of a legal proceeding in which 39 other witnesses were heard. Not long before Shea's name was called by the court crier, Attorney General Gordon

Conant dropped in on the trial and was seen to confer with Cecil Snyder and with James McFadden, who was assisting in the prosecution.[7] Mr. Conant was afterwards questioned by the *Globe and Mail*, to which he explained that his presence there was "of no significance." "I like to drop in on important cases like this to see that they are running smoothly," the attorney general answered.[8]

Shea's purposeful rendition of what he claimed were the events of the evening of Saturday, January 7, showed him a bit ill at ease. Responding to Cecil Snyder's questions, he now told the same story as at the preliminary hearing, with his characteristic convincing sincerity and evident forthrightness. Again, the segment of Shea's evidence that mattered most began with his telling of the unexpected arrival at 209A Ossington about 6 p.m., of Mickey, Alex, and Cecil Clancy and, soon after, as Shea told the story again, Mickey and Alex went out the door, as one of them said, "to do a job." One brother had what Shea termed a .45 revolver and the other a loaded .38, both taken from a bureau in Shea's own living room. The Crown would allege the MacDonalds went away in Clancy's Dodge Cabriolet with Alex, who did not drink liquor, at the wheel. Later, Clancy would testify that Alex had retained possession of the keys to his car.

Shea, as his evidence went, was stuck minding Clancy, who was, at the very least, an inappropriate and unwanted guest. Shea said he and the drunken bookie, whom he had met only once previously, drank some more, then he started to cook a meal, in which, inadvertently, he burned the bacon. Eventually, about 8 p.m., as Shea continued, the brothers returned:

Mr. Snyder: *What then?*

Shea: *The first one that came in was Mickey; he was quite excited, and he told me he had just killed a man.*

Mr. Snyder: *Use his own words.*

Shea: *"I have just killed a man," he says.*

Mr. Snyder: *Mickey said this to you?*

Shea: *To both Clancy and I.*

Mr. Snyder: *"I have just killed a man." Go on.*

Shea: *I said, "What are you talking about?" He said, "He got tough, showed fight, I had to let him have it." Alex followed in immediately, that is, within the space of a minute or two, and I turned to Alex and asked what Mickey was talking about, that he killed a man? Alex says, "He is crazy, he didn't kill him, he only shot him here."*

Shea explained that Alex pointed with his finger at his own left thigh — and did the same himself. He was asked by Cecil Snyder to step out from behind the witness stand and make the same indication so the jury could see it plainly.

Mr. Snyder: *Repeat again what Alex said?*

Shea: *"He is crazy, he never killed him, he only shot here,"* pointing to his leg. Mickey said, *"I did not."*

Mr. Snyder: *Mickey said, 'I did not'?"*

Shea: *"I shot him here."*

Mr. Snyder: *Pointing where?*

Shea: *Pointing to the stomach. He said, "I know when a man's dead. I saw his eyes roll."*

Mr. Snyder: *"I know when a man's dead."*

Shea: *"I saw his eyes roll. I saw the white of his eyes."*[9]

Part of this was Shea's story about Louis Gallow's supposed involvement — that Mickey had said Gallow got the bookie's diamond tie-pin and his diamond ring, and that Mickey, while escaping the scene of the crime, had thrown Windsor's diamond-studded watch out the car window. He said, as well, that Mickey complained that all Windsor had was "a lousy seventy bucks." Then, so Shea's evidence went, Mickey ended these foolish confessionary admissions by saying, "Let us get down to Jarvis and Dundas Street, so we can have an alibi in case the police are out looking for us." Mickey, Alex, and Clancy, in Shea's version of what happened, then left for The Corner.[10]

There was lots more, of course, but Shea's most damaging evidence was in Mickey's supposed acknowledgment of murder and the short argument with Alex, in which the younger brother's attributed part tacitly admitted his own participation in the robbery and, therefore, according to the law, the murder. Windsor's name, Shea said on cross-examination, was not mentioned by Mickey or Alex during the episode he described. Shea testified that he heard a radio report later that night and at first understood that the victim's name was "Genser," not Windsor.[11]

Shea's one great error was a story that he told of an alleged visit Mickey had made to his apartment on the afternoon of Tuesday, January 10, and of a series of supposed after-visits that week. Two of these visits came complete with issues and dialogue.[12] The difficulty was that Mickey had been before Judge Parker on the James Elder robbery-with-violence charge coincident with the time of the alleged January 10 visit, and he was in the Don Jail waiting to be shipped to Kingston during the following week, and long after that. Caught out by Frank Regan on cross-examination, Shea tried to claim that these events had happened at a previous time, but he could not make their spoken content fit within the framework of other known events, and, finally, had to admit, "I can't reconcile the facts."[13]

The key part of Shea's testimony was weakly corroborated by Cecil Clancy, who, in an at times barely audible voice, gave the jury to understand that, on the fatal evening of Saturday, January 7, though "groggy" from drink, he had seen Mickey take two guns from a chest of drawers in Shea's apartment, that the MacDonald brothers had then left saying they would be "back in half an hour," and that, when they returned nearly two hours later, Mickey had immediately made the abrupt announcement, "I just killed a man." Clancy testified he had caught some, not all, of the after-talk between the MacDonalds that Shea said happened. The others had purposely excluded him, Clancy evidenced, by taking their dangerous conversation into the adjoining room. He agreed with Shea that he, Mickey, and Alex had afterwards left the apartment together for Jarvis and Dundas streets "to get an alibi." He said that, at first, he thought the whole thing was "a joke" the others were playing on him.[14]

Clancy did add one important bit of information that was exclusively his own. He testified that the day before the murder he had bumped into Mickey near The Corner and that Mickey had then specifically asked "if I knew a bookie named Windsor" and "Was Windsor a friend of mine?" "Yes, a very good friend," Cecil Clancy testified he had answered.[16]

One problem with Clancy's evidence, as was plain after he was cross-examined, was that he remembered almost nothing else of what had happened between Friday night, January 6, and Monday morning, January 9, except that which was of value to the Crown in its prosecution of the MacDonalds. Another real difficulty was that the lawyers for the brothers had been allowed a copy of a statement Clancy had made to the Toronto Police on February 2, in which he groggily remembered things quite differently than at the preliminary hearing and at the present trial. He had, for example, named Teddy Wells as the driver who drove Mickey and himself in his Dodge to Shea's apartment and had then added, "Alex may have come in" later. Similarly, Clancy's statement showed a tendency to agree with Shea's previous statements after at first saying he did not remember.[15] What the defence lawyers saw in this was that Clancy had constructed his current version of what happened in response to police suggestion of Shea's account of what took place — that, in effect, he had been coached to corroborate Shea's evidence.

As he had done at the prelim, John V. "Jack" McDermott, the first of the five eyewitnesses to the murder to testify, now following Cecil Snyder's questions, took the jury through the events of James Windsor's murder, providing a chillingly effective narrative of the crime. Then he identified Mickey as the killer and Alex as the blue-eyed gunman who had held the household at the point of a rusty revolver. The other four identification witnesses came on during the second week of the trial, their testimonies being similar to, if to varying degrees mildly less effective, than that of McDermott. Each retold the story with minor differences, the three women all breaking down in doing so. Lorraine Bromell specifically noted that the killer had a "spot," or a mark of some kind, on his left cheek, where, indeed, Mickey's face wore a small mole.[17] As did Jack McDermott, all spoke of recognizing the MacDonald brothers in the line-up of Sunday, January 22 — the fourth of five police line-ups they had attended.

Revenge, not robbery, was the defence theory of the motive behind the crime. The lawyers for Mickey and Alex characterized the perpetrators as being Italians, as they had been first described by the witnesses to the murder, not as MacDonalds, as they were initially identified by the eyewitnesses in the line-up of Sunday, January 22 — the day after Jack Shea had told his story to the police.

On cross-examination, Frank Regan and Isadore Levinter worked to undermine the testimony of Shea by emphasizing his obvious motive as an untried, unsentenced felon to seek the Crown's favour by lying

Mickey and Alex up the steps of a gallows, and both counsels more than suggested there was "a deal" that would let Shea walk away a free man in return for his testimony. Shea and the Crown, of course, denied this, as an admission of any such deal would serve to neuter Shea as a witness. The suggestion was more than made that Shea himself was a part of the gang that invaded Windsor's home. Cecil Clancy's corroborative evidence was attacked as that of a blind-drunk alcoholic who had merely been convinced later by the police of what Shea said happened and, so, out of fear, had parroted Shea's story.

Isadore Levinter would get Lorraine Bromell to agree that the actual killer seemed to know Windsor and, from the brutal way he treated him, "to have revenge in his heart."[18] Jack McDermott admitted the same possibility.[19]

At different times during the trial, both Mssrs. Regan and Levinter questioned the eyewitnesses while themselves wearing a handkerchief mask and a peaked cap pulled down over their foreheads — this, in ridicule of their identifications of Alex and of the notion that all five of the witnesses — all five! — had been able to identify Alex in a police line-up based only on their previous sight of the gunman's blue eyes and his nice eyebrows, as well as his height. Repeatedly, Frank Regan asked the Windsor household about the four Italians from the Windsor Bar-B-Q who were then under indictment for extortion, and demanded to know whether or not their descriptions did not more closely conform to those of the killers as given by the witnesses on the night of the murder.

On cross-examination, Detective-Sergeant Harry Glasscock, the first policeman to question four of the witnesses on January 7, admitted to Regan he could not swear that all of them had not then said that the killers were Italians.[20] As well, their five separate identifications were subjected to attack as having been wrongly made as a group identification. All of these witnesses had testified that they were shown police photographs on Sunday, January 8, and Monday, January 9, and most had claimed to have picked out two different likenesses of Mickey only from about 200 pictures.[21] If these identifications really happened, why then was Mickey not put in a police line-up long before Jack Shea named him? the defence lawyers wanted to know.

As was still considered both courageous and unusual in 1939, the MacDonald brothers both took the stand to testify in defence of themselves, both making vehement and definite denials that they had any part in the murder of James Windsor, or that they were anywhere near the Briar Hill Avenue house on the night of the crime, or at any other time. They both denied that Alex was in Shea's apartment on the night of January 7, as Shea, the Crown's star witness, had claimed.

The defence for Mickey, such as it was, was an alibi that, in its telling, highlighted his essentially dissolute lifestyle. He went into the box, jauntily, self-assuredly, politely, and almost off-handedly testified that he and "Doc" had been drinking whisky all that Saturday afternoon in the vicinity of The Corner, when Alex had unexpectedly turned up and, being an abstainer, was in condition to be asked to drive Clancy and himself to Ossington Avenue and Dundas Street in Clancy's Dodge. Unknown to Alex, said Mickey, the purpose of the trip was to take groceries to Jack Shea, who was then a fugitive, and both brothers testified that they stopped at a grocery store on the way. Mickey claimed that, since he didn't want his supposedly-square brother to know where Shea was hiding out, he instructed Alex to go home for supper in Clancy's car and to meet them later at The Corner. Then, as Mickey continued, he and Clancy went into Shea's apartment and all three shared Clancy's fourth or fifth bottle of Scotch of the afternoon. Shea, Mickey testified, took him into the back room and, understandably, demanded to know, "What did you bring that drunk here for? He might talk," to which Mickey now told the jury he responded, "Clancy is all right. We are just going to have a few drinks and we are leaving."[22]

And that was all Mickey said happened at 209A Ossington on the night of James Windsor's tragic demise. Mickey wasn't entirely sure but he thought that he and Clancy had caught a cab on Ossington Avenue and had repaired to The Corner. By this time, so Mickey's evidence went, he was too drunk to remember much, and, thus, his only real accounting for the time of the murder, and the hours after, was provided by others who worked at, lived near, or frequented Jarvis and Dundas streets. Teddy Wells, a twice-convicted safecracker and alcoholic fixture of this sodden crowd, testified that he saw Mickey on The Corner, in

front of the Imperial Bank, with Clancy, "about 7:30." A waiter named
Andrew Cira swore that he served Mickey a drunkard's meal of vin-
egar and eggs in the nearby White Cap Restaurant between 7:30 and
8:00 p.m., and Bruno Panza, a barber, first saw Mickey about 8:45 p.m.
and then cut his hair after 9 o'clock. Panza testified that Mickey didn't
need a shave or a haircut, as some of the eyewitnesses had observed the
killer did. A frequenter of the Windsor Bar-B-Q, Panza said that word
of Windsor's death was about The Corner by the time Mickey came
into his shop and that he and Mickey spoke of it briefly, Mickey saying
that it was "too bad." In fact, as was apparent, Mickey's only actual alibi
witness for any time near to, or coincident with, the time of the murder
was Wells, who, as an ex-convict and a well-known Gangland figure,
was something less than totally and utterly credible.

Then Mickey got a break of a sort.

His hazy recollection of the all-important time period, as told to
his lawyers before the trial, included a chance meeting with a teenaged
girl named "Madge," who, years before, when she was "a little girl,"
Mickey remembered he had sometimes teased and given candies as
she rode her bicycle in the vicinity of The Corner. After much legwork
by G. A. "Arthur" Martin, Frank Regan's young assistant, Margaret
Mary "Madge" Hoskins, aged 17, was finally located at 8:30 a.m., on
Tuesday, May 16, the morning of the last day of Mr. Regan's defence
of Mickey in court. Regan put the girl in as a witness, in dramatic
fashion, that afternoon. One effect of this was that Madge Hoskins
afterwards acquired the tag-name "The Mystery Woman," and, to her
dismay, would be pointed out as such on the streets of Gangland during many days to come.

On the witness stand, Madge, "doll-faced and bare-legged," told that
she had lived almost all of her life with her parents at the King Edward
Apartments, at 194 Jarvis Street — virtually on The Corner. She was then
employed by the Royal Canadian Tobacco Company and did a lot of
roller-skating at nearby Mutual Arena.[23] On the evening of Saturday,
January 7, she was, she testified, in Nicholl's Drug Store, on the northeast
corner of Jarvis and Dundas, when the clock over the soda fountain told
her it was five minutes to seven. It was just then, for the first time in years,

so she said, that she spotted Mickey in the drug store's telephone booth and noticed he was "very, very drunk." Then out of the booth came the candyman of Madge Hoskins' girlhood:

> I just turned my back around and asked him if he was Mickey. He said, "Yes." I said, "Don't you remember me?" He says, "I remember your face." I said, "Don't you remember Madge?" He said, "Oh, yes." He then grabbed a handful of jelly-beans and gave me some."[24]

Madge testified she told Mickey, "You don't look so good," to which he answered that he had been on a "bender" for three days. She stated that she looked again at the clock when Mickey left the store and it said 7:05 p.m.

"I only saw him go outside, and there was a kind of stout man standing there, and a lady with a black hat, and black coat, and blonde hair," Madge informed the court.[25] She said she thought the man and the woman were waiting for Mickey. Her teenaged interlude with the accused murderer of James Windsor ended there.

Alex's alibi was not quite so unordinary, but it did, of course, accord with his brother's story. As he testified, after leaving Mickey near Ossington and Dundas around 6 p.m. on the night of the murder, not then aware of who Mickey was going there to see or why, he next drove to the Red Spot Hamburger on Avenue Road, where he had a light supper. Then he went home to Poplar Plains Road, where he interacted in normal fashion with much of the MacDonald family during a half-hour that overlapped the time of the incident at 247 Briar Hill Avenue. Then, as Alex continued, as was his Saturday evening habit, he went to the Hillcrest Shoe Repair on Dupont Street to meet his friends, Sandy Killah and Tom Wettlaufer. Thus, Alex's version of the facts was supported by the testimonies of seven alibi witnesses whose sworn evidence accounted for his movements during the all-important hour between 7 and 8 p.m.: Alex's father, his mother, three of his sisters, Killah and Wettlaufer, none of whom had a criminal record, none of whom were known to frequent Gangland or The Corner. On cross-examination, the matter of Maggie MacDonald's purchase of stolen clothing from Jack Cosgrave in October 1935 was raised by Cecil Snyder to attack her credibility as a witness. None of the others who appeared for Alex were subjected to any such indignity.

CHAPTER TEN

Hanged by the Neck Until You Are Dead
(May 18, 1939–May 20, 1939)

AT 2:43 P.M., THURSDAY, May 18, Isadore Levinter began his almost five-hour address to the jury, said to be "the longest ever heard in a Toronto courtroom on a murder case."[1] Mr. Levinter scrupulously dissected the Crown's case against Alex and he strongly assailed the core evidence of Jack Shea, whose story he characterized as "the most fantastic that I have ever heard."[2] As Frank Regan would do, Levinter scored again and again the danger in Shea's evidence: that he might well have a deal with the Crown to testify against Mickey and Alex in the murder trial in return for his going free on the Port Credit bank robbery charge; that he might have fabricated evidence to achieve this end; and that Shea, himself, could well have been a part of the gang that killed James Windsor.

"Why wasn't Shea brought before a magistrate and sentenced to 10 or 15 years for his crime?" Isadore Levinter asked, rhetorically. "Because if he had been sentenced he would not have lied. That is the inducement that the Crown held out to him," he answered himself, before giving the opinions of prominent jurists who were in agreement that it was "infamous" to put an unsentenced felon into the box as a prosecution witness.[3]

While pointedly stating that he was not suggesting Donald was guilty of anything, Mr. Levinter necessarily hit the theme "Let not the sins of Mickey be visited upon Alex." He rightly insisted that much of the evidence in the Crown's case did not apply to Alex at all and that Alex "stands or falls alone."[4]

Frank Regan's address to the jury, which began the afternoon session on Friday, May 19, was preceded by Attorney General Gordon Conant's second visit to the proceeding. Mr. Conant stayed for at least part of Mr. Regan's address.[5]

Regan explained his case for more than three and a half hours, picturing Jack Shea and his tale in much the same light as had Isadore Levinter. Clancy and the eyewitnesses, he said, had fallen in with Shea's story under police suggestion or pressure. He reminded the jury that Clancy, hopelessly drunk all of that weekend, could recall almost nothing else of what happened except what was of value to the Crown's case. The Windsor household, he argued, were in obvious contradiction of themselves, identifying Italians one day, MacDonalds soon after. They had, he said, "changed their story" under police pressure.[6] He charged that, after Shea had named the MacDonalds, "the police had determined to fasten the crime on them," that "the methods adopted to convict these men are a disgrace to a court of law and call for a sweeping investigation after this case is over."[7]

"For weeks the police decided to pin a crime on these two men, not by direct evidence alone," he continued, "but by seeking to destroy any possible alibi evidence they could secure."[8] He cited the testimony of several associates of Mickey's, who had told stories on the witness stand that were meant to say the same. Foremost among these was Leo Gauthier, who had angrily testified that after he had refused to be bribed or intimidated into giving evidence against Mickey, he was rewarded with a phony charge of the armed robbery of the Dominion Shoe Repair, followed by the Crown's asking for, and getting, seven remands in Toronto Police Court, without any evidence against him ever being provided, and without his being granted bail. Which meant that Gauthier had stayed 42 days in the Don Jail, before, finally, the charge was thrown out.[9] Waving the police information against Gauthier at the jury, Frank Regan rantingly exhorted, "I say this information is evidence of criminality on the part of the police."[10]

Delivered on the evening of Friday, May 19, the only evening session of the trial, Cecil Snyder's Address to the jury took only an hour and 25 minutes. It was a cold, factual, closely-argued exposition of the case presented against the brothers, and ended with Mr. Snyder's plea to the jurymen to "do their duty fearlessly," otherwise "the MacDonalds and others of their kind will leave this court laughing at you, laughing at the court, and snapping their fingers at the administration of justice."[11]

On this next-to-last day of her husband's trial for murder, as on two or three prior days, the press had time to notice that Margaret "Kitty Cat" MacDonald, making her last fashion statement of the event, was wearing "a stylish purple hat."

Justice McFarland's two-hour Charge to the Jury began at 9 a.m., Saturday, May 20, the trial's seventeenth and last day. After explaining the jury's duty, His Lordship told the jurymen that in this case "the head of gangsterism is raised in our community for the first time" and that this "must be stamped out" and "ruthlessly eliminated." He defended the police against the attack made on them by "one of the learned counsel for the defence," and said their actions were "in the main, were entirely reasonable." Then he explained Section 69-2 of *The Criminal Code of Canada* — the doctrine of common intention — and instructed the jury that they could find one defendant guilty and the other not guilty but, in order to do so, they had to find that one was in the Briar Hill Avenue house at the time of the murder and the other was not. If both were there, under the law, they had both formed a common intention to commit a crime and the second man was as guilty of murder as the man who had actually shot James Windsor to death.[12]

Then Justice McFarland discussed the evidence.

His Lordship organized his consideration of the facts of the trial into what he termed "a chronology of the events in their sequence" for the benefit of the jury.[13] In this, he arranged a view of the murder and the happenings that were said to have preceded it exactly as had Cecil Snyder, in what he had termed Part One of his two-part case, with much about the handling of guns by Mickey and much about the alleged trip to Ottawa to rob a bank. Then McFarland explained the testimony of John R. Shea at length, briefly endorsed Cecil Clancy's bleary-eyed evidence as corroboration of Shea ("That evidence given by Shea is corroborated by Clancy."), and went over the eyewitnesses' testimonies extensively, while mentioning little about the arguments of the defence concerning the evidential shortcomings of their testimonies.

Though he spent considerable effort discussing the most damaging segment of Shea's evidence, McFarland did not see fit to even mention Jack Shea's transparent fabrication of several make-believe visits by Mickey to his apartment-hideout on Tuesday, January 10 and after, and he expended only five mild sentences on what might be "the motive actuating Shea" and the possibility "that clemency in connection with the crime that is hanging over his head now is the price which he is to be paid for giving the evidence which the police wished him to give."[14]

He said nothing at all concerning the chance that Shea, himself, might have been a participant in the invasion of James Windsor's home and, thus, under the law, the murder. His instruction of the jury included his opinion that "the principal part" of the Crown's case was in the testimonies of the five eyewitnesses. He said that all five had "agreed in the main on the events which took place," and explained that all had made four separate identifications of the defendants: at the house at the time of the murder (when, in reality, they had identified Italians, not MacDonalds); by way of police photographs; at the police line-up; and in the courtroom.[15] He reminded the jury of an observation of "one of them," who said of the killer, "I shall remember that face as long as I live; I couldn't forget it."[16] McFarland only passingly mentioned the discrepancy in the eyewitnesses' initial contentions that the killers were "Italians," not MacDonalds, but did mention "the terrible mental strain, which might affect their observation as to the details of what took place." Neither did he notice that the witnesses' identifications after the January 22 line-up had been made in an irregular manner that suggested a group decision.

Justice McFarland spent more than three times as long organizing and explaining the Crown's case for the jurors as he did discussing the two defendants' alibi defences combined, and he began by inaccurately characterizing the first of Mickey's witnesses as "the only one of the group who has no criminal record; he was arrested only once and that for vagrancy." In fact, at least 5 of the 13 witnesses for Mickey did not then have criminal records.[17]

In short, Justice George Franklin McFarland did not quite instruct the jury to "Hang that pimp and his brother."

The jury retired while Objections to the Charge were heard. Amidst much more, Justice McFarland listened to Isadore Levinter's contention concerning his remarks about the danger in Jack Shea's evidence being inadequate, but when the jury came back, McFarland said nothing further regarding the evidence of Shea.

The jury went out again at 11:45 a.m., had their lunch, then deliberated only 25 minutes before the foreman gave notice that a verdict had been reached.

As the 12 jurymen filed into the courtroom, the brothers were both seen to visibly blanche at the sight of their stone-faces — thought to be a certain sign of a guilty verdict.[18]

Soon after one o'clock, on a signal from the bench, the court registrar asked the foreman of the jury, "Do you find the prisoner at the bar, Donald (Mickey) MacDonald, guilty or not guilty?"

"Guilty," came the word that meant a death by hanging.

Mickey reacted with only a faint smile. He said nothing. Then, briefly, he fingered his upper lip.

Alex was now seen to close his eyes while tightly gripping the rail of the prisoner's dock.

"Do you find the prisoner at the bar, Alex MacDonald, guilty or not guilty?"

"Not guilty," answered the foreman, the word "not" being spoken louder than the word "guilty."

The jury was polled by name on the question of Mickey's guilt, all twelve jurymen answering "guilty." The time was 1:05 p.m.[19]

It was noticed that Alexander MacDonald Sr. was the only family member in court this day — and that he sat "as if stunned" after the verdicts were announced.[20]

Alex Jr. was then discharged by the court. Before leaving, he spoke briefly, his voice choked with evident emotion. He gratefully thanked Mr. Levinter and the jury, then, all at once, broke down from the strain he had been under for months. Tears from his blue-grey eyes streaming down his face, Alex was then assisted from the room by sheriff's officers. Outside in the hall, he was promptly re-arrested by the police — taken back into custody by reason of the Port Credit bank robbery charge against him.

Turning again to Mickey, Justice McFarland then sternly ordered, "Stand up, Donald MacDonald."

Mickey slowly rose to his feet in the prisoner's dock.

The bench asked, "Have you anything to say why sentence should not be passed?"

Mickey had a lot to say — in fact, a veritable rant. He began to speak, as was reported, "in a firm voice and with just a slight quiver on his lips." His tone was defiant. Talking *at* Justice McFarland, he commenced telling His Lordship that his Address to the Jury was not fair, then he switched to saying that he was "the victim of a frame-up at the hands of the Toronto Police Department." There was a garbled part to the caustic remarks Mickey made wherein his voice rose as he attacked the attorney general's department, Justice McFarland again, and the Toronto Police again. Then he bitterly set upon the Windsor household, the members of which he claimed had said at the line-up on Sunday, January 22, that he was not the man who shot James Windsor, then all gave "manufactured evidence" (a favourite phrase of Frank Regan's) against him at the trial. He ended by saying that he had never killed a man, and that he was not a coward and was not afraid to die.[21]

When Mickey had exhausted himself, Justice McFarland pronounced the sentence that was his only option under the law:

> Donald MacDonald, the sentence of this Court upon you is that you be taken from here to the place from where you came, and there be kept in close confinement until the 20th day of July, 1939, and upon that date you be taken to the place of execution, and you be there hanged by the neck until you are dead. And may the Lord have mercy on your soul.[22]

As His Lordship reached the words "hanged by the neck until you are dead," Mickey interrupted his own death sentence by angrily shouting over Justice McFarland's words, "Give that to the police department; to have mercy on the people who framed me." He was by then sobbing, coming apart altogether.[23]

"All right, take him out," ordered McFarland.

The *Evening Telegram* of that same afternoon reported that Mickey, as he went from the courtroom in the custody of sheriff's officers, cried out loudly and dramatically, "After the Port Credit bank robbery case is over, you will know all about this, and why Shea framed me."[24]

CHAPTER ELEVEN

In the Death Cell
(May 20–September 26, 1939)

EVEN AS THE JURY foreman spoke the word "guilty," Frank Regan turned to Mickey and assured him there would be an appeal, and that they would win it. Later that afternoon, Mr. Regan went to the jail, spoke with Mickey at length and, afterwards, announced to the press that the conviction would be appealed "as soon as counsel have an opportunity of analyzing the evidence and deciding upon the various grounds for appeal, of which there are many."[1]

His lawyer's resolve to fight on in the Ontario Court of Appeal, and his conjectured favourable result, gave Mickey hope and thereby the strength to bear up to the watch on his impending date with the hangman. He soon surprised his keepers with his quiet and cheerful attitude in one of the Don Jail's newly-renovated Death Cells. During these days, he was, notwithstanding his ungainly histrionics at his sentencing, anything but down-hearted. In the face of his perilous situation, he continued to staunchly maintain that he had been falsely accused and wrongly convicted, that he had been "framed" by Jack Shea, the Toronto Police, and the Attorney General of Ontario, all of whom, for different reasons, needed a "patsy" to take "the fall" for the Windsor murder. He might have added what some others believed: that he was the right guy for "the fall," in view of his apparent low character, since he was perceived to be a fall-down drunk, a thief, a gunman, an armed robber, and a pimp — or something near to a pimp. Somebody who ought to be gotten rid of anyway...[2]

Now officially the condemned man's spiritual advisor, Brigadier Owen was the only visitor permitted to see Mickey in his cell almost any day. He kept his subject supplied with good reading to busy his mind, and a sympathetic presence attuned to the needs of both the fated prisoner and his worried family. The Brigadier was the one person in a position to carry daily news to the MacDonalds, who waited on it, Mickey's mother almost desperately.

On Wednesday, May 31, Cecil L. Snyder racked up yet another conviction for murder, after which Mickey had company in the Death Cell Corridor. In January 1939, William "Bill" Petrukowich, a 30-year-old White Russian, shot and killed Annie Geraznic, his former lover, in front of a house at 374 Bathurst Street. Justice Keiller MacKay sentenced Petrukowich to be hanged on August 10 — 21 days after Mickey was to die. Inevitably, Mickey and Bill, installed in adjoining cells, soon became friends. Since Bill spoke little English, Mickey began teaching him the language. The two played game after game of both checkers and dominoes through the bars of their cells, as Mickey did with their three around-the-clock guards, each of whom was paid an extra dollar a day to watch over the condemned men until their separate dates with the hangman.

The campaign to raise money to pay for Mickey's appeal was organized by Margaret "Peg" MacDonald, the oldest of Mickey's sisters still at home. The cause was not helped by several imposters, men and women both, who were reportedly going door to door purporting to be collecting for Mickey. The real fund saw none of this money. One faker, a man named Frank Zaza, eventually spent a week in jail after his plea for two dollars to aid the "Mickey MacDonald Appeal Fund" upgraded itself to verbal abuse and threats of violence. Peg MacDonald spoke byway of the *Toronto Star* on May 29. "We do not collect money at people's doors," she stated in frustration. "Anyone who wishes to help should send money to me personally."

By early June, the legitimate fund had raised $129, which was not a lot considering the projected cost of reproducing a single copy of several necessary transcripts of the evidence was $675. After that, other costs were estimated to be more than $1,000. Frank Regan had been negotiating with Richard Greer, a noted attorney experienced in appellate court, to conduct the appeal, but there was no money to pay him. By June 10, the attorney general's department had been served with a notice of appeal and, at the same time, made aware that "the accused is entirely without funds." In the face of this, Frank Regan and Arthur Martin informed I.A. Humphries, the deputy attorney general, that they were willing to argue the appeal "if the Court should see fit to appoint them." Records of the Department of the Attorney General tell that Mr. Humphries meant to take the appeal fund's $129, which was held in trust, and put it toward the cost of the department's paying the cost of the appeal. Frank Regan thought that, in the circumstances, Mickey's lawyers should at least have this money. Attorney General Conant overruled Humphries. "It's too small an amount to worry about; let him have it," Mr. Conant instructed.[3] A few days later, in what then seemed an act of fairness and generosity, the attorney general was quoted in the press as saying that, if Mickey could demonstrate need, the cost of his appeal would be paid for by his department. The lack of financial resource "should never deprive any citizen of access to our courts," Mr. Conant stated grandly.[4]

On Monday, June 19, Arthur Martin served notice of appeal at the Court Registrar's Office at Osgoode Hall against the conviction of Donald "Mickey" MacDonald for murder and made application for leave to appeal before the Ontario Court of Appeal. Initially, the petition submitted 10 grounds for appeal, and a further 18 were added before the case went before the Court. The practice was, and is, that the Court of Appeal would only hear argument on those grounds that the Court itself judged might have merit.

Eight days later, on Tuesday, June 27, Chief Justice Robert S. Robertson issued an order that fixed the date for hearing of argument as September 11 and, at the same time, ordered the execution of Donald "Mickey" MacDonald stayed until September 30. After the order was formally entered at the registrar's office, Arthur Martin went straight to the Don Jail and personally notified Mickey of the postponement of his death. The condemned man, who otherwise had only 23 days to live, was said to be "greatly relieved."

By now, Arthur Martin, the 26-year-old son of a prosperous Huntsville, Ontario merchant, had become critically important to Mickey's chances. Frank Regan was not an appellate court lawyer — and more or less knew it.[5] Richard Greer, after brief interest, was soon effectively out of the picture. Mr. Regan, whose alternative was likely to argue the appeal himself, smartly chose to go with his young and inexperienced assistant, whose extraordinary ability he surely had gathered long before.[6] Thus, it was Arthur Martin who coldly studied the 1531-page transcript of the trial, who set out numerous additional grounds of appeal, who would argue most of the appellant's case, and who would argue best.

By early August, Mickey had grown both sleepless and listless from the wearing situation he was faced with. Checkers, dominoes, and good reading were not occupying his mind as before. His outlook had now turned to serious matters. He was said to need something of relevance, something that he was able to convince himself gave meaning to his own 32 years of sordid existence. And so he decided to write his autobiography. Reportedly, Mickey began this project in the belief he could finish it by the day of his re-scheduled death, September 30. By September 7, the epic tale was said to be "almost completed," though by this date, the project was slowed by Mickey's newfound "deep interest in the European situation." On August 23, the infamous "Black Thursday," Hitler's Germany and the Soviet Union of Joseph Stalin had proclaimed their Non-Aggression Pact, which was virtually a joint announcement of the war to come. Germany invaded Poland nine days later, Great Britain and France declared war on Germany in consequence, and Canada, by an Act of Parliament, would do the same on September 10. Mickey was now reading all of the Toronto papers every day, as well as the *Manchester Guardian*, all of which were regularly brought to his cell by Brigadier Owen. Whether or not Mickey finished its writing, "The Autobiography of Mickey McDonald" — or whatever it was to have been called — was certainly never published.

* * *

Appeal courts do not deal in right or wrong verdicts. They deal in procedural rights and wrongs, in fair and unfair court practices, in whether or not an accused has been properly and fairly tried.

The appeal against the verdict of guilty in the trial of Donald John MacDonald for the murder of James Windsor was heard at Osgoode Hall on September 11, 12, and 13, before Chief Justice Robert S. Robertson and Justices Middleton, Masten, Fisher, and Henderson. It was "submitted for the appellant that he had not had a fair trial and that he was not convicted by due process of law."[7]

At the outset, Arthur Martin, who argued most, not all of the appeal, informed the five presiding justices, "The learned trial judge misdirected the jury on certain points and permitted certain other irregularities to creep in."[8] Of the several grounds that were put forward against the conviction, the Court would require the Crown, represented by Cecil L. Snyder, to answer only three.

The first "irregularity" that required an answer had to do with the fact that the jury had been allowed by "the learned trial judge" to visit the scene of the murder, 247 Briar Hill Avenue, at midday, on Saturday, May 6, accompanied only by sheriff's officers, who did not enter the house with the jury. Neither the defendant nor his attorneys were present to represent the interest of the accused. Mr. Martin reasoned that the jurors should have been taken to the house at the same time of day as the murder happened and suggested that the jury *might* have done experiments on the premises under wrong conditions, since the lighting and the furniture were different than at the time of the murder.[9] He argued that, in effect, such a viewing ought to have been seen as an extension of the actual trial, as if it were the examination of an exhibit, and that what was done was the same as "taking evidence without representation" — and that, even by itself, this "made it a mistrial."[10]

Another "irregularity," Arthur Martin contended, had to do with several instances of "evidence adduced by the Crown in relation to appellant's past conduct and associations." None of these instances were evidence against the appellant in the matter at trial, Mr. Martin maintained, but at the same time, they all unfairly tended to show the accused's bad character, were thus prejudicial to him, and were wrongly allowed to stand by "the learned trial judge."[11]

In this vein, Mr. Martin demonstrated several "improper references" that were discursively made by Cecil Snyder during the course of the trial. The most obvious example involved a series of questions in cross-examination about Mickey having been charged with burglary in August 1931, together with Louis Gallow, where, worse, the jury was not told that MacDonald was acquitted. Together with the strong suspicion of Gallow's involvement in the murder of James Windsor, this reference was highly prejudicial, maintained Martin, in that it tended to suggest a long-time criminal association between MacDonald and Gallow, and was otherwise irrelevant as evidence in the matter at hand.[12]

Another part of the Crown's case that was objected to on the same ground was the whole "trip-to-Ottawa-to-rob-a-bank story" that was purposely brought out in the testimonies of Jack Shea, Joe Smith, and others. This too was irrelevant as evidence in the murder trial and, again, tended to prejudice the jury against the appellant.[13]

Similarly, the Crown had scrupulously laid out Jack Shea's criminal record when he was put in as a witness, a wrong procedure, Arthur Martin argued, which again was prejudicial to MacDonald, since it tended to show that he associated with a habitual criminal, the Crown's own star witness, Jack Shea.[14]

Concerning Justice McFarland's misdirection of the jury as to the all-important evidence of John R. Shea, Arthur Martin's argument was the same as at the trial: that Shea might well have been an actual accomplice in the murder; that Shea, untried and unsentenced on the Port Credit bank robbery charge, was dangerous to believe since he might have an understanding with the Crown; that the jury should have been warned, expressly, carefully, in considerable detail, by the trial judge of these real possibilities and of the danger in Shea's evidence. Instead, no caution at all was given.[15]

Arthur Martin closed the case for Donald MacDonald on the afternoon of Wednesday, September 13. When Frank Regan's "assistant" sat down, Mr. Justice Fisher, apparently on behalf of all five Justices, observed warmly, "This Court does not customarily remark on the brilliant arguments of elder practitioners. Still we feel that we cannot refrain from commenting on the brilliant manner in which so young a man has handled his appeal."[16]

The Court reserved judgment in the matter, but the attorneys for Donald MacDonald left Osgoode Hall with every reason to believe that the appeal had been won.

On Tuesday, September 26, the result was made known. By unanimous decision, the Ontario Court of Appeal quashed the conviction of Donald John MacDonald for murder and ordered a new trial. The lengthy judgment was written and delivered by Chief Justice Robertson at Osgoode Hall. A majority of the Court endorsed all three arguments that were presented to them by Arthur Martin. Concerning the trial judge's failure to carefully instruct the jury regarding the evidence of John R. Shea, all five Justices of the Court were in agreement that this was a serious omission that required a new trial.[17]

In his Death Cell in the Don Jail, Mickey's hardest days were those immediately before the decision of the Court was made known. On Monday, September 25, five days before he was to die, and the day when the Court's decision was expected, the condemned man was pacing up and down in his cell and asking the guards every ten minutes if there was any word of the Court's decision.

News of the successful appeal was delivered to Mickey by Harry Denning, governor of the jail, less than four days before he was to hang. This ended Mickey's suffering for the moment. He may never have been told that it had already been decided at Ottawa, with the assent of Minister of Justice Ernest LaPointe, that if there was an eleventh-hour appeal for clemency, Donald MacDonald's sentence of death was "a clear case of No Interference."[18]

At 3 Poplar Plains Road, the MacDonald family learned of Donnie's new chance from Brigadier Owen, who telephoned the news to Mickey's mother as soon as it became known. The MacDonalds, all of whom had been living in a state of high anxiety for many months, were made briefly happy but then, as was their seemingly unending lot, had to steel themselves for the next struggle that was coming. Mickey's retrial was scheduled for the York County Fall Assizes, which were to begin in less than three weeks.

In consequence of the Court of Appeal's decision, Mickey was returned to the jail's general population — and, in leaving the Death-Cell Corridor, had to say goodbye to Bill Petrokowich, whose own appeal had been dismissed on September 13, the day it was made. Bill was hanged at 8 a.m., Wednesday, October 4, 1939. By all accounts, he died more than bravely. His death was the first task of a new hangman, whose identity was kept secret and who obviously performed his initial piece of work exceedingly well.

CHAPTER TWELVE

On Instructions from the Attorney General
(October 16, 1939–November 2, 1939)

ON THURSDAY, JUNE 22, 1939, five days after he high-mindedly announced that his department would pay for Mickey's appeal, Gordon Conant abruptly stopped the trials of John R. Shea, Leo Gauthier, and Alex MacDonald for the armed robbery of the Port Credit Bank of Commerce, with his own directive that the three must be tried before a judge and jury. No reason was given — and no reason had to be given. The attorney general's legal device was a little-known, little-used section of *The Criminal Code of Canada*, Section 825-5, which then gave his office the right to direct a jury trial where "an offence charged is punishable with imprisonment for a period exceeding five years."[1] The defendants were literally before Judge Archibald Cochrane, in Peel County Judges' Criminal Court at Brampton, when the surprise order was made known and, in one fell swoop, the trials of Jack Shea and the others were effectively deferred for another four months. Crown Attorney A.G. Davis informed the court that he had not received notice of the order until 10 a.m. that morning — an hour before the trial was to go on.

Why? Basil Essery, Gauthier's lawyer, wanted to know.

"Nobody here knows why this direction has been issued," answered Crown Attorney Davis.[2]

Mr. Essery saw "some ulterior motive."

"The time and place to have issued this direction was at the time of the prisoners' election in February," he stated angrily, "and not many months later." He further asked the court, "Can the attorney general override the rights of the accused in this matter because of another matter involving MacDonald and Shea but in no way involving my client, Gauthier?"[3]

Judge Cochrane was not sure. He declared a half hour adjournment while he consulted the law books. When court was reconvened, His Honour explained, "The section is quite clear. I have no discretion."[4]

The trial of the three accused was later re-scheduled for the Peel County Fall Assizes in October. Thus, as Frank Regan surely gathered the moment he heard of it, if Mickey, who was then still in a Death Cell, was to lose his appeal, he would certainly hang without ever knowing what, if any, consideration Jack Shea got for himself on the Port Credit bank robbery charge; but if Mickey were to win his appeal, his re-trial at the York County Fall Assizes and the bank robbery trial of Jack Shea and the others at Brampton were very likely to overlap in time.

* * *

The retrial of Donald John MacDonald for the murder of James Windsor opened before Mr. Justice J.C. Makins and a Supreme Court jury in the same Toronto City Hall Courtroom No. 3, at 11 a.m., Monday, October 16, 1939. Mickey, unfettered and uncuffed, wearing a neat blue suit and a wan smile, was brought into court on the arm of a sheriff's officer. When asked to plead to the charge of murder, he answered loudly, "Not guilty, sir," as, indeed, he and Alex had both done at the trial in May. In stark contrast to the previous proceeding, only four onlookers were seated in the public enclosure when the trial began. The onset of the Second World War had altered the public outlook on many things, including, as it seemed, Mickey MacDonald and his trial for the most frightening murder in Toronto's recent history.

In his Opening Address to the Jury, Cecil Snyder made much less of criminal events leading up to the murder night of January 7, 1939, than he had done at the May trial. The Court of Appeal decision had ended the Crown's extraordinary interest in such matters as Mickey's now-much-less-relevant criminal associations with Jack Shea, Leo Gauthier, and Joe Smith, and in his alleged involvement in a scheme to rob an Ottawa bank. Thus, Mickey was made to seem to the jury somewhat less of a general criminal menace than at the trial in May.

John R. Shea and Cecil Clancy both put forward their evidence much as before, both recounting yet again the improbable confessionary scene in Shea's apartment. As at the previous trial, a strange silence — a hush — fell over the courtroom as Shea gave testimony that was surely meant to facilitate the hanging of his former friend, Mickey. When, on cross-examination, Frank Regan asked Shea if he was testifying against Mickey for fear of being implicated in the murder, as Shea had previously said he was, Shea's new and better answer was, "I wasn't afraid of being implicated in it; I was afraid of being charged with it."[5]

In the witness box, on Tuesday, October 17, Shea made his first public admission of his participation in the Port Credit bank robbery, which caused Justice Makins to incredulously interject, "Do you know what you are saying? Do you know what this confession means?"[6]

Shea said that he did.

Right then Cecil Snyder jumped in to explain to the Court that Shea had previously confessed to the bank robbery, after which Mr. Snyder, not Shea, handled the discussion with the Court. Soon after, Frank Regan's cross-examination of Shea continued with a loaded question: "Do you know if the attorney general has ordered the hearing of the Port Credit bank hold-up case held in abeyance until after this case is heard?"

Shea said nothing, but Justice Makins then interrupted to observe, acidly, "It seems to me, Mr. Regan, that you are causing a great deal of unnecessary trouble in this case."[7]

But Frank Regan knew what he was doing and why — and he didn't care a whit who didn't like it. The trial of the Port Credit bank robbers would soon take place at the Peel County Fall Assizes, the criminal business of which would commence on October 27.[8] It was now manifestly clear to Regan, if it was not before, that Jack Shea would be the principal Crown witness against Alex and Leo Gauthier at Brampton. Regan knew he was in an inverse race through time with the bank robbery trial, in which his object was to come second. He was certain in his own mind that Jack Shea had "a deal," that Shea would never be held to account for the Port Credit robbery, that he would walk away a free man. He needed Shea to get his "wash" on the bank robbery charge, in public, *before* he addressed the Toronto jury on Mickey's behalf. He needed to be able to tell the jury that Shea had demonstrably been rewarded for his testimony, not only at Brampton, but against Mickey and Alex in the Windsor case, as he, himself, had been saying all along would happen — in the face of the sanctimonious denials of Cecil Snyder, of Jack Shea himself, and of the self-imposed silence of the Attorney General of Ontario, who Regan considered had surely made the decision to piece Shea off for his testimonies both at Brampton and at Toronto. The start of the Brampton trial, Frank Regan knew, ought to tell the tale — and, so, an important part of his strategy was to slow down the murder trial as much as was necessary. Which, of course, by natural inclination and long habit, he was very good at anyway.

Terrier-like, Regan cross-examined Jack Shea, Cecil Clancy, and the five eyewitnesses at length. Notwithstanding that there was now one charge of murder, not two, to be defended, Shea was on the witness stand for almost the same length of time as before — most of that under an intense questioning by Mickey's attorney. As seemed ridiculous, Clancy was cross-examined for "more than an hour" over whether or not he had nibbled at some burnt bacon that Shea had served him on the night of the murder. The thing went on so long that the court spectators, and even the jury, were laughing.[9]

Frank Regan opened the case for the defence immediately after the Crown closed its case at 4 p.m. on Tuesday, October 24, the trial's eighth day. He called the first of what he said would be 30 witnesses he would put on — an astounding number compared to the 13 that he had employed at the first trial. Whereas the trial of Mickey and Alex in May had lasted 17 days, the trial of Mickey alone would consume 15 days, which would make Mickey a defendant in what *The Daily Star* would tell its readers were "the two longest murder trials in Toronto's history."[10]

"Never in my life have I been in Shea's apartment," declared Alex MacDonald, who was then out on bail and would be tried in a few days' time for the Port Credit bank robbery.[11] Alex told the same story that he had testified to at the first trial. As he said, he was at his parents' home and at the nearby Hillcrest Shoe Shop at the time of the murder. Thus, he was not present at 247 Briar Hill Avenue to help slay James Windsor, or at Shea's apartment to hear Mickey's alleged confession, or to participate in any incriminating after-talk such as Shea claimed had happened. Shea's testimony was all a lie, Alex declared with great emphasis.[12]

Frank Regan then put on six of the seven alibi witnesses who had stood up for Alex at his trial in May: Alex's mother; Alex's sisters, Margaret, Alice, and Florence; and Sandy Killah and Tom Wettlaufer, Alex's friends. All six, of course, testified to the same facts as before — their testimonies all directly contradicting Jack Shea's story about Alex and, thus, by indirection, Shea's testimony about Mickey. Alexander MacDonald Sr. did not testify at this second trial of his eldest son, Donald, for murder, nor did he even once attend court, as at the previous trial. Florence MacDonald later said that he "couldn't bear to come." Kitty, Florence, and Brigadier Owen were usually, or always, in court as supporters. Marjorie Constable — the supposed "friend of the family" — had by this time looked in the mirror and attempted suicide. She was for a time in custody in a mental health facility.

The same four Corner witnesses for Mickey appeared as before: Madge Hoskins, Teddy Wells, Andrew Cira, and Bruno Panza, all telling that they saw Mickey dead drunk at Jarvis and Dundas streets between 6:55 and 9:15 p.m. on the evening of January 7, 1939. Madge and Teddy were, of course, the only real alibi witnesses, since the times they claimed to have seen Mickey were near to, or coincident with, the time of the murder.

Now described in the press as "a pretty blonde," Madge told her story as in May: that she had seen Mickey in Nicholls Drug Store at 6:55, and that he had left at 7:05 p.m. But Mickey's candy girl had by now grown a few warts, such that later, in his Charge to the Jury, Justice Makins would ask, "Did this girl look like a girl you could rely on, or did she look like a girl who had been touched by the underworld?"[13] Not seeming quite so young and fair as at her earlier appearance, Madge had admitted to Cecil Snyder on cross-examination that she had been convicted of passing a bogus cheque as payment for two dresses, and that she at times used the alias "Gloria North," because, as she claimed, she was tired of being made out as "The Mystery Woman."[14]

Teddy Wells, who appeared in the uniform of a private of the Army Service Corps, told the jury that he had seen Mickey and "Doc" Clancy in front of the Imperial Bank on the southeast corner of The Corner "at 7:25 p.m. on the night of January 7."[15] At the first trial, Teddy had said it was 7:30 when he saw Mickey and Clancy.

The courtroom went quiet when Mickey took the stand on Monday, October 30, to staunchly fight for his life. There was none of the jaunty, self-assured Mickey who had gone into the box in May and testified off-handedly, as if the case against him did not have consequences that in any way worried him. Following Frank Regan's questions, Mickey, his eyes shining, told the Court and the jury that he had not murdered James Windsor, that there was no such admission of guilt by himself as Shea claimed, and that there was no argument such as Shea had said happened between himself and Alex, who had not entered Shea's apartment. All of this and more was a fabrication of Shea's, Mickey predictably maintained. He denied his supposed motive — his desperate need for $50 that was held by Shea to be his underlying reason for the robbery and thus the murder — and he denied the tale Doc Clancy told about his asking if he knew a bookie named Jimmy Windsor on the day before the deadly incident at 247 Briar Hill Avenue.

At times during his testimony, Mickey almost shouted at the jury, who could see his clenched fists and his face red with anger. Gratuitously, he said that he had offered to take a lie detector test, or truth serum, or to be put under any test that might be devised "to prove my innocence of this crime." During his re-examination by Frank Regan, he histrionically cried out, "I'm as good as on that rope now!"[16] Then he went off on an uncontrolled rant of irrelevancies about his having spent 25 months in solitary in Kingston Penitentiary, about obscure reasons why Jack Shea and Cecil Clancy had framed him, and how he had "died a hundred deaths already in that death cell in the Don." Words burst forth from

Mickey's lips as though his mouth was a river in spate, his persecution complex apparent, while Justice Makins shouted, "Stop! Stop! This has nothing to do with the case."[17]

It was at the end of Cecil Snyder's cross-examination of Mickey on Monday, October 30, that Frank Regan got the word from Brampton that he had been waiting on. At the opening of the trial of John R. Shea, Alex MacDonald, and Leo Gauthier for the Port Credit bank robbery and the wounding of Ray Bryant, the bank's accountant, Peel County Crown Attorney A.G. Davis had risen to inform Mr. Justice Gerald Kelly:

> The Crown is not offering evidence in the case of John R. Shea. On instructions from the attorney general, I ask the indictment be so endorsed and that all further proceedings against Shea be stayed. It is an absolute discretionary power with the attorney general.[18]

This meant the charges against Jack Shea could never be brought up again, that they were null and void forever, that Shea was walking away a free man, as Frank Regan had said would happen from the outset. At the same time, Shea was charged as a material witness and, as Mr. Davis informed the court, he would be employed as a Crown witness in the trials of Alex MacDonald and Leo Gauthier.[19]

Later that afternoon, Shea went into the box and testified against his partners in the Port Credit bank robbery. Under cross-examination by Gordon Ford, Alex's lawyer, Shea lyingly stated that it was a "complete surprise" to him that he was not being prosecuted with the others, and that he had no secret understanding — no deal — with the authorities. He said that he had come to court that morning prepared to plead not guilty to the Port Credit robbery. What was not noticed in court at Brampton until after the trial there was over was that Shea's sworn testimony was wholly at variance with his sworn testimony at Toronto 13 days before, when he had admitted his participation in the Port Credit bank robbery and when Cecil Snyder, too, had told the Court that Shea had previously done so. So how could Shea have come to court at Brampton prepared to plead not guilty to the bank robbery? In the face of his 10 years of living by crime, punctuated by two substantial sojourns in federal prisons, Jack Shea, who had been a confidence man long before he was a bank robber, smoothly told the Brampton jury, "I have always refused to consider that I am a criminal."[20]

In Toronto, Crown Prosecutor Cecil L. Snyder, in his Address to the Jury, explained Shea's good fortune at Brampton in the murder trial by saying:

> There was another case in another county where most of the witnesses were forced to get down on their faces when the crime was committed. It was found necessary to use one of the men who took part in the crime to give the jury evidence.[21]

Thus, Shea, so Mr. Snyder said, was allowed his freedom, solely because he was needed as King's Evidence in the bank robbery case, not because of any testimony he gave against the MacDonalds in the murder trials in Toronto. "I have never made a deal with a prisoner in my life," Snyder told the jury on the Toronto murder trial's fifteenth and last day, Wednesday, November 1, 1939.[22]

The previous afternoon, Frank Regan, his face drawn with tiredness and strain, had addressed the jury for five hours and forty minutes consecutively.[23] His main theme was Jack Shea's deal with the authorities — a deal that, he said, demonstrably allowed Shea to go free in return for his testimonies against Mickey and Alex in the two murder trials. He hit that theme over and over again and, near the end of his presentation, he loudly framed the question that was at the heart of his case: "Gentlemen, there was or there was not a bargain made by the Crown with Jack Shea. Shea was paid, or he was not paid."[24]

The Toronto Police had "manufactured" evidence, Mr. Regan charged. Ideas had been planted in the drunken, incompetent mind of Cecil Clancy, as well as in the minds of the frightened eyewitnesses, all of whom had ideas "drummed into them by some outside force." The line-up on Sunday, January 22, was "a phony," in which the witnesses knew beforehand who would be on display and who to pick out as the murderers. And, as he had done at the previous trial, Regan termed the conduct of the Toronto Police "dangerous to the community."[25]

But the plot Regan saw went right to the top. It involved no less a figure than Gordon Conant, the Attorney General of the Province of Ontario, whom Regan said had visited the first trial twice, the appeal once, this trial, too, on Friday, October 20, and who was "the only man who can direct that charges against Shea be dropped."[26] It was Gordon Conant who had ordered the charges against Shea stayed and who had delayed the bank robbery trial at Brampton till the last possible moment in hopes of keeping the murder trial jury from knowing that Jack Shea was to go free.

When asked on Monday, October 30, to comment on the charges against John R. Shea being dropped, Attorney General Conant only said, "I can't add anything."[27] So far as is known, Mr. Conant would say nothing at all about the matter for public consumption, then or later. He merely left the explanations, such as they were, to Cecil L. Snyder, the most-successful Crown prosecutor in Ontario's history, who, by repute, had never up to this time failed to get a conviction in a capital trial.

CHAPTER THIRTEEN

Two Verdicts
(November 1, 1939–November 22, 1939)

JUSTICE J.C. MAKINS' TWO-HOUR Charge to the Jury was completed at 2:20 p.m., Wednesday, November 1, after which the jury went out a few minutes later. Frank Regan was not satisfied with His Lordship's remarks about John R. Shea's evidence, which, not unlike those of Justice McFarland in May, did not see extraordinary danger therein and discounted the likelihood of Shea's having a "deal" with the authorities. Incredibly, Justice Makins had said:

> It is not new that a man turns Crown's evidence. No doubt the man who does expects preferential treatment. But that is quite different from the defence submission that Shea made a bargain with the police.
>
> It could be argued, I suppose, that Shea could perjure himself and implicate others in something he committed. But what point would he have in doing that? Confine yourself to the evidence he gave.[1]

After the jury first retired, Mr. Regan put it to Justice Makins that his remarks had "thrown a halo around brother Shea. You asked why

Shea would lie. The answer is, to save his own good-for-nothing carcass from imprisonment of 14 to 20 years."[2] The jury was brought back in for further instructions and finally went out to consider the evidence at 3:20 p.m. Nobody was expecting a 25-minute verdict of guilty this time.

During the 15 days of the trial, spectators gradually filled up the courtroom, to the extent that, notwithstanding the general preoccupation with the war in Europe, the public seats were now each day packed to capacity. After the jury went out to deliberate, most of the watchers were soon turned out of the courtroom. That left many curious thrill-seekers and a good part of the city's underworld loitering about the corridors of City Hall. Mickey's Gangland friends and acquaintances gathered in small whispering groups spaced out about the halls, till, at 6 p.m., all of the loiterers were turfed from the building entirely. Policemen and sheriff's officers were set to guard the doors, while most of those who were evicted were left to hang about the James Street entrance, hour upon hour, waiting for the jury's decision on whether or not Donald John MacDonald would live or die.

Kitty, Florence MacDonald, and Teddy Wells were among those close enough to the issue to be allowed to stay inside. As the hours passed, Kitty mixed in among "the laws" — the interested detectives — discussing and arguing the case with them. She also took it as her right to wander in and out of the press room where the reporters were waiting on the verdict while playing cribbage, gossiping, and pulling on a bottle of Wiser's Special Blend. Many years later, Gwyn Thomas recalled Kitty as "a good-looking but rather hard-boiled girl in her early twenties" who was "always beautifully dressed" and who that night "wore a silver fox fur around her neck." She took a liking to young John Bassett, later the publisher of the *Telegram*, who was then reporting for the *Globe*. "She sidled around to where he was playing cribbage, got as close to him as she possibly could and flicked the fur at his face, saying, 'Here, big boy, play with some tail,'" laughed Mr. Thomas, who never forgot Bassett's face going red in embarrassment.[3]

Kitty's untoward behaviour had hit its apex when, on the evening of the first day of Mickey's retrial, she and Charlie Dorland, her "other man," were charged in connection with having opened "a joint" on quiet residential Rathnelly Avenue, perhaps 150 yards from the MacDonald family's home.[4] Six weeks after the trial's end, Kitty would again be open for business, this time in a nearby Avenue Road apartment. For the second time within two months, she made the papers when she was convicted of keeping a disorderly house in which another prominent lady-of-the-evening was also a found-in. This earned the notorious "Kitty Cat" MacDonald 60 days in jail.[5]

Meantime, the jury was still out.

At their home on Poplar Plains Road, the MacDonald family was anxiously awaiting word from City Hall as well as word from the Brampton Courthouse, where, by happenstance, the trial of Alex and Leo Gauthier had gone to the jury about 9 p.m., 5 hours and 40 minutes after the jury at the Toronto murder trial began its deliberation. Peg MacDonald and a girl who was then Alex's fiancée, were sitting on developments at Brampton. Periodic updates were being telephoned to the anxious family by those watching and waiting on both verdicts.

At 10:10 p.m., the murder-trial jury returned to City Hall Courtroom No. 3. The foreman asked that they hear again Justice Makins' exact definition of reasonable doubt as it was given in his Charge to the Jury earlier that day. The court reporter read out what Makins had then said, the gist of which was that reasonable doubt "must be an honest doubt, a doubt of reasonable honest men trying to do their duty."[6]

The jury then retired again to further consider the evidence. An hour and twenty minutes later, at 11:40 p.m., after having deliberated in all 8 hours and 20 minutes, the jurymen returned quietly with their verdict. Only a handful was in the public gallery to see and hear it. Kitty and Florence — Mickey's own family — were not permitted into the courtroom, as was the case with some others who, by whatever means, had gotten into the City Hall on legitimate business or on some pretext. Dozens, if not hundreds, of would-be spectators, many of them "police characters" who had been pushed out of the building at 6 o'clock, still waited outside by the James Street door.

At the direction of the Bench, the Court Registrar soon asked, "Gentlemen, what is your verdict?"

"We find the prisoner — not guilty," the foreman answered in a deep voice, with a noticeable pause before the last two words.[7]

For a long moment, Mickey merely stared at the head juror with unblinking eyes. Then he gave out with a great sigh of relief that was heard throughout the courtroom. After which a smile appeared on his pale face and the weary look that he had worn like a suit of clothes throughout many days — a look of anxiety and disquiet — disappeared from his person.

Cecil L. Snyder did not look happy. This was the first and only defeat he would ever suffer in a capital trial.

For a few seconds there was noise and confusion in the court. People murmured and a half-dozen reporters went clattering out the door into the hall corridor on their way to telephone their city desks with word of Mickey's acquittal.

After the Court Registrar affirmed the jury's verdict, Justice Makins directed his attention to the jury.

"Gentlemen, the responsibility for this verdict is yours and yours only. You are discharged from further duty," His Lordship said to the jurymen in a cold tone that left no room to doubt that he did not approve of their finding. Then, turning to the prisoner's dock, he curtly ordered, "Stand up, MacDonald."[8] After Mickey got slowly to his feet, Justice Makins continued:

> The verdict of the jury is that you are not guilty. It very well might have been otherwise. In fact, I am of the opinion that it ought to have been otherwise. You have escaped by a hair's breadth the severest penalty the law allows. I hope you have learned your lesson.[9]

That was the end of it. Court was adjourned. Mickey was taken downstairs, then, after a few minutes, out to the courtyard at the rear of City Hall, where he was loaded into a large black sedan that whisked him away to the Don Jail. For the first time since February 24, Mickey did not have to make the trip wearing leg-irons and handcuffs.

Kitty got word of the trial's result from a reporter who ran out of court to telephone the news of Mickey's acquittal to his paper. When told of the verdict, Kitty yelled Mickey's name and ran off down the corridor to vicinity of the courtroom, where friends and foes of the now-exonerated Mickey were milling about amongst each other. Kitty leaped into the arms of Florence and Teddy Wells, all of them made joyously happy by Mickey's good fortune. Then, after a few minutes, Kitty and Florence rushed by taxi to the Don Jail, as they had done other days of the trial, so they could exchange a few shouted words back and forth with Mickey as he was taken inside by way of the front door.

"How do you feel, honey?" Kitty queried loudly.

"I feel like a million dollars!" Mickey answered jubilantly.

"You can't keep a good man down," Florence shouted at her eldest brother, Donnie, as yet again the "good man" disappeared through the massive front door of the dreary Don Jail from where he would soon be transported to Kingston Penitentiary to serve the unexpired portion of the time he still owed on his two-year sentence for the blackjack beating of James Elder.[10]

Representatives of all of the Toronto papers went to Poplar Plains Road "to get comment from the family," who had had the news telephoned to them by both Teddy Wells and Brigadier Owen. By the time the press got there, a joyous celebration that involved much of the large, tight-knit MacDonald clan was in progress. "Thank the Lord," Mickey's mother repeated again and again. Family members clasped each other in their arms, crying happily, "Isn't it wonderful!" The shadow of the rope that had hung over Mickey for many months in a very real sense had hung over the rest of the MacDonalds, too. The suspense and the strain of having to live with the possibility of the awful consequence of a guilty verdict had been theirs on a daily basis since February 23. Now they were free from the family agony — or so it seemed for most of an hour.[11]

Then the telephone rang again.

While the MacDonalds were rejoicing over Mickey's acquittal, the jury at Brampton had come in at 12:07 a.m., Thursday morning, with guilty verdicts on both the bank robbery and shooting with intent counts against Alex MacDonald and Leo Gauthier. The jury had believed Jack Shea's testimony rather than that of "interested witnesses" — Alex's mother and Anne Smith, his older sister — who both had testified Alex was at his restaurant at the time of the robbery.[12] Nor did the jury embrace the arguments of Basil Essery, Gauthier's lawyer, who, much like Frank Regan, saw a plot against the defendants by "those in authority" — the attorney general and the police. At 12:35 a.m., after hearing pleas for leniency and other arguments from their lawyers, Justice Gerald Kelly ended the three-day trial by sentencing both Alex and Gauthier to 10 years in prison. Word of this was telephoned to the MacDonald family less than an hour after the good-news verdict on Mickey. It was then that Alexander and Margaret MacDonald were made painfully aware that their most intelligent and most-promising son, Alex, now aged 20, would be going off to Kingston Penitentiary, sentenced to more time than Mickey had then served in all his days in prison. Gordon Ford, Alex's lawyer, pleaded with Justice Kelly, arguing, "A long term in the penitentiary will make a confirmed criminal out of him."[13] His plea was truly an augury.

The telephone call from Brampton ended the gaiety on Poplar Plains Road. One by one the family members soon detached themselves from the gathering. Maggie MacDonald, tired and worn-down by it all, was left alone with the reporters, who at last got the message and left the house themselves.

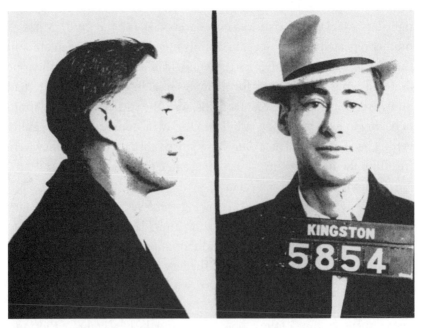

Mickey as he looked in November 1939, soon after being acquitted of the murder of bookmaker James Windsor. (Library and Archives Canada)

BOOK II

Mickey McDonald, Canada's Public Enemy No. 1

CHAPTER FOURTEEN

The Mad Dog of Jarvis Street
(October 5, 1940–March 28, 1944)

MICKEY MCDONALD'S ARREST FOR the murder of Jimmy Windsor, and the many months of almost-unrelenting publicity that followed, were the beginning of a watershed in Mickey's life and career in crime. Basically, these events amplified Mickey, made him bigger than he had been, bigger than he was or could ever be. They altered the way Mickey was to be seen in the future by many other criminals, by the press, by the public, by the Toronto Police and, ultimately, by himself. Many "police characters" of a sort became impressed with Mickey, who they now saw as a killer who had gotten away with murder — a perception Mickey is said to have done nothing at all to dispel. Mickey himself would take a little time to see it, but he too would come to understand that he now had a greater cachet in illicit circles and that he could use his new standing as his ticket to better-paying crime.

To elements of the print media, if Mickey had not then made himself into a big-league criminal, he could certainly be made into a big news story — and his impending leadership role in "Toronto's Greatest Crime of World War II" would make him seem to be almost worthy of such notice. To the Toronto Police detective department, Mickey was still the minor-league thief and pimp, or near-pimp, who he had always been, but now he was considered to be both extremely dangerous and a criminal who, in escaping the rope, had made the Toronto Police look to be at fault. He was seen by detectives as an erratic, gun-carrying thug who had decided to live by crime, who might well kill again and who, one way or another, Toronto would be well rid of.

Mickey completed his sentence for robbery with violence on October 5, 1940, and returned to Toronto, where he briefly moved into a furnished apartment on Avenue Road. There he spent some time with Kitty, but he had no intention of ever living with her again. Kitty had become a liability in Mickey's professional life. The fact that she had testified for the Crown against Johnny "The Bug" Brown and the others in January 1939 meant that he had to choose between Kitty and his criminal associates — in effect, to choose between his wife and his life in crime. If he had tried to live with a known "rat," Mickey would have completely lost caste among his own kind. He would no longer have been regarded as trustworthy. He would have had to get a job — and, notwithstanding his sundry declarations and occasional feints in that direction, Mickey was not truly ready for anything like that.

Kitty had also become a problem in another way. She had become a heroin addict — and in the short time he spent with her in the fall of 1940, Mickey began to "crank up" too. This was potentially ruinous and, as foolish as he often was, Mickey was smart enough to figure this out.

In his first month of freedom, Mickey was getting regular visits from Detective-Sergeant John Nimmo and Detective Edmund Tong, both of whom clearly regarded him as a civic undesirable. Why don't you go somewhere else? was their basic message to Mickey, who they already knew was making almost daily trips to Hamilton. The question in the minds of the detectives was why? A likely answer was that, even by this time, Mickey was both buying and selling heroin — and Hamilton was where his connection-of-the-moment was. How else could he then pay for the "smack" he was using? Steal, sell your body, or sell heroin yourself. That's how users get by.

Then on December 8, 1940, Mickey vacated the Avenue Road apartment and for a time dropped off the radar of the Toronto Police.

December 1940 was the real end of Kitty in Mickey's life, though she would resist her exclusion till May 1944, when she herself would file for divorce, charging Mickey with adultery and naming Mickey's then love-interest, Kathleen Donovan, as co-respondent.[1] Mickey now simply moved to Vancouver, supposedly to remake his life, and Kitty was not asked to go along. But the remake did not take and, as was generally the case, Mickey saw the fault as other than his own. In a Toronto court, in April 1941, he would whine to a judge: "I went 3,000 miles away, to Vancouver, to try to get away from my old life and start a new one, but as soon as I got there I was picked up by the Vancouver Police. I learned afterward that the Toronto Police sent a circular saying that Mickey McDonald was in Vancouver."[2]

So Mickey was soon back at "work" at The Corner in the old ways. Perhaps he simply missed his kind of "action." In the early war years, he peacocked around Gangland, as though he were Red Ryan or John Dillinger, basking in an importance that he had had none of before.[3] Now he was pointed out on Jarvis Street, not as a garden-variety shopbreaker or clip artist, but as a rounder of real note. "Look, there's Mickey McDonald! The guy who iced Jimmy Windsor!" the cognoscenti murmured to each other — and, notwithstanding the fact that Mickey was barely eating, a class of low-end criminals began to see him as a kind of legend on "the Boulevard of Broken Dreams."[4]

Early on the morning of March 8, 1941, Mickey was charged in connection with what was apparently an instance of the old Badger Game, where a woman sets up a "mark" with money to be robbed by one or more other men. The event happened near The Corner, where Robert McQuaid of Havelock, Ontario, looking for a "good time," was shunted into an alley, beaten up, and relieved of all of $12!

But unlike most victims of such "a score," McQuaid wasn't willing to let it go. Five weeks later, in York County Court, Mickey, again as Donald MacDonald, was convicted of robbery with violence in the McQuaid incident and sentenced by Judge Ian Macdonell to 30 months in Kingston Penitentiary. Andrew Cira, Mickey's alleged accomplice in the robbery, who in 1939 had been a witness for Mickey at his two trials for murder, was similarly convicted and sentenced to six months in reformatory. "I haven't committed a single crime since I left the penitentiary," Mickey bleated to the judge, to no avail.[5]

The McQuaid conviction does not appear on most versions of Mickey's lengthy police record by reason of the fact it was quashed on appeal in June 1941. Chief Justice Robert S. Robertson of the Ontario Court of Appeal saw merit in Arthur Martin's argument that there was simply insufficient evidence to convict the accused. Justices Masten and Gillanders concurred. Thus, Mickey went free.

Now, on Jarvis Street, Mickey — the unpunished killer — was much more of a force than before. Two punks named Borden and Turner brought him in as a "mediator" in their dispute with a hotel waiter named Cecil Guyette, who, after he was viciously set upon on his way home from work, persisted in pressing charges against them for assault and wounding. In consequence of his efforts on behalf of this dubious pair, Mickey himself was at first charged with threatening, then with attempting to persuade a witness not to prosecute — but both charges fell down in court.

Years later, Roy Steinberg, who operated a taxi from a stand at Jarvis and Gerrard Streets, remembered the Mickey of these days as "a pretty nice guy, who would sometimes ask for credit but who would always pay double the fare later."[6] Policeman Art Keay liked Mickey too, at some times but not others. He was, said Mr. Keay, "a nice guy when he wasn't drinking but real bad when drunk."[7]

*   *   *

By the summer of 1942, Mickey was living with Kathleen "Kay" Donovan, a girl he had met in Vancouver, who, badly smitten, had pursued Mickey back to Toronto. Born Kathleen Pavlena in Hamilton of Italian parents, Kay had first married a Hamiltonian named Mike Donovan and the couple had gone out to the West Coast. There, either before or after the marriage collapsed, Kathleen had resorted to prostitution and as a result had acquired two convictions for being found in a bawdy house. Later, in 1941, in Toronto, Kay was convicted once for soliciting on the street.

The couple took Apartment 4 at 514A Yonge Street, with a large third-floor front window that overlooked Toronto's main thoroughfare, just northwest of Maple Leaf Gardens. There, without benefit of clergy, Kathleen began calling herself "Mrs. Donald J. MacDonald." Kitty, who dearly wanted Mickey back, made it her business to frequent the White Spot Restaurant, at 530 Yonge Street, a few doors north of Mickey's and Kay's apartment.[8] There, Kitty would cattishly talk down Kathleen on an ongoing basis, to anyone who would listen. During these war-time days inside the White Spot, Kitty engaged in at least two vicious fights of the kind for which she was long-since locally notorious — scratching, biting, spitting, swearing — in both cases the unfortunate opposition being a soldier in the Canadian armed forces. "The restaurant management was afraid of her, afraid to throw her out," remembered Robert Lackaey, a White Spot Restaurant patron, many years later.[9]

For a short time in September 1942, Mickey tried to run a booze can out of a venue at 297 Parliament Street. No sooner had he opened than he was raided by the police twice within a few days. Upon his second conviction for Breach of the Liquor Act, Mickey was required to serve a 90-day sentence in the Burwash Reformatory.

* * *

Then came the incident that, more than any other, conjured up the public image of Mickey as "The Mad Dog of Jarvis Street." It happened on the night of December 23, 1942, at the Royal Cecil Hotel — Gangland's notorious "Bucket of Blood" — on the northwest corner of The Corner.[10] About 10:30 p.m., Johnny Hill, a heroin-addicted jailhouse friend of Mickey's, was refused admittance to the "Ladies and Escorts" room of the hotel by William "Old Bill" Blair, the Cecil's 88-year-old doorman.[11] Hill's wife was inside with another man — and Hill didn't like it. There was some sort of struggle between Hill and the waiters in the "Men's Entrance" taproom, after which Hill was physically ejected, but not before he issued a threat. "You better not be here when I come back. I won't be alone," he told the always rough-and-ready waiters of the Royal Cecil Hotel.[12]

An hour later, five men with blood in their eyes came back to "The Cecil" looking for revenge for the terrible slight that had been visited upon Johnny Hill: Hill himself; Mickey McDonald, who was already long-since barred from The Cecil; and three others who were not certainly identified and thus were not later charged. After knocking the elderly doorman into a snowbank and kicking him, the gang fought their way inside, where a melee that was said to have lasted 20 minutes erupted. "It's the Old Jarvis Street Gang," someone shouted, and most of the patrons ran out. The invaders were joined by fellow ex-convict, Albert Johns, who got up from a table to help Hill's supporters beat up the hotel's staff. Mickey and the rest left before the police arrived, leaving waiters Sam Neveau and Steve Cibo flat on their backs on the floor, tapman Neil McIntyre unconscious from the smack of a wooden chair over his head, and "Old Bill" Blair, the aged doorman, suffering from an assortment of injuries, including a badly cut forehead, a badly swollen and discoloured left eye, and numerous bruises about his body, some of them 5 inches in diameter. In addition, Johnny Hill had stolen Steve Cibo's watch.

"Hitler would give me better treatment than that," Mickey shouted at Magistrate Robert J. Browne on Thursday, December 30, 1942, when His Worship refused to consider bail for the thug the press was now calling "The Mad Dog of Jarvis Street."[13] Mickey sat in the Don Jail, unable to get bail in any of three different courts till February 23, 1943 — 62 days after the Royal Cecil brawl — when Mr. Justice Chevrier of the Supreme Court of Ontario allowed him out on a $5,000 bond. Mickey was perhaps released on compassionate grounds; his father, Alexander MacDonald, who had been in poor health, died at home of heart failure within a fortnight of Mickey getting free.[14] Before long, Mickey's mother, who had long suffered with "bad nerves," would be committed to the Ontario Hospital at Whitby, a mental health facility. And most of the six MacDonald girls would be married and gone by the end of 1943. The family of Alexander and Margaret MacDonald, always strong for their own, was growing up and dispersing. Thus, support for Mickey and his two younger brothers, Alex and Edwin, who were in different stages of emerging as significant criminals themselves, would be somewhat weaker in the future.

The County Court trials of Mickey McDonald and John Hill for conspiracy to assault Sam Neveau, for the assault of Neveau, for conspiracy to assault William Blair, and for the assault of Blair, as well as the trial of

Hill only for the theft of Steve Cibo's watch, began on Thursday, March 18, 1943. Two days of testimony were heard before the trials were at first suspended for a week, then the jury was discharged and the case traversed to the next session of the court. The reason was that Cibo, an important Crown witness, had suffered a heart attack on the witness stand. The case would not finally be heard until March 18, 1944 — 15 months after the incident happened. The Cecil's staff, a soldier named Gordon Jones, who had got into the brawl on the side of the waiters, and several patrons of the hotel, would testify to the violent actions of McDonald and Hill on the night of December 23, 1942. The defendants, Albert Johns, and several inmates brought from jails and prisons, including a woman brought from the Mercer Reformatory, testified for Mickey and Hill.[15] The star witness for the defence was Steve Rodall, an ex-Kingston inmate, whose testimony contradicted the testimonies of the Crown witnesses.[16] After asking for the protection of the court, Rodall claimed that he, not Mickey or Hill, had been the one who roughed up "Old Bill" Blair. Rodall's unabashed story was that he had hit Blair "with an open hand" and the elderly man fell into a snowbank.

A County Court jury, on Tuesday, March 28, 1944, found the two defendants guilty of conspiracy to assault Sam Neveau, and of assaulting Neveau. Hill was convicted of stealing Steve Cibo's watch. Both Mickey and Hill were acquitted of conspiracy to assault William Blair, and of assaulting Blair.

According to what he later said, Mickey made "a fairly decent living" in 1942–43 "running dice games and liquor" from his Yonge Street apartment.[17] But there was more he did not tell. Now he often had to meet people in the daytime, and late at night he would sometimes call a taxi to 514A Yonge — and he would go out doing deliveries. The product he dropped off was often not liquor. It was heroin. Mickey was selling small, but he was selling. The war, which provided lots of opportunities both lawful and illicit for those who had had few or none during the Depression, made many things possible that would not otherwise have been so. At some point, as peculiar as it might seem, Kay, who had domestic inclinations, came to see "Donnie" as the man who would get for her The Little House with the White Picket Fence. With Kay, almost anything Donnie did was just fine, in part because, as she later said, he was supporting her! Now Donnie had difficulty being wrong about anything. He was looked after, catered to, loved, as if he were something precious. Kathleen mothered him and spoiled him with affection and attention. She made him elaborate home-cooked meals and knitted sweaters for him. For Mickey, it was almost like being at home with his own dear mother! Perhaps because of Kay herself, perhaps because he saw possibilities that were not there before, perhaps because his time had almost ended in July 1939, Mickey too now dared to want more out of life than The Corner, more whisky, and the next dirty little scam.

And now there was a way!

Like many thieves and racketeers of the day, Mickey had begun to see heroin as his road to big money — and his and Kay's mutual means to a happy and prosperous future together. The two things that were most necessary were a reliable and safe supplier, and enough start-up cash to buy and sell in quantity. With these, he could make a prosperous living while insulating himself from the worst of the serious risks in the heroin game. To this point in his life, so far as is known, Mickey McDonald and big-money crime had never gotten past the talking stage. But now Mickey knew that he had to take a big chance, maybe more than one. And if he lost it would cost, not only because he now at last thought he had something to lose but because big crime gets long time in prison.

CHAPTER FIFTEEN

Toronto's Greatest Crime of World War II
(December 13, 1943)

"TORONTO'S GREATEST CRIME OF World War II" happened on the bitterly cold morning of Monday, December 13, 1943.

About 6:30 a.m., George Butcher, a driver for Western Freight Lines, arrived at the company's yard at 235 Wellington Street West with an overnight load of 600 cases of whisky and gin from the Hiram Walker Distillery in Walkerville, Ontario, consigned to the Gooderham & Worts Distillery, Trinity Street, Toronto.[1] There was no one at Western Freight's warehouse to receive the shipment, and Butcher, the regular driver on the Monday morning run, knew there would not be until 7 a.m. It was still dark and cold and Butcher was tired, so he began to nod off in the cab of his tractor with the motor running.

After a few minutes, the driver's door was abruptly yanked open, and a startled George Butcher was confronted by a man who held "what looked like an automatic gun" pointed directly at him. There were two others in company with the man with the automatic.

"Get out of the truck," the gunman roughly ordered.

"All I could distinguish was that he had a thin face and wore a light-coloured overcoat," Butcher later said.[2] He did not guess that the man with the gun was Donald "Mickey" McDonald, one of Canada's best-known criminals.[3] But he soon knew that his truck and its load were being forcibly hijacked and that he was being taken prisoner.

The three robbers frog-marched Butcher out a gate at the northwest corner of the yard, then east along Wellington Street to Windsor Street, where there waited what Butcher later described as both "a grey sedan" and "a light-coloured sedan." They put the hapless trucker into the back seat, made him lie on the floor, then stuffed a pillow over his head, and told him to take care not to look up. The three men then got into the car, the man with the pistol in the back seat on the right side, then the sedan — a Nash — started to move off. Butcher at first only guessed that they were in convoy with his truck and its $35,000 cargo as it went west on Front Street, then south, then west again along Fleet Street West.[4] Two other men, one an unemployed cartage driver, had gotten into the tractor's cab at the Western Freight Lines terminal. In fact, there were five men involved in the actual hijacking, and at least six others who had some part in the larger criminal scheme.

By Butcher's later estimate, there followed a half hour ride, much of it through city streets. He heard the iron-wheeled clatter of passing streetcars and noticed that the man who was sticking a gun in his ribs was "sniffing and coughing with a bad cold."[5] Near the ride's end the Nash turned onto a gravel road and soon reached its destination. Then Butcher heard the truck coming. "All I could hear was that it was working pretty heavy, as though it were going up a grade," he later testified. "Then after running a little longer, I heard something crash, together with what I thought were barn doors being closed."[6]

The gravel road was Richview sideroad near Royal York Road and Eglinton Avenue in Etobicoke Township, a mostly-rural outlying area of Toronto.[7] The hijackers had moved the truck about 10 miles west and north from where it was stolen.

Waiting at the Lazy L Ranch, a riding stable about 800 feet west along Richview sideroad, were three men who were there to receive the truck and its load: James Shorting, the proprietor of the Lazy L, who during the daytime sold used cars from a lot near Dundas and Keele streets in Toronto's west end; Howard Wilkinson, aged 19, a $15-a-week stablehand Shorting employed to do the work of the riding stable; and Benny Zanelli, a small-time bootlegger, gambler, and occasional labourer, who was the hijack gang's man at the scene of their intended liquor cache.

The previous Saturday afternoon, Zanelli, who knew Shorting casually, had brought Sam Mancuso, a bootlegger and professional fence of stolen goods, to the ranch. Introduced to Shorting, and later to Wilkinson, only as "Sammy," Mancuso was looking for a place to store what Zanelli had termed "a few cases of Christmas liquor," and Shorting greedily agreed to let them use the barn's haymow in return for $20 up-front and "a couple of cases." Shorting, as he later testified, had no inkling that the liquor was to be stolen at gunpoint; instead, he imagined, without really knowing, that it would be untaxed liquor brought from Quebec. Later, he and Wilkinson "shook out some hay," to be used to camouflage the liquor while it was in the barn. Sam Mancuso paid Wilkinson $5 for this.

A police photograph of the Lazy L Ranch barn from the southwest, showing the ramp to the second-floor haymow and, on the right, the home of Mrs. Kathleen Jackson. (Archives of Ontario, file 4-32 #1498)

Monday morning, when he heard the tractor trailer coming up the hill on Richview sideroad, Shorting rightly sensed the danger in the bargain he had made. He was expecting a light delivery truck and "a few cases of Christmas liquor." Straining up the grade was a fully loaded tractor trailer. Then the driver made the mistake of pulling onto the property to the east, that of Shorting's landlady, Mrs. Kathleen Jackson, who didn't like Shorting at all and had previous reason not to trust him. After the truck backed out of her lane, though it was still dark, Mrs. Jackson began to curiously watch the hijackers from her parlour window. When there was more light, she would send her son-in-law, Ted Hogan, to surreptitiously take the license plate number of the Nash sedan that accompanied the truck onto the Lazy L property. The car's plate, 8-E-391, would inescapably tie William "Billy" Baskett, an unemployed Hamilton factory worker who was Kay's brother-in-law and a gambling friend of Mickey's, to the hijacking of the truck and the kidnapping of George Butcher.

Mrs. Jackson was unable to see what happened after the truck driver circled Shorting's barn. The tractor trailer was backed up the short, steep ramp on the barn's west side leading to the second-floor haymow. The first time it went up the ramp the back of the trailer didn't reach the doorway. The second time the driver hit the gas too hard, such that the trailer and its load — 17 tons in all — went right into the barn, where its rear wheels smashed clear through the planks of the second-floor. The flooring on a part of the west side of the barn collapsed, which meant that "the truck was right down on the timbers of the barn," the trailer was impaled, and the tractor immobilized.[8]

This was an outright catastrophe for the hijackers. It was immediately obvious to them that the truck could not be freed, that it would soon be discovered, and that the stolen liquor was lost to them unless they could find a way to get it out of the barn quickly. Over and above that was the important question of what Shorting and Wilkinson would say to the police when the truck was discovered. Shorting's loyalty to the scheme was minimal — and Wilkinson's was non-existent.

Then, after a brief conference among the hijackers, someone said, "Okay, let's get the truck unloaded."[9]

More than half the men went to work at unloading the truck in the dark barn by the dim light of a lantern and a flashlight. The driver of the hijacked tractor trailer may not have gotten out of the cab until it was time to leave. Apparently his face was never seen by Shorting or Wilkinson. Mickey McDonald was still out in the Nash sedan guarding George Butcher, the hostage driver. Shorting, after moving several frightened horses that were stabled too near the collapsed section of the barn, escaped dealing with the grim situation by going to give neighbourly help to Ted Hogan, whose car was frozen up and wouldn't start.

Then, after a time, a gunshot was fired!

Bill Baskett, who had replaced Mickey as the man guarding Butcher in the Nash, was cold and wanted a bottle of whisky to help warm himself and his prisoner. Apparently, the shot was Baskett's foolhardy way of getting the attention of those in the barn.

Kathleen Jackson and Ted Hogan heard the gunshot — and were alarmed by it. Mrs. Jackson, still watching through the morning darkness from her parlour window, saw the simultaneous flash of a gun in or near the Nash, and then she saw three men come out of the barn to investigate. She watched them speak briefly with "the man in the car" and then go back inside the barn.

Shorting heard the shot, too. His qualms about "the few cases of Christmas liquor" now further aggravated, he stopped helping Ted Hogan and returned to the Lazy L and the Nash sedan, to see what was going on. He just missed seeing the three men who had gone back into the barn. Shorting pulled open the Nash's back passenger door and, as he later said, was surprised to find "a man sitting there with a gun in his hand and another man half lying on the seat and half on the floor, with his head covered up."[10] He would later testify that he knew then that the truckload of liquor was stolen — and that the man who was held prisoner on the floor of the Nash was the truck's driver.

Baskett's response to Shorting's interruption was to forcefully tell the proprietor of the Lazy L Ranch, "Get out of here, you son-of-a-bitch, or I will blow your brains out. Get into that barn and help unload that stuff."[11]

Shorting did as he was told.

Inside the barn there were "about six men unloading in a chain." Shorting joined them. The unloading, which took more than an hour, was finished a few minutes after the gunshot. In the interim, as Shorting and Wilkinson both later testified in court, a man in a light-coloured trenchcoat, who had not participated in the unloading, and who they had not previously seen at all, came into the dimly-lit barn, took a bottle from a broken case, and began to leave. Whereupon an unseen voice in the barn instructed, "Mickey, don't take that now. Wait until later."[12]

The man called "Mickey," as quoted by Shorting, answered dismissively, "The man in the car wants a drink. He is damned near freezing."[13] Then, bottle in hand, he either went down a ladder or slowly disappeared out the barn door. Wilkinson and Shorting's later testimonies gave him separate exits.

When the truck was fully unloaded, the hijackers held a brief conference, which, as Shorting later said under oath, ended with one saying, "Oh, hell, this truck will be nothing to get out of here; Mickey knows everybody, and he will find somebody to get it out in a few minutes."[14] Shorting said nothing for fear of the consequences — but for $20 and the promise of two cases of liquor, he was obviously being left holding the bag. Then the five men who had arrived with the stolen truck, quickly piled into the Nash sedan and, with George Butcher still on the floor and now forced to wear a green-coloured lady's kerchief as a blindfold, the Nash briskly departed the Lazy L Ranch.

Butcher himself would later testify that the car "drove quite aways over a gravel road," then it stopped and he was "thrown out into a ditch" and told not to take the blindfold off for five minutes. After the hijackers drove away, Butcher disregarded his instructions and soon came to know that he was on Brooke Avenue, a residential street southeast of Wilson Avenue and Bathurst Street in North York Township, about ten miles northeast of the Lazy L Ranch. He walked to the Wellwood Dairy at the corner of Bathurst and Brooke, where he telephoned Western Freight Lines to let them know why their truck and its driver were not yet at the Wellington Street terminal. The time, Butcher noted, was 9:10 a.m. A police car arrived at the dairy soon after.

CHAPTER SIXTEEN

Jock and the Chinaman
(December 13, 1943)

WHEN DETECTIVE-SERGEANT JOHN "JOCK" Nimmo and Detective Edmund "The Chinaman" Tong, who was Welsh, not Chinese, arrived at Toronto police headquarters to start work about 12:30 that Monday afternoon, they learned of the hijacking and of its attendant kidnapping. As had become their practice on almost any major crime of a sort, Nimmo and Tong, who were regarded by some as the Toronto Police "heavy squad," went straight to Mickey McDonald's apartment over a store at 514A Yonge Street. The two detectives' doggedness was about to pay off in the most important arrest of either of their careers — and the major catastrophe of a lawless lifetime for Donald "Mickey" McDonald, the gunman the two policemen most wanted to "get."

About one o'clock, Kathleen Donovan let the detectives into Apartment 4 when Nimmo asked to see "Donald McDonald." Once inside, the detectives sensed immediately that they had happened on a meeting that was about the crime they had just been assigned to investigate.

Gathered in the living room, trying to sort out their end of the botched caper of a few hours before, were Mickey, Sam Mancuso, and a Gooderham & Worts salesman named Max Applebaum, who was, at the

same time, one of Toronto's biggest bootleggers. These were the princi-
pals in the hijack — the three who had organized it and who intended to
wholesale most of the stolen liquor to others in the underground trade,
just as if it were an ordinary load of bootleg from Quebec. When the
detectives entered, Mickey, who was obviously suffering with a bad cold
or some similar ailment, was sitting on a footstool in his pajamas, and a
serious conversation was in progress. The others were standing.

"What's going on here?" Nimmo demanded to know.

"It's just a family gathering," Mickey answered calmly.

In the meantime Detective Tong had entered the apartment's small
bedroom and found a second collection of unlikely Monday afternoon visitors to the couple's living quarters. Kathleen was entertaining
Bill Baskett, as well as Edwin MacDonald (Mickey's then 18-year-old
brother) and Vic Taylor, an unemployed cartage driver and small-time
bootlegger, whose brother, Fred Taylor, not by coincidence, had recently
been let go from a job at Western Freight Lines.

A police photo of the trailer of the hijacked liquor truck being lifted out of the
barn on the evening after the armed robbery and kidnapping of driver George
Butcher. (Archives of Ontario, file 4-32 #1498)

Since there was limited space in their police car, the detectives rounded up the four suspects they knew least well — Baskett, Edwin, Applebaum, and Taylor — and took them to 149 College Street. Twenty minutes later, they returned to get Mickey and Mancuso, who they imagined would still be at the apartment. Sam, however, had simply left. Nimmo and Tong then took Mickey to police headquarters, where he and the four others were put into an identification line-up viewed by George Butcher. Later that day, in a second line-up, all but Mickey, who had been allowed to leave, were looked at by Kathleen Jackson and two of her daughters, who had also seen some of what happened at the Lazy L Ranch. None of these witnesses identified any of the men put on parade in consequence of their being found at Mickey's apartment.[1]

It was Ted Hogan, who, about 1:30 p.m., after reading of the hijacking in the early edition of the *Evening Telegram*, had reported to the Etobicoke Township Police the truck's whereabouts at the Lazy L Ranch, as well as the license number of the Nash sedan that had been used by the men who had done the crime. That meant Shorting and Wilkinson were later picked up at Huddlestone Motors on Dundas Street West, where Shorting sold used cars. After the hijackers had left the Lazy L, Shorting, with Wilkinson's help, had covered the 600 cases of liquor in the loft with hay then had closed up the barn doors as well as could be done with the truck's tractor protruding from the west door. Then Shorting had spent half the day sweating and dickering with Zanelli over possible help to get the truck out of his barn. By 4:30 p.m., a half hour before the police arrived and took him to headquarters, Shorting knew he would get no help from the hijackers. "You will be taken care of," Shorting was assured by Zanelli, who felt entitled to dictate to him what he should tell the police: that two nameless men had rented the barn on Saturday, that he had been away from the ranch on Monday morning and had returned to find the truck through the barn floor. This weak story failed to take into account the fact that four witnesses in Kathleen Jackson's home had seen otherwise.[2]

That evening Nimmo charged Jim Shorting with receiving the stolen truck and its load, after warning him he would do so if he didn't "come clean." Shorting didn't, and wouldn't, until late January 1944, when, in hopes of getting out from under the charges against himself, he would make the decision to testify for the Crown. Howard Wilkinson, who at first tried to back Shorting by telling the police a lying story consistent with Shorting's, fessed up an almost entirely true version of the facts on the evening of the crime and was charged by Nimmo as a material witness — meaning he was seen as a person who would likely give evidence for the Crown, but might not unless compelled to do so. A $500 bond posted by Wilkinson after a court appearance the next morning was meant to guarantee his testimony at a later trial. Max Applebaum, Vic Taylor, and Edwin MacDonald were, for the time being, charged with vagrancy, which allowed the police to hold them for a few days while they gathered information.

Bill Baskett was the suspect who was already in hot water, and his situation had obvious future implications for the others. The following morning, Baskett was charged with armed robbery. The police had discovered that the 1939 Nash sedan, license number 8-E-391, used in the hijack was registered to Joseph Pavlena, Bill's father-in-law and Kay's father, a labourer at the Burlington Steel Works, resident at 21 Lyndhurst Avenue, Hamilton.[3] Mr. Pavlena worked nights that week. Baskett, aged 30, and his wife Zora lived in Pavlena's home, where the keys to the Nash were often left on the hall table — and they were, in fact, taken and returned without Pavlena's knowledge or consent on the early morning of Monday, December 13. Baskett had two previous convictions for taking other peoples' cars without permission — in fact, his entire crime sheet.

Only Donald "Mickey" McDonald, thought to be the linchpin of the criminal scheme, was allowed to go home uncharged. John Nimmo later explained that Mickey had been let go because he was disruptive sitting in the detective office waiting to be questioned and "because I could always get him, if I wanted him."[4] Mickey, "The Mad Dog of Jarvis Street," was, of course, then out on bail in the Royal Cecil matter. That evening, Nimmo took the news of Baskett's connection to the Nash sedan to Mickey at his apartment. Seemingly, he wanted Mickey to have the experience of fretting over a stay of many years in prison in consequence of the gang's incompetence in several ways, but especially in using a family vehicle, wearing its own license plate, for such a piece of "business."

CHAPTER SEVENTEEN

The Chief Wants to See You
(January 5, 1944–May 1944)

TWENTY-THREE DAYS AFTER THE liquor truck was stolen, on the morning of Wednesday, January 5, 1944, John Nimmo and Edmund Tong returned to 514A Yonge Street to tell Mickey, "The Chief wants to see you at police headquarters."[1]

That was Nimmo's cute way of getting it across to the likes of Mickey that he was not under arrest but that he had no choice but to accompany them to 149 College Street. Mickey knew they would be coming. He, Jock, and the Chinaman, according to what Mickey later said, then shared a drink of Mickey's whisky before leaving.[2] As they went out the apartment door, Kathleen followed them with the imploring words, "Bring my honey back to me."[3] Though she didn't want to know it, Kay had lived her last day with the empty hope whom she had always called "Donnie," as did his mother, or "Donald," as did his father — but never "Mickey," as did his criminal friends.

As the result of a $100 payment to an informer, Benny Zanelli had been arrested while trying to hide under a bed in a rooming house at Allandale, near Barrie, Ontario. Nimmo and Tong got him there at 4 a.m., Monday, January 3. Sam Mancuso was arrested by the same zealous detectives the following afternoon at a Barton Street gas station in Hamilton. Sam had gone on the lam after leaving Mickey's apartment 22 days before and, to all appearances, was now set up for the cops by a snitch who posed as a friend. Likely this arrest also meant yet another payment out of the well-used pecuniary resource known to Toronto detectives as the Stool Pigeon Fund.

Thus, an identification line-up at police headquarters on the afternoon of January 5, 1944, was made up of Mickey, Mancuso, Zanelli, Edwin MacDonald, Vic Taylor, Max Applebaum, and eight other men from the health department office upstairs at 149 College Street. Though Bill Baskett was at the apartment when the detectives came for Mickey, he was not in the line-up. He had already been charged with armed robbery and had claimed in court afterwards that the police had beaten a statement out of him. He was then out of jail on $20,000 bail. Thus, the detectives had no legal right to put Baskett in a line-up and considered his presence unnecessary anyway; they already had him well-connected to the matter under investigation.

The viewers of the line-up were James Shorting, who was rightly figured by the police to eventually make the decision to testify for the Crown, and Howard Wilkinson, who already had. This day, Shorting went up and down the line, carefully studying each of those on parade, and finally identified only Benny Zanelli. Later, Shorting would admit in court that he was fearful of the hijackers but not of Benny. He would say on the witness stand, "I knew that I was not mixed up with any schoolboys, and I did not want to carry any lead around in me."[4]

Howard Wilkinson's feet were not quite so cold. He walked briskly up the line and fingered Mickey, Mancuso, Edwin, and Zanelli, all of whom he recognized as having been at the Lazy L Ranch on Saturday, December 11, or Monday, December 13. Mickey, Mancuso and Edwin were then charged with armed robbery and kidnapping, as Bill Baskett already had been. Zanelli had been previously charged with receiving the stolen truck and its load, as Shorting was on the day of the robbery, and later he would be charged with armed robbery and kidnapping as well. Unidentified by any witness in three line-ups, Max Applebaum and Vic Taylor were now effectively off the hook. They could only be proven guilty of being in Mickey's apartment in suspicious company at a suspicious time. Their names would be barely mentioned at the impending trial of the five who were charged.

* * *

When Mickey and the others came up in Toronto Police Court the following morning, Magistrate Robert J. Browne set high bail for Mancuso, Edwin, and Zanelli but only responded to Mickey's lawyer's repeated pleas by firmly answering again and again, "No bail for Donald McDonald."[5]

Starting now, on Thursday, January 6, 1944, Mickey was locked up in the dirty, dreary Don Jail for the next 561 consecutive days — until July 20, 1945 — while all of the charges he faced wended their ways through various delays in the courts. He was not well when he entered the jail, since he could not shake the sickness that he first had in December 1943 at the time of the hijacking, and he was still unwell throughout his trial on the Royal Cecil charges in March 1944. Coincident with that trial's end, he developed a chronic throat infection and a high temperature that required his transfer to the jail's hospital. It was not until April 13, 15 days after he was convicted of conspiracy to assault Sam Neveau and the assault of Neveau, that the much-publicized Mad Dog of Jarvis Street was well enough to be sentenced. Mickey, his throat swathed in flannel, stood before Judge Ian Macdonell, who told him, "I could give you ten years, McDonald," before awarding him yet another two and a half years "down East" — Mickey's fifth federal prison term for various mean little offences.[6]

But there was bigger and worse in the offing.

On May 4, 1944, Kitty filed for divorce, charging Mickey with adultery, which in itself in the Toronto of the day was good for a scandal. A few days later, the Toronto Police, armed with a drug warrant, searched Kitty's apartment but, instead of heroin as they expected, found evidence of her receiving $1,500 in stolen Victory bonds. This corresponded with the opening of the trials of the five accused of the Western Freight Lines armed robbery and kidnapping, so that sordid details of the life of "Kitty Cat," as well as of Mickey's own self-seeking criminality, were featured in a lurid story that appeared in John Blunt's *Flash*, a Toronto scandal paper.[7]

County Court Judge James Parker listened carefully on Monday, May 29, while G.C. Elgie, Mickey's latest lawyer, argued that the *Flash* article had unfairly "blackened" Mickey's character, to an extent that was "detrimental to a fair trial for the accused." About *Flash's* portrait of Mickey, Elgie said, "It indicts him as being a man whose love affairs are of such a character to be notorious. It also indicts him as being a boastful person and a man of legendary exploits in the realm of crime."[8] Kitty was depicted, to Mickey's obvious detriment, "as being equally renowned among Gangland's circles." Most objectionable, Mr. Elgie declared, was the story's snapshot of his client as "Mickey McDonald, notorious underworld character."[9]

Judge Parker agreed that the article's effect on Mickey's legal chances was likely as claimed. He ruled that the hijacking trial should be traversed to the next session of County Court, when the story "would not be so fresh in the minds of the jurors." Thus, like his first trial on the Royal Cecil matter, what was later referred to as the hijackers' "Flash trial," or "May trial," was aborted on its third day.

This delay did not sit well with some of the other defendants, who were inconvenienced by it. Issues existed between the hijackers that arose out of the several criminal blunders that had been made before, during, and after the theft of the truck. There was apparent mutual recrimination between Mickey and Sam Mancuso — more so than among the others — and this would worsen during their common trial when the two would fail to present part of their shared story in synch. Mickey would testify that he was not aware of the hijacking until Nimmo and Tong showed up at his apartment and told the "family gathering" about it. But Sam would say on the stand, "I went over to McDonald's apartment and told him there was a truck hijacked, and he asked me all about it, and I went out and got a paper and showed it to him."[10] This was a serious discrepancy in their sworn testimonies and it would greatly foster the Crown's purposes. It was Mickey's version that seemed much less likely. Mickey, Mancuso, Applebaum, and Vic Taylor all palpably made at least part of their illicit livelihoods by the sale of bootleg liquor. Would not Mancuso, who, as both agreed, had previously discussed the hijacking with Zanelli on the telephone after both had seen the *Telegram*'s early edition story about the theft, have mentioned it to the others? Would they not all have been interested, whether they were involved or not?

Still, the five defendants, notwithstanding their differences, would gather under an umbrella defence. They would stand together, all pleading not guilty to the formal charges of robbery, robbery while armed, and kidnapping, all intending to tell their own stories in such a way that they were consistent with the innocence of the others. Each defendant had his own lawyer. Mickey, Edwin, Mancuso, and Baskett had individual alibis for where they were at the time of the hijacking and all had alibi witnesses, some better and more believable than others. As well, Edwin, Mancuso, and Baskett had plausible or semi-plausible reasons for being at the unlikely meeting in Mickey's apartment on the afternoon of the hijacking. Zanelli, who was only belatedly and spuriously charged with armed robbery and kidnapping, mainly had to worry about the charge of receiving the truck and its 600 cases of liquor. He would claim at trial that he only went to the barn on the morning of the hijacking because Shorting asked him to be there. His story was to a great extent dependent on Mancuso's absolving him of guilty knowledge of the hijacking. "I would have given him a couple of cases, but he was not part of the deal," Sam would testify.[11] As a device to get out from under the armed robbery and kidnapping charges, Sam would claim that the liquor had been bought by himself as bootleg liquor, not stolen liquor, from a dangerous criminal he feared to name in public. "My life could be at stake. I don't want to say his name," Sam testified.[12]

Mickey would cause a sensation in court by later naming Rocco Perri, once Hamilton's "King of the Bootleggers," as the illicit vendor.[13] Likely Mickey and Sam both knew by way of the underworld grapevine what most others in the courtroom did not: that Perri was already dead as of late April 1944, that his body had been secretly disposed of, and that his known enemies were by then in charge of the Steel City's underworld. The story for many years after was that Rocco Perri was in a barrel of cement at the bottom of Burlington Bay.[14]

CHAPTER EIGHTEEN

A Parasite Like Who?
(October 17, 1944–November 7, 1944)

FIVE MONTHS AFTER "THE Flash trial," at 10:15 a.m. on Tuesday, October 17, 1944, Mickey and his co-defendants got the first of their 12 days of Justice, as the five accused went on a second time before Judge James Parker and a County Court jury. All faced charges of robbery, armed robbery, and kidnapping, while, in addition, Benny Zanelli was charged with receiving. Notwithstanding the war, the trial was a major interest in the city and drew large crowds of watchers to City Hall.

The Crown's case included the testimonies of James Shorting, Howard Wilkinson, George Butcher, Kathleen Jackson, Ted Hogan, Joseph Pavlena, Alexander McCathie, and John Nimmo. Oliver Borland, identification officer of the Toronto Police, also testified and showed photographs, especially of Joseph Pavlena's Nash sedan, license 8-E-391, which were taken at a Hamilton garage on the day after the truck theft. Together with the key testimonies of Ted Hogan, who had taken the plate number at the Lazy L Ranch, and Joseph Pavlena, the photos and Borland's testimony unalterably chained Bill Baskett to the Nash and to the hijacking, and Baskett's presence at 514A Yonge Street, Apartment 4, on the afternoon of the occurrence indirectly linked the other defendants

— and a self-incriminating group it was in its composition — to Baskett and the crime.

Mickey's hopes of acquittal were most seriously hurt by the testimonies of Shorting and Wilkinson, both of whom exhibited no doubt in identifying him as the hijacker in the light-coloured coat who came into the dimly-lit barn while the truck was being unloaded and walked off with a bottle of whisky from a broken case.[1] Both told of that man being addressed as "Mickey" by another of the hijackers, whom they did not see and could not identify. "Mickey, don't take that now. Wait until later," were the words the jury heard were spoken to the man in the light-coloured coat.

George Butcher testified that the hijacker who first guarded him in the Nash was "sniffing and coughing with a cold." And he quoted the same man as gratuitously telling him that he had already" served 10 years in prison over liquor."[2]

John Nimmo testified to the details of the investigation: to discovering the unlikely gathering at Mickey's apartment on the afternoon of the crime; to his soon after visiting the Lazy L Ranch where the hijacked truck and the liquor had been found; to locating the Nash sedan at Joseph Pavlena's home in Hamilton late that night; to the various arrests, line-ups, identifications, and court appearances involving the five defendants and others.

On cross-examination, G.C. Elgie asked Detective-Sergeant Nimmo if he had pitched a deal to Sam Mancuso "that if he would make a statement involving McDonald that you would see he got off lightly?" Nimmo registered surprise.[3] "You know who we want," Mancuso would later testify that Nimmo said to him, and then had propositioned him that if he gave him a statement implicating Mickey, he would see that he was "kept out of the penitentiary."[4] Judge Parker let the cross-examination of Nimmo go into the record before he admonished Mr. Elgie for "the aspersion he is casting against the administration of justice in the County of York, in the City of Toronto."[5]

Mickey's story was that, at the time of the hijacking and of its after-events at the Lazy L Ranch, he was at home, sick in bed, with an illness that gave him a temperature and caused him to sweat his way through several changes of pajamas from 2 p.m., Saturday, December 11, till Nimmo and

Tong came walking in on the gathering in his living room on the following Monday afternoon. Usually mild-mannered and polite in his presentation, Mickey denied all of the charges and allegations, in effect saying, "I know nothing about this." And as ever, he let the jury know that he was being persecuted by the Toronto Police:

> Every time something big happens in Toronto, like the bank on Royce Avenue — fifteen minutes later, Nimmo and Tong are there. At the time the bank at Mount Dennis was robbed, the police were in my apartment an hour later, and wanted to know where I was at such and such a time.[6]

Because of this, Mickey maintained, there would have been no such meeting in his apartment if he had been involved in anything like the crimes he was charged with.

Kathleen testified to the illness of her "Donnie" — full of detail and with lots of heart-tugging particulars about this and previous sicknesses of his that had twice required his hospitalization. She supplied Mickey's necessary alibi for the morning of the truck theft — and especially for the key hours between 6:30 and 9:30 a.m. After a doctor's after-midnight visit to their apartment, Donnie got off to sleep about 2 a.m. on the morning of the crime, Kay told the jury, and he didn't get up until around 10 a.m. She slept beside him all through the night. She herself got up shortly after 7 a.m. Neither of them, she said, left the apartment during any of that time.[7]

A doctor named Howard Jones, whose office was on The Corner, who kept no records, who did his business in cash, testified to having treated Mickey at his apartment in the early hours of Monday, December 13. Dr. Jones said he diagnosed Mickey as having influenza and administered three grains of phenobarbitol, a sedative that he said would put Mickey to sleep "for five or six hours," except if he drank alcohol. The doctor testified that Mickey was "fairly ill" and that he "wouldn't expect him to be up and outside from the seriousness of his influenza."[8]

Two visitors, who were separately admitted by Kay to the apartment between 7:30 and 8:30 a.m. on the day of the truck theft, both testified they had seen Mickey McDonald, sick and asleep in his bed, coincident with the time the hijackers were at the Lazy L Ranch. Robert "Buck" Adams, a convicted armed robber who had been a witness for Mickey at a previous trial, now told the jury that he went to 514A Yonge Street in quest of an early-morning bottle of whisky and thus had caught sight of Mickey sick in bed. Mary Pecanic, the wife of a man who had been in the Don Jail in May 1939 when Mickey was being tried for murder, came by to pick up Christmas presents to take to Kathleen's family in Hamilton. She gave evidence that she saw the accused "in bed, soundfully asleep," and was certain that the date was December 13, because she spoke with Kay that evening and was told of the detectives' visit and of their taking "Donnie" and the others to police headquarters. Mrs. Pecanic said from the witness box, "I cannot forget it. It was from that day I would know I was going as a witness for Donnie, because I did see him that morning."[9]

James Shorting also named Mancuso, Baskett, and Edwin as being at the Lazy L Ranch on Monday, December 13, and Mancuso as being the man who came with Zanelli on Saturday, December 11, and made the deal to store "a few cases of Christmas liquor." Zanelli, he said, had arranged the Monday morning details with him over the telephone late on Sunday night, December 12, and came to the barn about 6 a.m. to wait for the truck. Howard Wilkinson identified all of the same conspirators but wasn't certain that Mancuso was at the Lazy L Ranch on Monday, December 13. He was sure Sammy was there two days before, "dressed smart" in a blue suit, collar, and tie.

"That's a lie," Mickey's brother, Edwin, shouted out in court when Shorting identified him as the hijacker who first opened the right-side door of the truck at the Lazy L Ranch.[10] Edwin was also said by Shorting and Wilkinson to have gone about wiping possible fingerprints off the truck's door handles.

Butcher, who had at first not identified anyone, wrongly named Edwin as the thin-faced robber in the light-coloured coat who first pointed the automatic at him in the Western Freight Lines yard. The trucker was slow to identify anyone and perhaps knew that the police investigators, for a time, remained unconvinced that he too was not in on the hijack plot.[11] The thin-faced man with the automatic was Mickey, not Edwin, whose lantern-jaw was his face's most notable feature. It was Mickey, not Edwin, who was sick and coughing, who had already done nearly 10 years in prison, and who was wearing a light-coloured trench-coat such as the gunman wore. Edwin, aged 18, had no police record at all, though he was then under indictment on a charge of shopbreaking.[12]

Edwin's story was that he was at the MacDonald home, then at 110 Balmoral Avenue, at the time of the hijacking. His sister Florence, and his fiancée, Mary Wilson, whom he had married in the interim, testified to this as well. Edwin claimed to have gone to Mickey's apartment at 11 a.m., December 13, to pick up a heating pad for his mother, who was not well. As Mickey had done, Edwin told that Wilkinson and Shorting had had Mickey pointed out to them as he sat in the detective office at police headquarters on December 13, 1943, and that three weeks later, on January 5, 1944, Wilkinson had fingered Mickey, Edwin, Mancuso, and Zanelli in an identification line-up, after which he and Mickey had been charged with the hijacking and kidnapping.

Lantern-jawed Edwin MacDonald. George Butcher, the Western Freight Lines truck driver, wrongly identified him as the "thin-faced man" with the gun. (Library and Archives Canada)

Sam Mancuso's story was that he was playing an all-night bridge game with his girlfriend, Dorothy Campbell, and another woman at the time of the truck theft. Miss Campbell, a seamstress, gave Sam his alibi. The other lady did not appear and neither Sam nor Dorothy Campbell would give her name. The stated reason was that the other woman's mother would not have liked her being there.

Of the defendants' alibis, Bill Baskett's was the weakest. He claimed he was in bed at 21 Lyndhurst Avenue, Hamilton, with his wife Zora, who did not come to court to testify in support of her husband's story and, to appearances, did not come to court at all. Her stepfather, Joseph Pavlena, testified for the prosecution — his evidence clearly aimed at his stepson-in-law, Baskett, in particular. Baskett's only alibi witness was Tom Belan, a gambling friend, who imparted that Bill had knocked on his door in Hamilton at 9:30 a.m. on the day of the truck theft to ask for a ride to Toronto. This was supposedly so he could look for work at the John Inglis Plant. Instead, they went to Mickey's apartment where the hijack post-mortem was in progress, because, as they both said, there was no heater

Bill Baskett, the hijacker who brought his father-in-law's Nash sedan, wearing its own license plates, to such a piece of "business." (Library and Archives Canada)

in their car and they were freezing. After a cup of tea, Belan went home to Hamilton. Baskett's testimony jibed, of course, with Belan's evidence. He denied that he had taken his stepfather-in-law's Nash sedan, that he had ever been at the Lazy L Ranch, and that he had been part of any armed theft of a liquor truck or kidnapping of its driver.

The defence lawyers made much of the fact that Shorting had been remanded in police court 12 times since December 14, 1943, without his ever being asked to plead to the charge of receiving the truck and its load.[13] It was a situation similar to Jack Shea's testimony against Mickey in the Windsor Murder trials. Shorting was characterized by the defence lawyers as a likely accomplice who had not been dealt with and might say anything to get out from under the charges he himself had yet to face. The suggestion was that Shorting had been promised immunity on the receiving charge — which he denied. As in Jack Shea's case, the charge against Shorting would be withdrawn, but in this matter, long after the trial of the five accused was completed.

All of Monday, October 30, and much of Tuesday, October 31, were entirely taken up by the addresses to the jury by Crown Attorney W.O. Gibson and the five defence counsels. Judge Parker's Charge to the Jury was completed in only 38 minutes. The jury retired and returned at 5:10 p.m., October 31, with their verdicts. Mickey, Mancuso, Baskett and Edwin were all found guilty of robbery, armed robbery, and kidnapping, and Zanelli of the receiving charge only.

Judge Parker told the jury "I agree with your verdict," discharged the jurymen, and put over the sentencing of the accused until 10:30 a.m., November 7. The convicted hijackers were all remanded in custody.

That Tuesday morning, November 7, 1944, His Honour spoke about the hijack gang's crimes and the need for "adequate punishment." Benny Zanelli was then sentenced to two years less a day in reformatory, and Sam Mancuso to 15 years concurrent on each of the three counts. Edwin MacDonald was given five years on each count, the sentences to run concurrently, together with Judge Parker's empty hope that he would not have to serve his sentence in Kingston "with older criminals, but that you go to Collins Bay." Bill Baskett got three concurrent sentences of 10 years.

Donald MacDonald was sentenced to three concurrent 15-year sentences, consecutive to the two-and-a half-year sentence that he was already serving.

When Kathleen heard Mickey's sentence, her stricken cry was audible throughout the courtroom. Then she burst into tears and ran out into the hall, sobbing uncontrollably, her unlucky dream of a halfway normal life with the likes of "Donnie" all but gone.

"That is what I expected from a parasite like you," was Mickey's now less than polite shouted reaction to Judge Parker's 15-year sentence. "A deceitful bunch of bastards, that is all you are," he thundered at the generality of his listeners — the judge, the lawyers, court officials, reporters, courtroom spectators, sheriff's officers, and the many detectives and plainclothes policemen who were there in case there was a major disturbance.[14] Mickey got that much out before he was "removed" by two sheriff's officers.

CHAPTER NINETEEN

You Have Decided to Live a Life of Crime (November 7, 1944–October 25, 1945)

MICKEY AND SAM MANCUSO naturally chose to appeal their 15-year sentences and thus were not transferred to Kingston in November 1944, as were Edwin and Bill Baskett. One advantage to waiting out the process in the Don Jail was that Kathleen and those of the MacDonald family who cared to do so could more easily visit Mickey in the Don Jail than in the penitentiary.

G.C. Elgie would not conduct Mickey's appeal.[1] Instead, Miss Vera Parsons, Toronto's first woman criminal defence lawyer, argued Mickey's case before the Ontario Court of Appeal at Osgoode Hall beginning on Monday, February 19, 1945. Mickey and Sam Mancuso's appeals were heard together — the five-day hearing then reported to be one of the longest in the history of the Ontario Court of Appeal.[2] The Court reserved judgment in both cases.

The Court of Appeal decisions were announced at Osgoode Hall on the morning of Tuesday, May 8, the same day that the Second World War in Europe ended officially at 9 a.m. E.D.T.[3] The convictions against Mickey were unanimously set aside by the Court and a new trial was ordered for him. In his Charge to the Jury, Judge Parker had warned of the danger of accepting the uncorroborated word of an accomplice and had then cautioned that James Shorting might be considered as such. The rub was that the judge had not given the same caution concerning Howard Wilkinson. The three Justices of the Court of Appeal all thought that the warning should have been given with reference to both witnesses and that the question of whether or not either or both was an accomplice was for the jury to decide, after they were given proper instruction. At the same time, Sam Mancuso's appeal was dismissed.

*　*　*

Meantime, during his long days in the Don Jail, Mickey was playing a lot of bridge and fomenting what trouble he could. In early January 1945, he was observed to be the principal instigator of an incipient riot over the jail's "rotten food," and particularly over the "rotten pudding" the inmates were given to eat on a particular day. Jail "sources" later advised Gwyn Thomas that Mickey had gotten up on a table and was giving a rousing speech to a gathering of inmates when guards pulled him down and whisked him off to "the hole."[4]

Mickey was rightly unimpressed with his chances of acquittal at his impending retrial, to the extent that an escape attempt now seemed his best option. In July 1945, again as told by Gwyn Thomas, two unnamed detectives came to the jail in possession of information obtained from an informer and found more than one hacksaw blade "hidden under the quarter-round of the washroom baseboard." Their information was that the blades were "brought in for McDonald's use."[5] That meant Mickey soon found himself waiting his re-trial inside Kingston Penitentiary. Without his signing a waiver, he was abruptly shipped to Kingston on July 20 and admitted to the prison for the last time as inmate #8213. He was brought back to the Don Jail sometime before his retrial in order to be available to Vera Parsons for her preparation.

On Monday, October 15, 1945, Mickey's third and last trial over the Western Freight Lines caper began at Toronto City Hall before Judge Ambrose J. Shea and a County Court jury. Robbery, armed robbery, and kidnapping were again the charges.

The retrial was very much a replay of the previous trial. The Crown's case went on with James Shorting, Howard Wilkinson, George Butcher, Oliver Borland, Ted Hogan, and Detective-Sergeant John Nimmo testifying almost as they had done a year before. The most important difference was that Shorting, after 34 remands in Toronto Police Court, had had the receiving charge against him withdrawn five weeks prior to the commencement of the retrial. Thus, his status with the Crown was now clarified so that it was no longer possible for the defence to claim Shorting was tailoring his evidence to his own future benefit, as he had already benefited and the benefit was known.[6] Other changes were that Kathleen Jackson was called to testify by the defence, not the Crown, and Joseph Pavlena was not required to appear at all. Bill Baskett was not on trial now, so there was less about the surreptitious borrowing of the Nash by the owner's son-in-law. This time the Crown was willing to initiate discussion of Max Applebaum and Vic Taylor being at the "family gathering," and of the fact that Taylor's brother, Fred, also a

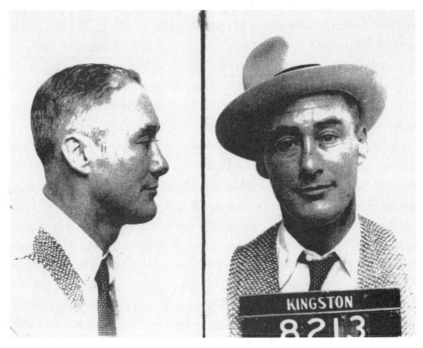

Mickey on July 20, 1945, the day of his last induction into Kingston Penitentiary. (Library and Archives Canada)

truck driver, had been fired by Western Freight Lines a short time prior to the theft of the truck. The point was that the people found in the Yonge Street apartment on the early afternoon of December 13, 1943, were incriminating in and of themselves — and the meeting's timing and composition was meant by the Crown to be seen as corroboration of the all-important testimonies of the two principal Crown witnesses.

Again Shorting and Wilkinson identified Mickey as the man who, in the dark barn, picked up a bottle of whisky from a broken case and thereby elicited the anonymous instruction, "Don't take that now, Mickey. Wait until later."[7] Again, after the unloading, there was the conference among the hijackers after which one of them said, "Oh, that won't be nothing; we will get that out in a few minutes. Mickey knows everybody. Mickey will get it out."[8]

As before, Mickey stuck to his story that he knew nothing of the hijacking until Nimmo and Tong told him of it.

Of the four previously-convicted conspirators, only Benny Zanelli, who had gotten a mere reformatory term, appeared for Mickey at his retrial.[9] The intended effect of Zanelli's testimony was to contradict the crucial identifications of Mickey by Shorting and Wilkinson. Benny testified that he did not see Mickey at the Lazy L Ranch and that it was too dark in the barn to recognize anyone except the man beside him. He gave evidence that seemed to say Shorting was more involved in the criminal scheme than he claimed and in some regards had definitely not told the truth. There was no conference among the hijackers after the truck was unloaded, evidenced Benny and, as he claimed, it was Shorting, himself who had said of the truck and the liquor, "Let's get the damn thing unloaded; it has got to be unloaded before we can take it out anyway."[10]

Kathleen, now employed at Brown's Bakery, testified as "Mrs. Kathleen MacDonald." She testified as she had done in October 1944, as did the cast of witnesses her testimony once again introduced: Dr. Howard Jones, Robert "Buck" Adams, and Mary Pecanic. In alibiing for "Donnie," Kathleen painted her man in glowing terms with regard to his effect on her life. With evident emotion, she told the jury, "I am living a perfect life since I have been with McDonald. I have nothing to be ashamed of since I have been with Donald."[11]

Vera Parsons' direct examination walked Mickey through his longstanding health problems; his illness of Saturday, December 11, through Monday, December 13, 1943; Doctor Jones' early morning visit; the "family gathering" in his apartment that Monday afternoon; the arrival of Nimmo and Tong; the line-ups "with the floodlights and the mesh" of December 13, 1943, and of January 5, 1944; and his claimed exposure to Wilkinson and Shorting in "the big detective room" three weeks prior to the January 5 line-up in which Wilkinson fingered him as one of the hijackers. His face set in a tight smile, Mickey delivered all of his answers in his most usual sunny manner. His testimony finished with his firmly stated denials of the charges against him.

But Mickey's cross-examination by Crown Attorney W.O. Gibson ended badly when he blundered into the trap of trying to pretend a high-minded criminal morality on the witness stand. He admitted that he would have bought the stolen liquor except that it was stolen with a gun and the driver was kidnapped.[12] Crown Attorney Gibson soon punished this by straightaway walking Mickey through his many criminal convictions, including several crimes of violence and a gun conviction, ending with the Royal Cecil "hotel fracas," for which Mickey was already then serving a two-and-a-half-year sentence.

Mr. Gibson finished by asking, "How old was the man that got into the fight, about eighty?"

"I think he was close to ninety," was Mickey's answer.[13]

Gibson left it there, with Mickey undressed again as The Mad Dog of Jarvis Street and thought to be a part of the beating of an elderly man, a crime of which he had been acquitted but which he did not specifically deny when asked by Mr. Gibson in court.

Judge Shea's Charge to the Jury began shortly after 10 a.m. Friday, October 19, 1945, and was not completed till 1 p.m. It was, to be certain, considerably more thorough than Judge Parker's charge of the previous year and was afterwards described by a Justice of the Supreme Court of Canada as "unimpeachable." It was 4:15 p.m. when the jury came back with its verdict of guilty on all three counts — a verdict that Mickey must have known was coming.

Only a small gathering was in court six days later when Judge Shea spoke of the crime and the criminal:

> This robbery was deliberately planned and executed. By the firing of the shot, we know the gun used to cow Butcher was loaded.
>
> Donald McDonald, apparently you have decided to live a life of crime. I can see no reason to change the sentence given at the previous trial. You will go to the penitentiary for 15 years, and this will be consecutive to the two-and-a-half-year sentence you are now serving.[14]

This time Mickey took his medicine in stoic silence. Kathleen again ran out of the courtroom sobbing and sat down on the bench in the hall, where she continued to weep. She would soon recover to solicit monies in support of two future appeals, first in the Ontario Court of Appeal, then in the Supreme Court of Canada. Neither would be successful.

CHAPTER TWENTY

Ulysses Lauzon and the Detroit River Gang
(February 23, 1945–November 2, 1945)

DURING MUCH OF 1945, while Mickey McDonald was marking time in the Don Jail, a daring 23-year-old Windsor youth who would be crucial to Mickey's last chance at freedom was stealing big money from banks all across southern Ontario.

His name was Ulysses Lauzon.

The son of a hard-working millwright, Lauzon was termed "incorrigible" in open court at age 15 and sentenced to a year in St. John's Training School. After that, Uly, as he was known, began compiling a rap sheet that included multiple convictions for theft, auto theft, break and enter, and receiving. Thick-lipped, hook-nosed, with reddish-brown hair, Uly's appearance was as distinctive as his burgeoning ambition to avoid a life of honest labour. Sentenced to Guelph Reformatory at 19, he soon startled the institution's psychologist, who, after interviewing him, wrote in a report:

> Says he has always been a crook and will always be one. Admits that the whole series of affairs was carefully planned and is proud of it. Says that he would never

have been caught if someone hadn't "Squeeled."(sic)
Says Kingston is his next stop. Will have to be watched
carefully.[1]

Three months later, Uly and three others escaped Guelph Reformatory and made for the east end of Windsor. They were recaptured when the police surrounded a Drouillard Road garage, but only after Uly, without fear or warning, gunned a stolen car through the padlocked garage door, crashing it into a police car parked in front. All four escapees, Lauzon included, were smart enough to meekly give up in the face of six police revolvers levelled at them.

The next day, Uly was sentenced by a magistrate to two years for escaping lawful custody. The day after that, he was admitted to Kingston Penitentiary as inmate #Y-6765.[2] Not yet 20, he now had to serve the unexpired portion of his reformatory sentence, 20 months and 26 days, plus two years. Uly surely saw his time in prison as being akin to career training. Like many before him, he listened intently to the prison's hardened bank robbers, who talked of their big "jobs," of their clever methods, of the good times stolen money had bought for them, and of all they planned to do when their next chance to "play the game" — rob banks — came to pass. By the day of his release, December 22, 1944, Uly knew he wanted to "take a chance" in the dangerous world of the professional bank robber. Perhaps he needed the risk to feel alive.

Ulysses Lauzon's "notorious summer of 1945" really began on the afternoon of Friday, February 23, when he and three other youths, one carrying a sawed-off shotgun, robbed the Imperial Bank of Canada at 1666 Tecumseh Road in Windsor of a paltry $830. Five days later, Lauzon and 19-year-old Joe Poireau, who was already Uly's most daring associate, were arrested in a downtown Windsor hotel and charged with armed robbery, after which a judge let them both out on $10,000 property bail put up by their families. Uly cunningly used his time on bail to romance, then to marry, a 20-year-old girl named Eileen Cornell, who, not by chance, was the principal Crown witness against him in the bank robbery. Their March 26 wedding meant Uly's certain acquittal as, under the law, a wife can't be compelled to testify against her husband.

The sleepy village of Ayr, Ontario, was made hectic on May 9, 1945, by a conference of the Brantford Presbytery, which brought hundreds of ministers and their cars to the village. This made it easy for two well-dressed bandits to go unnoticed as they robbed Ayr's Canadian Bank of Commerce just before its 3 p.m. closing. The pair entered the bank carrying briefcases, forced three staff members and three customers at gunpoint to crawl under a counter, then pulled down the bank's window blinds. While Joe Poireau stood guard, Lauzon gathered $19,600 in cash and $53,700 in negotiable bonds from the tills and from the already-open vault. "The Detroit River Gang," as the Windsor bank robbers were later dubbed in legend, got away with what was then described as "the largest amount in cash and bonds taken in any bank hold-up (in Canada) in the last 10 years."[3]

Six days later, OPP Criminal Investigation Branch (CIB) investigators charged Ulysses Lauzon with the Ayr bank robbery and, that same day, removed him to the Waterloo County Jail in Kitchener to await trial. Meantime, Joe Poireau had failed to appear in answer to the charges against him at Windsor and with a girl named Leona Kelly had taken it on the lam for Vancouver. The couple got as far as Winnipeg, where, on the morning of May 17, they were arrested, Joe in a downtown hotel room, where he was found to have in his possession three loaded revolvers and $2,830 in cash. "Takes Eight Detectives to Remove Prisoner" was the heading of a Page One June story in the wake of Poireau's pleading guilty to the February robbery of the Imperial Bank. Joe was not happy with the nine-year sentence he got.[4] The same charge against Uly was withdrawn for lack of evidence brought on by his clever marriage.

Reunited in the Waterloo County Jail, Lauzon and Poireau plotted escape. The two high-profile inmates were celled together in their own corridor and took exercise in the yard by themselves. In some manner that was never determined, they obtained a hacksaw blade. Then, early in the morning of Thursday, July 18, 1945, the Detroit River boys sawed their way out of their cells, then out of the prisoners' common area, from where they got past a door made of "escape-proof" steel by way of a levered widening of the gate that was later described as "no bigger than a rabbit hole." Then they went out the window of the guards' patrol area, through an opening 8 1/4 by 12 inches. Uly and the 6-foot, 175-pound Poireau were able to wriggle their way through this space too then to drop 9 feet down onto the jail's exercise yard. Their last obstacle was the 24-foot-high enclosure wall of the jail's yard, which they climbed on a half-inch lightning arrestor wire, tested for 40 pounds. In the early-morning darkness, the two "catwalked" 60 feet along the top of the jail wall, from which they were able to slide down the pole of a streetlight onto the property of the Kitchener Lawn Bowling Club. They left behind Leona Kelly, who was all by herself in a basement cell in the women's cell block.[5]

The escape was discovered about 6:20 a.m. by the only night guard at the jail. A general alarm went out to police in western and central Ontario in which both escaped men were described as "extremely dangerous."

Sometime between 3:30 and 6 a.m., a blue 1940 Ford Tudor, license 12-J-61, had been stolen from in front of nearby 229 Victoria Street North, Kitchener. Three days later, the same Ford was found ditched in Windsor. Then a car stolen in the Border City was dumped near Tillsonburg, where a farmer reported that his auto was commandeered and he was forced to drive two men over back roads for a considerable distance. That was how it went. Kitchener, Windsor, Tillsonburg, London, Dresden, Delhi, Chatham, one car dumped, another stolen or a crime committed, or both, as the fugitives, Joe driving, Uly navigating, raced all over the southwestern end of the province by way of concession roads. Interspersed among car thefts and reported sightings were a series of minor crimes for small money. To appearances, the jailbreakers had neither cash nor guns and were desperately trying to steal enough to stay at large until they could connect with substantial help. Windsor was where the help was, but it was also the most dangerous place for them to be. Who could they trust? Who, in such circumstances, was a friend, and who was a "rat"? Who might be able enough, dependable enough, and greedy enough, to help them for what money they could make on the deal?

Evidently, they found the help they needed.

On Monday afternoon, August 6, Lauzon and Poireau were "back in the banking business," as they robbed the Canadian Bank of Commerce in Port Perry, Ontario, north of Oshawa, of a reported $2,834.73. The bandits, masked and armed with revolvers, forced the accountant and two female tellers to lie on the floor while they scooped up the cash in the teller's cage. They made their getaway in a car driven by a 23-year-old Windsorite named Walt Koresky, a cigar-smoking former zoot-suiter who had been the leader of a wartime gang that dealt in stolen automobile tires.

Two weeks later, at closing time on Monday, August 20, Uly and Joe Poireau, both armed and unmasked, relieved the Royal Bank of Canada at Bath, Ontario, 15 miles west of Kingston, population 297, of $351,000 — all but $10,000 in negotiable bonds. The robbery would be described as "the biggest bank holdup in the Dominion's history."[6] Uly and Joe left the manager and a female ledger keeper tied hand and foot with wire before fleeing the scene in a blue-painted auto with Walt Koresky at the wheel.

By this time, the Detroit River boys had established a hideout a few miles north of Chicoutimi, Quebec, a cabin at a remote and heavily-wooded place called Lafrerriere, and Eileen Lauzon joined them there. Their idea was that they would live there year-round and use their "home" as a jumping off point from where they would rob faraway banks. They lived there for a little more than a month before it all came apart.[7]

Lauzon and Poireau made several trips into Montreal to cash stolen bonds in banks up and down St. Catherine Street. On Friday, August 31, about 10:15 a.m., Joe Poireau entered the Royal Bank at St. Catherine West and St. Mathieu streets, where he attempted to cash what was reported to be $6,000 in stolen Victory bonds. The bank's accountant, Hatton Longshaw, was immediately suspicious of both the youth before him and the bonds tendered, which bore serial numbers of a group that was by then known to be stolen. Sensing Longshaw's doubt, Poireau pulled a .45 revolver and ordered the accountant to get down on the floor. Instead, Longshaw grabbed for the revolver in the cage — causing Poireau, gun in hand, to bolt for the door. Longshaw followed on the instant and, at a distance of only a few feet, shot Poireau in the back. Joe fell out of the bank's door onto the St. Catherine Street sidewalk. The bullet had hit him in the lower spine. He would never walk again.[8]

Parked nearby in a stolen 1942 Chevrolet, Ulysses Lauzon saw his partner hit the sidewalk and decided it was time to leave. He jerked the Chev from a St. Catherine Street curb, drove a short distance, then rid himself of the vehicle and departed on foot. He left behind in the Chev another .45-calibre revolver and about $20,000 in Victory bonds. The Montreal Police instituted a massive search for Lauzon, involving scores of policemen, in the futile hope that he might be bottled up on the Island of Montreal.[9]

For Uly, Eileen, and Walt Koresky, the shooting and capture of Joe Poireau meant the end of the cabin at Lafrerriere. In a succession of stolen cars, the three fled across the back roads of Quebec, Nova Scotia, and New Brunswick, from where they crossed by ferry from Cape Tormentine to Borden, Prince Edward Island. At the Covehead Racetrack, 10 miles outside Charlottetown, on the afternoon of Wednesday, September 12, a sharp-eyed girl tipped the RCMP that three suspicious-looking "outers" — mainlanders — were plunging heavily on the harness races.

In the parking lot, Constables W.H. Warner and T.C. Keefe asked to see the strangers' wartime registration cards. After a scrutiny of the false identifications handed over by the three suspects, the officers' suspicions were not diminished, such that they informed the three that they would have to accompany them into Charlottetown for further investigation. About four miles out of Covehead, with Eileen in the front seat and Constable Warner in the back, Uly suddenly put their latest stolen car into the ditch. Constable Keefe, following in a police car with Koresky, pulled up behind.

Out of the car, Eileen cutely fainted and fell to the ground.

While the policemen went to her assistance, the criminals pulled revolvers.

Ignoring the danger, Constable Warner, a large and powerful man who had spent five years overseas, quickly grabbed hold of Lauzon, began to grapple with him, and soon caused Uly to involuntarily drop his gun, after which Uly began yelling at Koresky, "Shoot him! Shoot him! Shoot him in the head!"[10]

At this, Warner literally picked Lauzon up and used him as a shield. Koresky fired once at Warner and missed by inches, as almost at the same time, Walt was attacked by Keefe. Warner, who had just then thrown Lauzon to the ground, picked up Uly's gun, which caused Koresky to immediately drop his revolver and surrender.

A police chase that had lasted almost two months and traversed five provinces was at that moment over.

Ulysses Lauzon, in a remark that was widely published across Canada, was soon after quoted as saying, "I'll get 17 years for what I've done, but when I get out I'll have $300,000."[11] He was also quoted as insisting that they would have got away "if that yellow bastard Koresky had not lost his nerve and thrown his gun away."[12] Reportedly he bragged that he would have shot Constables Warner and Keefe, stuffed their bodies into the trunk of his car, and thrown them overboard from the ferry on the way back to New Brunswick. Asked pointedly by police if he would commit murder, Uly, grinning crookedly and sporting what a pressman termed "a superb black eye," replied, "Why not?"[13]

None of this was very smart.

On November 2, 1945, at Kingston, Ontario, Ulysses Lauzon, once described "as the cleverest criminal in Canada," along with Walt Koresky and a stretcher-ridden Joe Poireau, reaped the rewards of too much cleverness. The previous day Uly and Poireau had pleaded guilty to the Ayr, Port Perry, and Bath bank robberies as well as to breaking jail at Kitchener. Magistrate James B. Garvin handed them a total of 35 years each, which for Joe was consecutive to the nine years he had gotten at Windsor. Walt Koresky had pleaded guilty to the Port Perry and Bath robberies only and was given 15 years by the magistrate, who described all three as "callous criminals." To various degrees, the men of the Detroit River Gang primped and smirked for the photographers. Uly frequently laughed, or at least broke into a smile in court, when his criminal misdeeds were being described, to the extent that one Kingston reporter derisively labelled the cocky, arrogant, boastful criminal as "Laughing Boy." In the end, the three felons weren't laughing, as they were taken away in chains, the lives of Lauzon and Poireau apparently ruined into the everlasting future, Koresky's situation not much better.[14]

Three days later, Eileen Lauzon appeared in the same court charged only with vagrancy. The Crown merely asked that the charge be withdrawn. Pregnant and distressed, Eileen was allowed to go home to Windsor.

Months later, in the prison hospital at Kingston Penitentiary, Joe Poireau, who had been described in court as having "only a few cords of his spine intact," and as "a human wreck who would never again commit crimes," was despondent enough that, as a help to his stricken mental outlook, he was allowed occasional visits from his former partner-in-crime, Uly. This was highly unusual and a major concession by the prison administration.

"We didn't talk about crimes. We talked about other things, about Windsor, our relatives, things we did as kids, how it was going for us both, things between us," recalled Joe 60 years later.[15] "Uly was a real friend," affirmed Poireau, who remembered that Lauzon paid tobacco to other cons in the hospital to look after him well. And after he got free of Kingston, Uly sent Joe a typewriter, which Joe badly wanted, but which the prison authorities would not allow him to have. "When Uly and the others made their escape, the warden and the guards were mad at me. They took away my school books and I didn't get the typewriter," remembered Joe with some bitterness.[16]

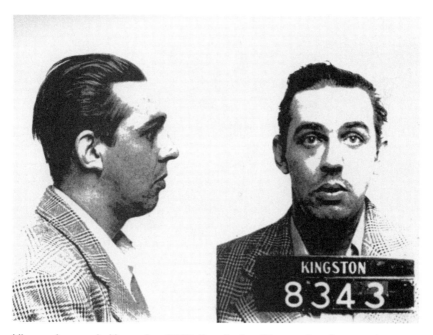

Ulysses Lauzon in November 1945, then facing 35 years imprisonment.
(Library and Archives Canada)

Joe recalled that in the early part of 1947, when he was in the Christie Street Hospital in Toronto undergoing treatment that was meant to help him walk again, he got a call from Kathleen MacDonald, by then Mickey's legally-married wife, who he didn't even know. She asked if he needed anything, if she could do anything to help him. This might have been because Kathleen knew Uly, Joe's buddy, and her husband, Mickey, were by then working on a project together.

CHAPTER TWENTY-ONE

Seventeen and a Half Years
(October 25, 1945–August 1947)

THE SOUND OF KINGSTON'S North Gate slamming behind him in October 1945 must have been one of the worst sounds Mickey McDonald ever heard. He had spent much of his adult life locked up in prisons, reformatories, and jails, but except as a young man at Michigan City, he had never before had to confront even the possibility of serving more than three years at once. Now Mickey was nearly forty — and he didn't have as much time left. Seventeen and half years meant he was looking at not getting out of prison till his early- or mid-fifties. There were not a lot of convicts over the age of forty in Kingston. Long before his projected release, Mickey knew, he would be one of the oldest inmates in the "pen."

Kathleen was still determined that she and Mickey would be together forever — and she had wanted to marry Mickey before he went away. Brigadier L.H. Smith, the Salvation Army chaplain at the Don Jail, refused to have anything to do with this. Mickey's lengthy sentence made the marriage wrong for Kathleen, he said. Nor, for a different reason, would the Protestant chaplain in Kingston marry them. Rev. A.J. Anderson was forbidden by an ordinance of the Anglican Church to marry divorced persons. Still, special permission was obtained from the Justice Department at Ottawa for them to marry inside Kingston, and a clergyman was found who would perform the ceremony. On the dull, drizzly Wednesday afternoon of April 10, 1946, the Reverend H.J. Bell, minister of the Zion Union Church, Kingston, joined Donald John MacDonald and Kathleen Donovan in a marriage that had little chance to end well. Warden Allan, two guards who stood on each side of the groom, and a bridesmaid who came with Kathleen from Toronto, were all who were present at the ceremony in the warden's office.[1] Kathleen and Mickey were not allowed to speak to each other. It was an eight-minute wedding, after which the couple were permitted a brief kiss before Mickey was led away. Kay later said she went through with the marriage so she could visit Mickey in prison. But she would wait in the apartment at 514A Yonge Street for almost eleven years, with Mickey's name on the door for most of that time, legally married to a long-term inmate, then to an escapee, then to an escapee who for years she desperately hoped was not dead, as he was said to be by those who she knew ought to know.

Mickey was assigned to work in the prison stoneshed where the inmates made concrete blocks and stacked them up in a large yard that surrounded the shop for shipment elsewhere. The stoneshed was sometimes described as "a prison within a prison," because it was inside its own wall — over a hundred feet in length — abutting on the east side of the North Wing of the Main Cell Block. Many of the 20-odd inmates who worked in the stone-cutting gang were considered security risks and, as it seemed, the wall around the shed was at least partly for security purposes. Absolutely, the prison system did not want those who worked behind the stoneshed's wall mixing up with the other inmates.

Paul "Biddy" Bedore was the only guard in charge of the stone-cutting crew, both inside and outside the L-shaped shed. This meant he had a lot to do keeping up with an often loose situation — and a lot went on in his shop and inside its walled enclosure that he did not know about. Bedore was, to put it mildly, easygoing. Roy "Binky" Clarke, a member of the stone-cutting gang in 1947 and 1948, saw Bedore as "an old farmer putting in his time who let a lot slide that other guards would not have."[2] Years later, in July 1978, Clarke remembered:

Bedore was an okay guard. He treated us pretty good. There was only an hour or two of work, maybe three some days, and then we could play cards or relax. The food in the 'pen' was awful and there wasn't enough of it. In the stoneshed, we could cook stews and the like in a washtub in the shop. Once, before the escape — because Mickey was in on it — we cooked a stew that included a squirrel, a rabbit, a pigeon, and the cook's cat. It tasted pretty good — much better than what we regularly got to eat. Then we tacked the cat's tail to the door of the cook's kitchen. Was he ever mad! We hated him because of the bad food. Bedore ate some of the stew along with the rest of us...[3]

It's easy to see, from this and other similar tales, that the guard in charge of the stoneshed was generally prepared to look the other way, as long as there was no apparent trouble. The stoneshed was a loose situation run in a loose fashion — and later, after the escape, when there were questions about the deputy warden having permitted "laxity" in the enforcement of discipline inside the prison, the situation in the stoneshed was a prominent example cited.[4]

Among the other convicts, Mickey was a natural extrovert. He was a talker, a guy with lots of arguments against the prison's system — which tended to make him, if not popular, then at least noteworthy among the other inmates. He took credit for all he could — his role in the Kingston riot of October 1932, for example, and all of the "big jobs" he was supposedly in on for which he was never charged. Mickey was smart without being too smart, and, in the time and place, he was listened to by many. The Windsor Murder — and the perception that he did it and got away with it — made him more important in the eyes of the other convicts than he would otherwise have been. But he was never the great criminal legend that he imagined himself to be. Familiarity breeds contempt. There were those in the prison who would call Mickey down as "nothing but a pimp" — especially after he was gone and never coming back.

Mickey made it his business to do as many favours for other cons as he could. He tried to keep on everybody's good side. That was his way. He had lots of friends in the prison. He made himself useful to others who needed him. That meant he had help when he needed it, or could arrange it and pay for it later. He was also on good terms with some, or many, of the guards. His dislike of the prison system did not extend to all, or most, of the staff. He was said to have charmed some, the kind who could be charmed, as he had previously done with some guards in the Don Jail, one or two of whom had found themselves out of work after being caught doing things for Mickey they weren't supposed to do, like smuggling contraband articles into "the bucket."[5]

Until December 20, 1946, when the Supreme Court of Canada finally dismissed his last appeal of the hijacking conviction, there was still a chance Mickey could get free of his sentence by legal means. But after the court decision at Ottawa, Mickey knew he had to "do his time." That surely made him much more susceptible to the blandishments of one of the hardest-bitten convicts who worked on the stone-cutting gang, who was determined to get out of Kingston any way he could. Ulysses Lauzon, then aged 24, was just beginning his 35-year sentence for three bank robberies and a jailbreak. Uly was one of the most watched inmates in the prison. Not only his daring and dangerous character made it so, but from his first days in Kingston, he went about telling everyone he felt like, including some say Warden Richard Allan — "Little Dick" to the inmates — that he would be leaving the high-walled prison as soon as he could arrange it. Another inmate on the stoneshed crew, a violent man himself, recalled his first meeting with Lauzon:

> ... The first time I talked to Lauzon, I asked him how long he was doing. He said 35 years. I was startled. He said, though, 'Don't worry, I'm not planning on doing it,' and I believed him.... Lauzon exuded violence. You felt it just talking to him. It wasn't just what he was saying, it was how he said it. It was something you felt more than anything. It was right inside him. Nobody got in this guy's way. He was just dangerous, that's all. You just knew it...[6]

Lauzon, still a young man, had already notoriously broken out of Guelph Reformatory and the Waterloo County Jail. Mickey, in many more years of imprisonment, had broken out of nowhere. Thus, Uly selected Mickey to escape with, not the other way around. Mickey was the easy choice on the crew to be asked in by Uly, because he had the best reason to say yes. Except for Lauzon himself, Mickey had the longest number of years yet to serve on the gang. He was also the inmate with the connections in the prison. That was important with regard to getting hold of the necessary tools and materials for the escape.

Some time before February 1947, Lauzon told Mickey a tale about a trap door in the North Wing of the Main Cell Block that led to an attic and said it was their ticket out of Kingston Penitentiary. Mickey was surely at first skeptical, but given the alternative, could not have taken long to warm to the idea. Up to this time, every known escape from the enclosure of the prison had happened, not from where the inmates slept, but from where they worked, or from some place in the prison where they were in transit. The legend of the Main Cell Block for years before August 1947 was that it was unbeatable: that no prisoner had ever escaped from there, that none ever could or would. This attitude would help the plotters. Things that might have been seen as suspicious elsewhere in the prison weren't noticed on H-range of the North Wing, where the stoneshed crew slept. There was a lesser perceived threat there. Nobody could get out of the prison from there. Or so almost everyone thought.

*　*　*

On February 24, 1947, Nick Minelli, an Ottawa burglar with a long record dating back to the age of eleven, was admitted to Kingston as inmate #8929. A feral-looking little man whose face often wore a scowl, Minelli was a professional criminal of a sort, but he was not a criminal of the same magnitude as McDonald, and certainly not as Lauzon. He had twice before been in the Guelph Reformatory and this was his third term in Kingston, but as he later always stressed, he had never before been convicted of a crime of violence. Lauzon and McDonald, needing another hand to help effect the plan they were working on, not seeing anyone else more suitable on the stoneshed gang, approached Minelli, who years later remembered:

> We were all long-term prisoners, and we knew each other from previous terms in Kingston, though I had never had much to do with either McDonald or Lauzon.
>
> They were 'regular.' I knew that. That meant they were trustworthy....
>
> The first week I arrived McDonald and Lauzon sounded me out. 'We've got something going,' they said. 'It looks good. Are you interested?'
>
> I said I was.[7]

Minelli was not as daring, as clever, or as dangerous as the other two, but in his own later words, he was "bitter and resentful." Like the others, Nick was looking at the front end of a long sentence. He thought he had been handed "a bum rap" in the Supreme Court of Justice Keiller MacKay over the violent kidnapping of an Ottawa taxi driver, a crime, he maintained then and years later, that was wholly perpetrated by an ex-footballer-turned-armed robber named Henry Ceretti.[8] Ceretti agreed that it was so, but then he had been already sentenced, so why did it matter to him? Now, being so aggrieved, Nick was ready to take a big risk with the others. But he cut a different deal with them. He was a partner in the escape only. After that, he would go his own separate way. They all agreed to this and Nick Minelli became part of the escape conspiracy.

Helping the plotters, perhaps even before Minelli became involved, was Harold Jamieson, also known as "James Labard," inmate #5939, who Mickey had known since 1933 during both of their first terms in Kingston. A full-blooded Mohawk, originally from the Six Nations Reserve near Brantford, Ontario, Harold was known in the prison as "Chief" Jamieson or as simply "The Chief." Very much of a loner who kept to himself most of the time, he was observed to be strangely friendly with both Mickey and Uly, to the extent that, after their breakout and Jamieson's release, prison authorities named Jamieson as a likely contact of the escapees, especially McDonald, during their time in hiding.[9] Finishing up 14 years for three armed robberies and an attempt to break jail, The Chief had been involved in three failed escape attempts himself, one each from the Guelph Reformatory, the Oxford County Jail, and the Manitoba Penitentiary at Stony Mountain. He was an iron-willed inmate who truly hated confinement and the prison system and who was determined to fight back against those he saw as his persecutors any way he could. As painted years later by another stoneshed inmate, The Chief was "tough like Hell, a dangerous man, in the class of Lauzon."[10] And he had spent a lot of time in "the hole." Removed to Stony Mountain in 1938, Harold had sawed his way out of his cell in September 1939 and then, when confronted, repeatedly bashed a guard over the head with an iron bar. He was lucky the guard lived, or he would have been charged with murder.[11]

Easily identifiable by city witnesses in the Ontario of the 1930s due to his swarthy complexion, Jamieson had not been overly successful at robbing banks, payroll offices, gas stations, and stores. The story is told that Mickey, who had had previous mild success selling narcotics, who was by this time expecting to have much more of the same, discussed

Nick Minnelli, the least violent of the three Kingston escapees, termed by Superintendent of Penitentiaries Ralph B. Gibson as "the weak link in the chain." (Library and Archives Canada)

with Harold a new line of "work" that might keep him in style when he was back on the street: heroin distribution. In the post-war era, the fat profits in the illicit drug trade were causing all sorts of gangsters and thieves to abandon other rackets in favour of pushing heroin. Harold listened greedily. Mickey let Harold know that, when he himself was out and properly set up in an American city, as he was expecting to be, he was looking forward to being able to supply his friends with heroin, in quantity, on a regular basis.

The reason The Chief didn't escape with the others was that he was due to be released on January 8, 1948. For the time he had left to serve, 143 days after the breakout of August 17–18, being a hunted fugitive, as the escape plotters would be, was not worth it. So Harold merely aided them as he could, with the expectation of profiting from this after they were all on the outside.[12] It helped all of this in-custody friendliness that The Chief was the occupant of cell 4-H-20, next to Mickey's cell, and next-but-one to the small corridor between G and H ranges and the fateful trapdoor.

Harold "The Chief" Jamieson, said to be "a dangerous man, in the class of Lauzon," helped the escapees in the hopes of later profiting from doing so. (Library and Archives Canada)

CHAPTER TWENTY-TWO

A Clear Path Out the Door
(February 1947–August 1947)

THE MAIN CELL BLOCK of Kingston Penitentiary, built by convict labour in the years 1834–61, was constructed to allow a handful of guards to securely control hundreds of inmates during the 120 or more hours a week they spent in their cells. In 1947, as now, it was the dominant building within the nine-acre enclosure. Its centre was its massive circular rotunda, known in the prison as "the Dome," the cupola of which then rose nearly 200-feet above the prison compound.[1] Its walls were a yard thick, its windows all heavily barred. Four four-storey cell blocks fanned out from the Dome in the shape of an equal-armed cross, to the four directions. The Dome itself was only a cement ground floor, with flights of stairs up its sides to galleried balconies at each of the four cell block levels. Each level of the cell blocks had two mutually exclusive corridors called ranges, back to back, 21 cells to a range, the cells all facing outward towards the outer walls. On each range was a narrow balcony in front of the row of cells, a hand-railing on the opposite side of the balcony, then beyond that a sheer drop to the ground floor between the railing and the outer wall of the cell block. The balconies led to the Dome at one end and dead-ended at their opposite extremities. There was a double set of barred gates through which, when opened, each range of inmates could enter or leave their cell block, to or from the Dome. Thus all inmates had to enter or depart the building by way of the Dome. The loud, clanging bell that controlled inmate movement in the prison was in the Dome, ringing out its various instructions more than 120 times a day, a constant irritant to the inmates, all of whom had to inure themselves to it. The guards operated a system of bars, locks, and the omnipotent bell to contain the inmates, to move them as need be many times a day, and to protect the Dome itself. The prison's system was hyper-security-sensitive. Only so many inmates were allowed out of their cells or their workshops at one time. Only so many were allowed to pass through the Dome at once. All movement in the prison was at the pleasure of the Dome's angry brass bell. Everything in Kingston Penitentiary, said to be Canada's oldest, coldest, dirtiest, noisiest, and most secure federal prison, was about inmate control. The Dome was the focal point of that control — and of the security of the institution.[2]

The interior of the rotunda of Kingston Penitentiary's Main Cell Block, commonly referred to as "the Dome." (Queen's University Archives)

* * *

It may have been that Ulysses Lauzon actually asked to be assigned to the stoneshed gang, where Deputy Warden Len Millard might have thought he would be less of a risk working behind another wall and sleeping on H range of the North Cell Block.

The cunning mind of Lauzon had already found the flaw in the Main Cell Block. He had previously worked in the prison as an electrician and as such had become aware of the trapdoor leading into an attic above the top floor of the North Wing. The trap door was at the extreme north end of the North Cell Block, in the ceiling of a small corridor between the ends of G and H ranges. This corridor was as far from the Dome itself as it was possible to be in the building and it was readily accessible from H range, where the stoneshed gang was celled. The trap door was unique in the prison. The other wings didn't have one — or a corridor for one. At work in the attic, Uly had noticed a small window, barely big enough for a medium-sized man to squeeze through onto the roof of the North Cell Block. These two discoveries together — the trap door and the garret window — were the genesis of a plan that would lead to what Assistant Commissioner of Penitentiaries G.L. Sauvant, in his later report on the escape, would term "the worst defeat Kingston ever had."[3]

For Lauzon, it became a matter of figuring out what was sometimes spoken of in the prison as "a clear path out the door."[4] Obviously, any plan of escape would involve getting past a number of obstacles, not only two. But Uly had gotten the most difficult piece of the puzzle when he saw the garret window — a window few guards or inmates had ever seen or even knew was there.

Most or all of the stoneshed gang slept on H range — their cells facing east on the top floor of the North Wing. They worked together and they celled together. These circumstances were important to the exit plan of the plotters. The loose situation in the stoneshed and its yard allowed them to manufacture then secret among the many hundreds of stone blocks piled up outside materials that were necessary to the escape. Though they worked with potentially dangerous tools — mallets and chisels — they were rarely frisked as in some other shops.

Most importantly, being celled on H range gave them ready access to the trap door and the attic.

Any escape from the Main Cell Block by way of the attic necessarily had to take place at night and had to begin from the range where the stoneshed gang was housed. Thus, the escapees would have to break out of their own cells, and that made the first obstacle their own cell bars. To cut the 3/4-inch, chromium-centred bars, formerly thought to be "uncuttable," they needed a hacksaw blade for each of those in on the plot — three handleless blades. The blades used were, as Superintendent of Penitentiaries Ralph B. Gibson later termed them, "precision instruments," and not of a kind to be found inside Kingston Penitentiary.[5] According to Nick Minelli, they were, as the prisoners say, "arranged." Arranged by way of whom, or what sort of whom, Minelli did not elaborate.[6] There have been at times a few underpaid prison guards who have been willing, for a consideration, to "traffic" goods, messages, or drugs in and out of the "pen." Approaching such a person to bring in hacksaw blades — an escape proposition — would be an especially dicey venture that, if it were rebuffed, could easily have serious consequences. Much more likely, seemingly, is the picture painted by "Binky" Clarke:

> I don't believe anybody paid anything to any guard. The farm gang and the excavation gang went outside the walls every day. All that would have happened is that some friend of Mickey's — a former inmate — would have hidden the blades at a pre-arranged spot and someone on the gang, knowing where they were hidden, would have picked them up and brought them inside. Once that happened, some runner or some member of the cleaning gang would have delivered them to Mickey.[7]

All of the other obstacles in their clear path out the door were only easy in comparison with the task of getting out of their cells. The trap door, the garret window, the roof, the long drop from the roof to the yard, the 250-feet-of-prison ground from the east side of the North Cell Block

188

to a dark spot under the wall near the northeast tower, and the perimeter wall itself, were all impediments to their gaining their freedom. Any of these might trip them up, and some might even kill them. But getting free of their cells would be the most difficult trick — and that, they knew, was where they were most likely to be stopped.

For six months the escape plotters worked on refinements of the plan and squirrelled away the materials and tools necessary for the break, all, or almost all, of which were scrounged within the prison. These items were mostly hidden among the hundreds of cement blocks in the stoneshed yard, or briefly in their cells, which the guards might take a notion to search at any time. In the last days before they made the escape attempt, some of these materials were moved to the attic, where there was some risk they might be discovered by a work crew. Some of the cleaning gang who were in league with the plotters sawed the lock off the trap door, substituted their own similar lock and, as need be, moved some of the materials to the attic during the daytime when the stoneshed crew was at work.[8]

From the canvas department ("the mailbags") inmate allies filched for them 6-foot lengths of mailbag jute cord to be painstakingly braided by the plotters, three cords to a section, into the strong 150-foot rope they needed to get them down from the roof of the North Wing to the yard. A 30-foot rope was similarly braided to be used to get them over the perimeter wall of the prison enclosure. In all, they required more than 500 feet of mailbag cord, which was gotten and trucked for them out of the canvas shop on Mickey's word it was needed. No reason given! No questions asked! The plotters and a trusted ally or two eventually carried all of this cord upstairs to H range under their clothing. Three heavy metal hooks — to attach to the end of the 30-foot rope — were surreptitiously made out of scrap metal in the stoneshed forge while Guard Bedore was outside the shop being "entertained" by other convicts, especially The Chief. Another ally was set to "keep jiggers" and called "Six," the traditional warning of prison inmates, if Bedore, or anyone suspect, seemed ready to come inside. Then the three would switch to making stew in a shop washtub. The stoneshed gang were always killing pigeons to make stew. Nothing odd about that. Guard Bedore allowed it.

The hacksaw blades, the mailbag cord, the hooks, and the key to the trap door were their most important acquisitions, but the plot required lots more. They got materials to make "dummies" to put in their beds at the time of the break — loaves of bread for the heads and human hair to be glued to the bread loaves. They needed soap to help smooth the cutting of the bars of their cells, graphite to camouflage the cuts, and small pieces of rubber to wedge between the cuts to hold the bars fast between cuttings. Also glue, mirrors, thread, spectacle lenses, white shirts, brown trousers, casual shoes — all of these to be used before, during or after the break — were obtained from the prison garage, the barber shop, the kitchen, the tailor shop, the library, or elsewhere, by way of friends and allies throughout the prison. No questions asked! As Nick Minelli would say years later, "an arsenal of escape equipment" was put together. Mickey obtained most of the arsenal.[9]

There were habits of their keepers and peculiarities of the prison that they had to learn and work around. The officer who patrolled the yard in the dark of night always walked counter-clockwise and appeared every 30 or 35 minutes. At night, there were only guards on two of the four corner towers — the northwest and the southeast towers. That and the fact there was a dark spot in the yard underneath the northeast tower meant that was where they would go over the perimeter wall. All of the plotters had a good view from their cells of the northeast tower and the darkness underneath the wall there. All had seen the yardman make his rounds many times. Mickey's brother, Edwin, inmate #7912, still serving time for the December 1943 truck hijacking, had a similar vantage point from his cell on F range of the North Wing, the third deck facing to the East, directly underneath H range, where the escape plotters slept. Edwin is claimed to have stayed up on the night of the escape to watch his most notorious brother take his final leave of Kingston Penitentiary.

CHAPTER TWENTY-THREE

The Escape of August 17th–18th, 1947
(August 12–August 21, 1947)

ON TUESDAY, AUGUST 12, Uly suggested that all was in readiness and that they ought to go the following Saturday night. The others agreed. Throughout this week, as they could, the three now took the risk of bringing the last necessary and most incriminating items up to their cells, from their hiding places within the stoneshed enclosure. The cleaning gang, with the key to the trap door's lock, transported the ropes, the hooks, and much of the rest from the escapees' cells up to the attic, where all was in readiness for the break. The three sections of 50-foot rope were joined there by the cleaners, not in Uly's cell as otherwise claimed.

It was during "the talking period" — the period from 5 to 7 p.m. when a radio broadcast played loudly and the inmates were allowed to talk among themselves — that the three cut the bars to their cells. They did small cuts on Thursday evening, more on Friday, and finished the job on Saturday. Each time they filled the cuts again with rubber and soap, then darkened the soap filling with graphite. One fear they had was that a hack — a guard — would suddenly turn up on the range and catch them in the act. Another was that, while they were at work in the stoneshed, a guard would take a notion to tap H-range's cell gates with a hammer, as was done on an irregular basis.

The Saturday night attempt to leave was a disaster that had to be aborted — and almost got them caught. First, when the bars were all or mostly cut, Lauzon tried to remove one of his cuttings and, oddly for him, made the mistake of dropping it noisily onto the cement floor of the balcony outside his cell, where it rolled till it almost went over the edge of the four-floor drop. The noise of its falling, as termed by one who was there, was "a tremendous clang that could be heard all over the range."[1] If the bar had fallen four floors to the concrete floor below, that would have been the certain end of everything. They would have all gone to solitary for many months.

The problem of getting the bar back had to be solved quickly — before the next nighttime visit of a guard on range duty. The answer was the prisoners' art of "fishing," usually used to pass books and small articles between cells, and even from one floor of a cellblock to another. Lauzon, with a string with some heavy winter underwear tied on the end, pulled the iron bar and Minelli pushed at it through his cell bars with a stick, till the errant piece of steel was drawn back along the balcony floor to Uly's cell.

That problem solved, the sawing of the bars continued till all was seemingly done. Their beds and dummies were arranged. Then the three convicts stripped themselves naked, greased their bodies with butter, and attempted to get through their cell gates.

Only Uly made it out of his cell.

Mickey and Nick had miscalculated and hadn't cut big enough spaces between the bars of their cells. Uly tried but couldn't pull either of the others through. There wasn't time to cut more bars — a guard might show up at any second, and "Six" wouldn't save them. The decision was made to put everything back together as best they could and to try again the next night. If that didn't work, they were beaten.

Every moment after this failed try was high risk. The bars of Lauzon's cell couldn't be put back together properly and were literally tied onto the cell gate with black thread, in a perilous way that meant Uly couldn't go in or out of his cell for fear the bars might fall off the gate. Food was brought to Uly by the others on Sunday — and it was only a hope that a passing guard wouldn't notice the condition of the bars of his cell gate, or of the other cells either. There was also the possibility that one in the widening circle of convicts who knew about the escape might sell them out for a parole or some other advantage. There were, before Saturday, at least eight or nine "solid" guys who knew — and more than that after the first noisy attempt. In years to come, it became a common Jarvis Street yarn of every other drunken ex-con to claim to have been inside Kingston on the night of Saturday, August 16, 1947, and to wonder out loud how it was possible that the guards didn't tip to the breakout. "Every con in the joint heard the racket. Why didn't the guards?" was the theme of a well-worn story one heard in the late 1940s, and for years afterwards, around Gangland and near The Corner.[2]

Again, on Sunday night, it was decided they would go just after "the final count" was taken.

Mickey and Nick both cut another bar during the Sunday night talking session. Later, in his report on the escape, Deputy Commissioner G.L. Sauvant would make it known that the opening caused by the cutting in Lauzon's cell gate was 9 1/2 by 11 inches; in McDonald's, 12 by 11 inches; and in Minelli's, 10 by 12 inches.[3] How could any medium-sized man get his body through an opening 9 1/2 by 11 inches? Amazingly, Uly did it three times in 24 hours. He had been part of a similar impossibility in slipping through the bars of the Waterloo County Jail in July 1945.

As Sunday evening passed into night, all three escapees, waiting in their cells, were becoming worried over an unforeseen factor that had been overlooked in their escape plan — which they all suddenly knew increased their chances of being caught or even killed. No one, not even Uly, had thought of the effect of moonlight on their chances. There was none the night before and many other nights, too. But now a full moon was pushing its way out from behind the clouds and was flooding the prison yard with its light.

At midnight, from the Dome, came the sounds of the guards changing shift. The escape plan was started. Using a homemade spyglass, peering from his cell, Lauzon now made dead certain there was no guard in the northeast tower. Then came "the final count" — the after-midnight count

— for which the three got under the covers of their beds and pretended to be sleeping.

Minutes later, they were arranging their cells in consonance with the plan — clothing and sticks of wood for bodies under the bedclothes, dummies with loaves of bread wearing real human hair for heads, heads towards the cell gates as all inmates were obliged to position themselves when sleeping.

Then, as on the night before, they stripped themselves naked, greased their bodies, removed the cut bars of their cell gates, and began to slowly inch themselves through the openings they had made in the bars. This time, they all made it through to the balcony.

Talking in whispers, they collected themselves and put on the street clothes they had had made in the tailor shop and had just then pushed through the bars. After replacing the cut bars as best they could, they crept the few feet along H range to the small corridor at the north end between G and H ranges — and the Main Cell Block's fatefully-flawed trap door. They clasped hands with The Chief and there were extended whispers of "Good luck" as they passed his cell. One or two others whispered the same.

For some reason, the plotters had not been able to get the key to the Yale lock on the trap door back from the cleaning gang. Instead, Uly had decided to deal with the heavy lock and hasp on the trap with a light crowbar. Lauzon, bar in hand, was boosted up by Mickey and Nick — more than 9 feet to the trap door — to the lock, which he broke open only after a signal to Harold Jamieson, whose cell was within the sound of their whispering voices, to flush his toilet. Again, Uly considered it would make too much of a racket to simply shove open the heavy metal trap, so they waited as they were until The Chief once more masked the sound by flushing his toilet again. When this flush happened, Uly shoved the trap open, climbed up into the attic and then pulled first Mickey, then Nick up after himself. Then there was a short wait for a third flush, made by the same toilet, before Uly closed the heavy trap door.

The attic was a long rectangular room — the shape of the North Wing — wherein there was electrical and boiler equipment, a concrete floor and heavy beams between the floor and the ceiling. At the far south end was a window that looked into the Dome, through which the escapees briefly peered down and watched the night guards playing cards. In the attic were several dim electric lights, which gave them sight of their surroundings. They soon found the garret window.

The small barred opening leading to the roof was equipped with a sturdy lock that went through a hasp and a metal chain. They broke the hasp and the chain with a heavier crowbar that had been purposely left in the attic by the cleaning gang. The 150-foot and the 30-foot ropes were already there, courtesy of the cleaners, Mickey's connections.

The three squeezed themselves through the window — said to be a foot and a half square — onto the roof of the cell block. They found they were midway up the roof, but as they knew they would be, they were on the west side and in the sight line of the guard on the northwest tower, who might chance to look up. Flat on their bellies, crawling as they had to, dragging the two ropes, one 150 feet long, the other 30 feet with the iron hooks attached to it, they painstakingly inched their way up and over to the east side of the cell block roof. Once there, they had to wait for

The North Wing of the Main Cell Block circa 1890. (Queen's University Archives)

the night yardman to make his next turn around the yard. Ten minutes passed before he showed up along the east wall of the enclosure, moving his flashlight here and there, as they had always known him to do.

After the yardman went by, they tied the long rope to the solid, heavy ventilation pipe that they already knew jutted out from the roof. Then they were ready to go down to the yard.

First Uly, then Mickey, then Nick went over the edge and down the side of the building, desperately trusting their lives to a 150-foot rope made of many lengths of braided mailbag jute cord — which was only as strong as its weakest link. After the first 12 or 15 feet they were able to use their feet on the bars of the cell block windows as a help in clambering down the structure. Nick, the last man, had to leave part of the rope dangling on the facade where he knew it might be seen in the morning. The bottom end he cut off and afterwards hid inside the compound.

Now came what they considered the most dangerous chance they had to take.

Moonlight bathed the prison enclosure and there were floodlights along the walls, all of which meant that, after they left the shadow of the cell block and before they gained the shelter of the prison vegetable patch, they would be easily visible to the guard on the northwest tower for a distance of about 90 feet. If the guard was awake and looking into the enclosure, he would surely see them and sound the prison alarm.

Ready to take a gambler's chance, the three convicts now linked arms, crouched low, counted to three and, all together, ran hard. Then, in a bunch, they dove headfirst into the garden — and waited.

Nothing happened. No alarm sounded.

"I was sure then that we were as good as free," Nick Minelli remembered years later.[4]

Now the three lay hiding among the tomato plants for a few minutes, waiting again for the yardman to make his next pass around the enclosure. After he went by, in the dark spot underneath the northeast tower, where they knew they were well-camouflaged by tall plants and by the shadow under the tower at the join of the two walls, they began tossing the 30-foot rope, with its iron hooks on the end, up to the top of the east wall. At first, the hooks wouldn't catch — and they were making noise hitting the stonework. Then they tried catching the hooks on a corner of the iron railing of the tower guard's catwalk. One of the hooks caught there and, to their mild surprise, the railing was easily strong enough to hold Uly's weight. So, first Uly, then Mickey, then Nick literally walked up the side of the 32-foot-high wall, pulling hard on the rope. Then each in turn slid effortlessly down the wall's other side and were suddenly outside the prison compound. The time was 2:15 a.m. The first-ever known-escape from the Main Cell Block of Kingston Penitentiary had taken just about two hours from the time the escapees had left their cells. As one of the three later remembered, there was an instant of exhilaration at being free of Kingston's high grey walls. This may have been what caused Mickey to foolishly tear off his blue prison shirt, #8213, and throw it away near the front of the institution.

They loped stealthily eastwards away from the prison — 1,200 feet as the official report on the escape later said — where, in front of 37 Livingstone Avenue, they came upon a suitable getaway car, an olive green 1940 Ford sedan, license number 73-T-21. As it happened, the Ford belonged to Ronald Haunts, a guard at Collins Bay Penitentiary. The doors were open and, for whatever reason, the car was reported to have a broken draft window on the driver's side. Uly got behind the wheel, the ignition was "hot-wired," the motor started, and the Ford was headed for Highway 2, where it was turned westwards toward Toronto. The convicts knew their absence was unlikely to be noticed before the 7 a.m. count. There was time to make "the Queen City" and beyond.

According to Minelli's remembrance, it was decided that one of the three would lie on the floor of the back seat as they drove, in case word was out that three convicts had escaped Kingston.[5] Uly did all of the driving — and nobody told him he couldn't. They stopped for gasoline and an hour's rest along the way. The feeling of exhilaration had passed. None of the three said much as they drove. They were exhausted from their efforts of the previous days — and there were new and dangerous obstacles before them. They had all missed a lot of sleep and all needed rest badly.

Nick's subsequent effusions imagined that none of the three had any plans about what they would do after they got out. "We had no cache of money waiting, no hideout, no disguises, no clothes, no food, no friends," he later said to a ghost writer.[6] If he really thought so, Nick had little understanding of the minds of the two men he was with, Lauzon especially. Uly planned everything. Joe Poireau, his former partner-in-crime, knew Uly better when he described him 62 years later as being "very calculating."[7] Uly had a plan. Likely he just didn't see any reason to tell Nick about it. Or Nick, in what he caused to be written in *The Star Weekly* in October 1959, didn't want to talk about Uly's plans, which involved Mickey, who, at the time of publication, was thought to be dead, but might not be.

Nick didn't remember it, but it seems likely that Uly, Mickey, or both would have made immediate collect telephone calls to trusted allies from whom, by pre-arrangement, they expected help and material assistance. Within a few days, the two more dangerous escapees would be heavily armed with, among other weapons, an automatic submachine gun. They would also be helped with transportation, clothes, and a hideout in or near the City of Windsor, for where Lauzon was certainly heading. All of this would have to be paid for — and that meant an armed robbery of a suitable bank would have to be done. In the underworld, the risk involved in helping such as Lauzon and McDonald generally costs big money.

About 8 a.m., as they got near Toronto, the fugitives listened to the car radio in anticipation of news of their escape — but there was none. An hour later, there was still no word that they were out and gone. But before 10 a.m., there was a news flash: *Three dangerous convicts have escaped Kingston Penitentiary!* In the Toronto area, where they then were, Mickey's involvement was, of course, the biggest part of the story. At first, prison authorities did not know how the three had escaped, only that they had done so. The police were putting up roadblocks all across southern Ontario. A province-wide manhunt had begun. Citizens were cautioned to be on their guard. "These men are noted desperadoes and are probably armed," the radio announcer warned.[8]

* * *

Back at the prison, Guard Reggie Roach had taken the 7 a.m. count in the North Cell Block, including on 4-H range. Moving briskly, he glanced quickly into the cells of McDonald, Lauzon, and Minelli and saw what he expected to see: not three dummies with bread loaves for heads, but, as was not unusual, three inmates feigning sickness, or perhaps catching a few extra winks, at the expense of their "jail mush" — breakfasts — before having to start another dreary day in the stoneshed. This was not out of the ordinary and didn't matter to Roach who, on the fly, quickly included the missing inmates in the morning count and passed on. After the breakfast period, the bell in the Dome rang yet again and the inmates on 4-H were marched off to work. It was then that The Chief and one or two others in the line rushed into cells 4-H-19, 4-H-15, and 4-H-13, hid the dummies under the beds, briskly straightened up the bedclothes, did a perfunctory clean-up of the cells, then closed the cell gates as if all was as usual.

Guard Paul Bedore, a 16-year veteran of the Penitentiary Service, made the mistake of accepting the stoneshed gang three men short. He always took his count inside the shop after work had started — which was not what he was supposed to do. This day, partly because other convicts in the L-shaped stoneshed were answering for the three who were not there, Bedore couldn't get his count right. Amidst the suppressed hilarity of the entire shop, he took a very long time to establish that three inmates were missing and even more time to establish which three were missing. Then, perhaps because he was very late in discovering a serious discrepancy and knew he would be in trouble over it, he made no report of the missing men to the North Gate — and, to appearances, just sat there hoping the problem would go away. Years later, Roy Clarke laughingly remembered Bedore saying in a worried aside, "I can't figure this out, why these three men are not here. Lauzon, McDonald, and Minelli. My three longest-termers, too."[9]

On the northeast tower, at 9:30 a.m., 75 minutes after he began his shift, Guard James Walsh had not yet noticed the rope that the escapees left dangling over the outside of the prison wall from the railing of the tower's catwalk. When the aged inmate who tended the prison garden pointed it out to him, Walsh was said to have at first dismissed the rope as having been left behind by the mason gang — which had done some work there weeks before! The same inmate, who also cleaned up in front of the North Gate on King Street then went outside the enclosure and found the discarded blue shirt of prison inmate #8213, Donald "Mickey" McDonald. When word of this was taken to Deputy Warden Len Millard's office, the escape was discovered. Seeing a rope made of mailbag cord hanging over the outside of the wall, Millard knew it had nothing at all to do with anything the mason gang had done. Millard took Mickey's shirt and the rope to Warden Allan at 9:40 a.m. News of the escape was then telephoned to the Kingston Police and soon after to radio stations at Ottawa, Toronto, and Montreal. Inside the prison, work went on as usual and the prison siren did not sound. Only the outside gangs — the farm gang and the excavation gang — were called back inside the enclosure walls.

* * *

In the meantime, according to Nick Minelli, Lauzon, a master at running the back roads, had decided to go around Toronto to the north and find a place on the western outskirts of the city where the three fugitives could rest for a couple of days and avoid the height of the police search. Twelve years later, Nick described how the escapees rode out this critical time:

> ... We drove down a dirt road until we found a grove of trees. We drove the car right into them, hiding it from anybody passing by. That's where we stayed.
>
> We were there from Monday until noon Wednesday when I broke away from the other two as I had intended. During that time we didn't do much except listen to the news reports and talk about where we would go. There was a pond nearby and we all went in for a couple of swims. On Monday I walked to a store about a mile away to buy bread and bologna. I didn't wear any disguise, just the white shirt, sports shoes and brown pants I had

escaped in. I didn't buy much food because we didn't have much money. We had had $12 to start with and we spent $3 on gasoline, leaving $9.

At night we could see the lights of Toronto and hear children's voices from a nearby farm, but nobody came near us during those two days and only one or two cars passed on the road. One of us kept watch the first night. After that we all slept in the car. The third man had to settle for the floor.

During this time Mickey and Uly were hatching plans I didn't want any part of. I won't say what they were, but they involved getting money. I was ready to leave and I did on Wednesday. They expected it. There were no hard feelings. I just said I was going and that was that.[10]

Ulysses Lauzon, who was unerringly generous with those he liked, handed Nick $5 of the $9 minus the cost of the food they had had, and insisted he take it.

"Don't worry about us. We'll do okay," he said.

Nick walked down the country sideroad to a highway where he hitched a ride going west. He would never see Mickey or Uly again.

CHAPTER TWENTY-FOUR

The Big Search
(August 18, 1947–September 16, 1947)

THE STORY OF THE Kingston escape was the banner headline of afternoon papers all across Ontario on Monday, August 18. *The Toronto Daily Star's* streamer shouted THREE ESCAPE 'PEN,' ONE IS MICKEY. The *Evening Telegram* had a similar headline. The *Windsor Daily Star's* banner blazed LAUZON, MACDONALD FLEE PEN. It was the same all across the province. The escape engendered fear, most especially in rural areas, where immediate help against attack was unlikely to be available. Three totally desperate men, all of whom had police records for violent crimes, were seen as a real and gripping threat by the worried public. Further afield, coverage of the event was big in some places, not so big in others. In Calgary, Alberta, *The Herald's* blackline was 3 DESPERADOES ESCAPE FROM ONTARIO PRISON. In Vancouver, *The Sun* gave the story only two column inches in the far left bottom corner of its front page. *The Halifax Herald* of Tuesday morning, August 19, had the story above the fold under the heading "Man Captured in PEI Is Among Escapees."

What was described as "one of the greatest manhunts in Ontario police history" began immediately after Warden Allan telephoned word of the breakout to the Kingston Police.[1] Reporters who initially questioned officials at the prison were given to understand that the three escapees were "the most dangerous prisoners in Kingston Penitentiary," and that all were to be considered "extremely dangerous." A day later, Warden Allan amended this by pointedly telling the press that Ulysses Lauzon was "by far the most dangerous of the trio." This opinion found support in Uly's hometown, where Inspector James Campbell told unsettling stories to *The Windsor Daily Star* about the December 1, 1941, arrest of a teenaged Lauzon:

> There were some others with him. They were locked in a garage in a stolen car, a padlock on the doors.
>
> We surrounded the place and then they drove right through the doors. On the way downtown, Lauzon said to me, "Campbell, it's a good thing for you that this didn't take place tomorrow. We were going to break into a hardware store for some 'rods' (guns) tonight. If we had them, it would have been different."[2]

Other Windsor policemen remembered the events of 1945 and warned that Lauzon was "just what he seems to be, a hardened desperado," who would put up a gun battle before he would surrender. Later in the week, Uly was being written of in the Windsor press as "Canada's Dillinger."

In Toronto, on Monday, August 18, the police were prosecuting "a widespread search for the three escaped prisoners" only a short time after the alarm from Kingston was heard. Cars entering the city from the east and the north were being stopped and examined, and the living quarters of some of Mickey's criminal allies, his wife, and some of the now-dispersed MacDonald family were already being watched. "It is probably the biggest manhunt in the history of the city," an unnamed senior police official was quoted as saying.[3]

As elsewhere, there were descriptions, recaps, histories, and anecdotes of the criminal careers of all three of the missing men in the Toronto press this day. Naturally, the name at the centre of local interest was Mickey McDonald, who was cast as "foremost of the escapees," as "justifiably famed as one of the most habitual criminals in the country" and, of course, as "The Mad Dog of Jarvis Street." Mickey was said to be "known internationally" because of the Windsor Murder trials. Robert Taylor's story in *The Daily Star* recalled that in November 1939, after being acquitted of murder, Mickey had gone off to Kingston with the lament, "Crime is a sucker's racket, and I'm the one who knows it."[4] "Today he is hunted, homeless and every man's hand is against him," Taylor wrote.[5] The escapees were now thought by some police and prison guards to be likely armed and ready to kill. "There'll be shooting when they are found. They won't be back here alive," a nameless Kingston guard was quoted as saying.[6] But Inspector John Nimmo, Mickey's old nemesis, told *The Daily Star* that there was no reason for any "shoot-on-sight" order on McDonald. "There's nothing tough about that guy at all. He's just a stupid baby," Nimmo stated flatly. "When a policeman sights him, all he'll have to do will be to say, 'Come here, Mickey,' and Mickey will come."[7]

Only in Ottawa did Nick Minelli get more than what was really passing notice. There, there was an informed rehash of the most serious conviction of Nick's career — the taxicab caper — and Ottawa Police Chief J.P. Downey was quoted in *The Citizen* as saying, "Minelli is a bad character to be at large and the men with whom he made his escape combine to make an extremely dangerous trio."[8] In many other places, Nick was reported to have the initials "N.M." tattooed on his "chin" — a press miscue that kept popping up for months. In fact, the tattoo was on Nick's "shin."

On Tuesday morning, August 19, a letter mailed in Toronto on the previous Saturday evening protesting living conditions in Kingston Penitentiary, especially with regard to the poor quality of the food, appeared on the front page of the *Globe and Mail* as the centrepiece of a copyrighted story. The 400-word letter, penned in "school boy's, precise, easy-to-read handwriting," bore the legitimate signature of "Donald Mickey McDonald No. 8213." It had obviously been smuggled out of the prison and was part of the ongoing prisoners' campaign to get public opinion on their side. Mickey's letter was accompanied by a petitionary letter, easily seen to have been written by an educated inmate. This was signed by 700 others — virtually the entire population of the Kingston prison — similarly protesting the quantity and quality of the food the inmates were required to live on. What the *Globe* termed Mickey's "covering letter" protested bitterly about the "starvation" of the inmates, complained as usual about his own alleged victimization at the hands of the Toronto Police, and even delivered an implied threat if the matter of prison food was not addressed.[9]

Already the Ontario Provincial Police and municipal forces all over Ontario were receiving large numbers of "hot tips" and reported sightings from the public, as well as information from underworld "sources." All, or most, of these had to be checked out. In Toronto and Windsor, all off-duty officers were called in, and there still wasn't nearly enough manpower. According to one senior detective, the police were looking into the most promising leads first and would get to the others as they could. In some cases that meant days later.

Typical of what officers were being told was a sighting called in by a farmer of the Napanee district, who reported that, between 9 and 10 p.m., Monday evening, he had spotted three men riding the top of a passing freight train. At a distance of 200 feet, in gathering twilight, the farmer recognized the three as the escapees. "I could swear they were the men the police want," he later told a reporter.[10]

About 10:30 the same night, a Queen Street hotel in Ottawa was all agog in consequence of a rash of police cars arriving in answer to a report that Mickey, Uly and Nick were in the hotel. A search of the premises was made, to no avail.

One afternoon that week, patrons of the Casino Theatre on Queen Street near Toronto's City Hall were surprised when a large force of policemen raided the burlesque show. Acting on a telephone tip that Ulysses Lauzon was seated in the back row, the police arrived suddenly, the theatre lights were abruptly turned on, the girl-watchers were carefully scrutinized, then a man who had been fingered as Lauzon was briefly questioned. He turned out to be a hard-rock miner from British Columbia who was visiting Toronto to attend a wedding.

It didn't take long for Mickey to be seen at The Corner — indeed, at The Royal Cecil Hotel. But he was not there. "We haven't seen Mickey here and we don't want to see him," was the manager's answer to a reporter who asked.[11] There were similar raids on other Jarvis Street hotels as a result of tips that were at times someone's hope of a reward but often mere pranks.

It was reported, too, that Mickey was working picking tobacco on a farm near Oakland, Ontario — but he wasn't there. Nor was he in Edmonton, Alberta, where he and the others were said to have been sighted only four days after the bust out. Nor were Mickey and friends in Maniwaki, Quebec, where the motorcar stolen at Kingston was allegedly pulled out of a ditch by a passing trucker.

It was a bad week in Quebec and Ontario to be driving a green Ford sedan of anything like 1940 vintage — or, in more than a few cases, any auto that was in any way similar.

But all of this paled beside what took place on the Quebec side of the Upper Ottawa Valley, beginning about 30 hours after the three convicts got free of the Kingston prison.

About 7 a.m., Tuesday, August 19, Alan Soucie, the young attendant at a gas station at Chapeau, Quebec, on Alumette Island, 80 miles upstream from Hull on the Ottawa River, had three men in an olive green car pull onto his lot.[12] The licence number of the car, Soucie was reported to have said with certainty, was 73-T-21. The men asked for directions to Waltham, Quebec, 9 miles away, and Soucie unsuspiciously obliged them. Two hours later, the daily paper arrived with the story of the Kingston escape — and Alan Soucie called the police. The Quebec provincial policeman who interviewed Soucie found him and his story to be credible — and thus began what would be the largest concentrated search for the three escaped convicts anywhere in Canada.

Soon Quebec provincial officers — many armed with automatic weapons and reportedly with orders to shoot on sight — were flooding into the rugged country of Pontiac County, Quebec, and all along Quebec Highway 8.[13] It was estimated 150 provincials came in police cars from Hull, from Montreal, and from elsewhere in Quebec. The City of Montreal Police sent three carloads of armed men. The RCMP joined the search, some of their cars having Ontario provincials in company with the Mounties. Roadblocks were put up and all manner of green cars were investigated. Hull and Ottawa municipal police helped by manning the Quebec ends of bridges over the Ottawa River. The police concentrated much of their search on the brushy, hilly trails that ran off Highway 8 between Chapeau and Waltham — these all being dead ends and the highway being the only way in and out of the district. Word of Alan Soucie's sighting of the convicts flashed up and down the highway, which meant that sundry other witnesses, who similarly thought they had seen the green Ford and the same three men, were interviewed by the police, and often by journalists with large imaginations. Some reporters wrote dramatic stories about how the police were "closing in" on the "dangerous desperadoes," when, in fact, the police had not even seen the three fugitives and had no certainty they were anywhere in the vicinity.

The idea being floated, at least in the press, was that the escapees were making for the Chicoutimi-Lac St. Jean area, where Ulysses Lauzon was said to have either $120,000 or $300,000 buried "in a hole beside a tree." This the Quebec criminal investigators knew was not so, as all but $7,000 or $8,000 of the loot stolen by "the Detroit River Gang" at Bath, Ontario, had already been recovered. Joe Poireau had told the police where to find the buried bonds, soon after he was convinced that Lauzon and Walt Koresky were in police custody at Charlottetown.[14]

By noon Wednesday, doubts about Alan Soucie's identification of the three escapees were being publicly expressed by Captain J.A. Quenneville, the man in charge of the search at Montreal. Speaking of Soucie that afternoon, Quenneville now said, "He is sure of only two of the five numbers of the licence plate on the car, and he is not sure what the person in the back of the car looked like."[15] In Chapeau, Alan Soucie was already sorry he had ever gotten involved.

The massive Quebec search — reported in Ottawa as "the greatest manhunt in the criminal annals of the Hull-Ottawa area" and in Windsor as nothing less than "one of the greatest manhunts in criminal history" — lasted a day and a night before, at noon on Wednesday, August 20, most of the officers were called off.[16] After that, only a few provincials from Hull stayed on the chase for another 24 hours. Some reporters hung around the area a day or two more, churning out last stories that were already redundant. No one was arrested. No one like the three fugitives was seen in the area by the police. It was all a necessary but futile exercise — the working out of what had seemed the best early lead the police of Quebec or Ontario had gotten. As one Quebec policeman put it, "They might have been here yesterday, but they are not here now."[17]

It would not be public knowledge until a story in *The Ottawa Citizen* of September 16, but the Quebec hunt had a strange trailer on it. A Kingston inmate — a member of the stoneshed crew — who had been released Saturday, August 16, approached OPP District Inspector T.W. Cousans, at Perth, Ontario, 72 hours later, with the offer of information that he claimed would produce the capture of all three escapees. Rheal Demers, aged 41, was believable enough that he was taken to the Justice Department offices at Ottawa where, on Friday, August 22, Superintendent of Penitentiaries Ralph B. Gibson promised him in writing a reward of $6,000, on the basis of $2,000 per escapee, if their captures happened in consequence of Demers' information, and if they occurred before midnight, August 31.[18]

Demers was an experienced woodsman who lived in Hawkesbury, Ontario, at the Ontario end of the Perley Bridge over the Ottawa River — only a few miles from Quebec's Laurentian Mountains. His story, always delivered in highly dramatic fashion, was that Lauzon had approached him inside Kingston with a proposition of "easy money" in return for his providing a backwoods hideout for himself and two others, all of whom would be escaping Kingston soon after Demers' release. The informer claimed he agreed to this, thinking Uly's escape plot was just so much talk of a kind not to be taken seriously. But, as he said, Uly, Mickey, and Nick had astounded him by showing up at his door on the evening of Tuesday, August 19, demanding the safe refuge they said he had promised. A stranger named "Bill," supposedly from Montreal, was claimed to be with them and to have soon impressed Rheal by producing a machine-gun from the trunk of a car. Thinking fast, Demers said, he took the four to an empty log cabin near Kilmar Mines, 18 miles north of Grenville, on the Quebec side of the Ottawa River. This satisfied them. Then, as Demers further related, the five went back to Grenville and drank beer in a hotel, where they cut a deal that would see Demers paid $25 a day and have the use of a "good used car" to run around after the escapees' needs while they were in hiding. All of this allegedly took place during the same time 150 dog-tired policemen were feverishly searching Pontiac County for the badly-wanted convicts.

The story of the "rat" got more bizarre. He took Inspector Cousans to a hill overlooking a log cabin, after telling him that Lauzon and McDonald had departed for Ontario to pull "a job," but that they were to afterwards come back for Nick and Bill. The inspector, watching the cabin from the top of a hill, saw no one. Demers urged that the police move in right then. "You can get one of them right now and I can earn $2,000," Rheal exhorted Inspector Cousans, who chose to wait on the return of the more dangerous others, especially Ulysses Lauzon. Demers was told by the policeman to play along with Nick and Bill, and to notify him right away when Lauzon and McDonald returned.

Days went by, during which events demonstrated that Uly and Mickey were far from the Province of Quebec, and they did not afterwards return to the watched cabin to pick up Nick and "the mysterious Bill." Time ran out on Rheal Demers' "contract" with the Justice Department. When the cabin was finally approached, no one was there. Then, in mid-September, for whatever strange reason, Rheal Demers foolishly told his story to the police of the Ottawa suburban town of Eastview — and escorted two Eastview officers, along with an *Ottawa Citizen* reporter named Joe Finn, out to the Kilmar Mines log cabin.[19] After which Finn did Demers the disservice of writing his strange yarn up in the *Citizen* of September 16 — and the police informer's story, or parts of it, was widely copied by other papers across Canada. Which might have got Rheal Demers — an outright nut and a danger to himself — killed.

Some time would pass before Ulysses Lauzon was in a position to communicate by way of "the underground route" with The Chief, and by way of him, others of the stoneshed crew on H range. In one of several letters, Uly told how glad that he and the others were that the main search for them had focused on the Province of Quebec. "We were never there or anywhere near there," Uly is said to have written to "Harold and the Boys," who, of course, thought the escape and the extent of the feckless police chase to be hilarious and a wondrous victory for their side over constituted authority.[20]

CHAPTER TWENTY-FIVE

The Windsor Bank Robbery
(August 22, 1947–August 25, 1947)

ON MONDAY AFTERNOON, AUGUST 18, a man cutting weeds on a concession road in Esquesing Township, Halton County, Ontario, was asked directions by the driver of what he later described to the police as "a 1937 or 1938 greenish-coloured Chevrolet or Ford." The man at the wheel of the 1940 Ford, stolen at Kingston early that same morning, wanted to know how to get to Guelph, Ontario, by way of concession roads, and definitely not by way of any highway. The next day Howard Garone, the weed cutter, identified photographs of Ulysses Lauzon as the wheelman who asked the questions and of Mickey McDonald as the passenger in the front seat. He also informed the OPP that there was a third man lying down on the back seat shielding his face with his hand.[1]

Off the Eramosa Road, now Highway 24, which goes northeast from Guelph to Highway 9 and Orangeville, there is a farm road beside which there was then, and may still be, a thick stand of trees known locally as the Monkey Bush. The escapees had information about this thick gorse before they left Kingston and saw its value as an interim stopover on their way to Windsor. As Nick Minelli remembered in 1959, "We drove down a dirt road until we found a grove of trees. We drove the car right into them, hiding it from anybody passing by. That's where we stayed."[2] The escapees rested there for most of three days. The important difference from Minelli's 1959 reminiscences was the thicket was near Guelph, where a crime was committed, not northwest of Toronto, as Nick would later claim.[3]

In the first dark hours of Thursday, August 21, with Nick, as he said in 1959, already gone his own way, Mickey and Uly left the stolen Ford hidden in the Monkey Bush, where it would be discovered a few days later by a group of teenagers out on a hike. The two fugitives legged it into Guelph, where they helped themselves to a 1946 Mercury Coach belonging to R.C. Cairns, a Guelph insurance agent, resident at 76 Eramosa Road. This took them to a safe hideout in, or near, Windsor, where, by pre-arrangement, Uly's underworld friends supplied them with a temporary refuge and the kind of equipment necessary to do a daylight armed robbery of a downtown Windsor bank.

Friday, August 22, was a payday, and the Royal Bank of Canada at the corner of Ouellette Avenue and Ellis Street in Windsor's business section was "a payroll branch" with lots of money on hand with which to cash the paycheques of its patrons.

At 2:57 p.m., three minutes before closing time, Lauzon and McDonald — bare-faced and wearing blue suit coats — simultaneously entered the bank, Uly by the front door on Ouellette Avenue, Mickey by the side door off Ellis. Uly carried a submachine gun, hidden beneath a coat draped over it. Mickey had a .45 Luger automatic and was toting a brown pigskin bag.

Right away Mickey — "the man in the gray hat" — jammed his pistol into a startled customer's back and loudly announced, "This is a holdup." Then he began herding the bank's patrons, 13 of them, against the south wall, where he made them kneel on the floor. He had to threaten into silence one or two women who became briefly hysterical.

At the same time, Lauzon, looking racy in a brown fedora, a red ascot scarf, and sunglasses, dropped the coat that masked the machine gun on the floor by the bank's front door, then he went briskly behind the counter and rammed the weapon into the back of John McIntyre, the bank's accountant. "This is a stick-up," Uly told McIntyre. Flourishing the machine gun and issuing threats like John Dillinger might have, Uly briefly cowed the bank's staff, then, after a few seconds, went quickly into the manager's office and fetched A.A. Kinahan, the bank manager.

Together, the two gunmen then forced the bank personnel — nine of them — to come out from behind the counter and to get down on the floor with the customers.

Most, or all, of the robbers' commands were laced with threats and foul-mouthed profanities. "Come on, or I'll blow your brains out," was the kind of menace that was so accentuated several times when compliance was slow or unstarted.

Next Uly walked carefully back around behind the bank's counter, making certain that all was as it seemed, then when sure that it was, he went back out into the customer area and, as if by a predetermined plan, exchanged weapons with Mickey. Then he forced John McIntyre and a female staff member to open the vault. He went briskly through the drawers, filling the pigskin bag with paper currency. He surprised the bank personnel who saw it by disdainfully tossing aside $60,000 in Victory bonds, many of them negotiable, that were all neatly tied up in an easily-stealable compact packet. The Montreal shooting of Joe Poireau had evidently made Uly leery of the value of bearer bonds.

While Uly was in the vault, two women customers walked in the front door, whereupon Mickey, in ungentlemanly fashion, wagged the machine gun at them and gruffly ordered, "Get over there against the wall and nothing will happen to you." That made, in all, 24 staff and customers, kneeling, crouching, or sitting on the floor.

To many of the bank's personnel and patrons, Ulysses Lauzon was easily recognizable. They had seen his prominent lips and nose in previously-published photographs in *The Windsor Star*. A.A. Kinahan, who later told the Windsor Police that the younger man "looked like pictures of Lauzon in the papers," was not particularly impressed with Uly — noticing especially how "nervous" he seemed to be. "They were not experienced bank robbers," Kinahan naively told *The Star*. "The chap who stuck the Tommy gun in my ribs shook so much that I was afraid it might go off from the vibrations."[4]

Finished in the vault, Lauzon walked back to Mickey at the front door and, again, as if by a plan, they switched weapons. Then Mickey went smartly out the side door onto Ellis Street, where he reappeared less than a minute later at the wheel of the Mercury they had glommed in Guelph. In firm possession of the machine gun and the pigskin bag, Lauzon now went briskly outside and got into the front passenger seat. The getaway car went four blocks north up Ouellette Avenue, Windsor's main street, as far as Erie Street, where it was seen to turn to the east. Someone looked at the bank's clock, which now said 3:10 p.m. The robbery had taken 13 minutes. First reports had the bandits getting away with just over $40,000, all in cash. Later, the bank's announced loss was upped to roundly $50,000.[5]

Within an hour, the Windsor Police had found the robbers' getaway car abandoned 15 blocks away, on Richmond Street between Hall and Pierre Avenues in east-central Windsor — Uly's old neighbourhood. A woman watching curiously from a window had seen the bandits ditch the Mercury and then walk smartly up a lane, one of them carrying the loot-filled bag. "They looked suspicious," she told detectives, who were able to establish that the two men had legged it for at least another three blocks after dumping the Mercury. Found in the Merc's back seat were a 12-guage sawed-off shotgun with shells, a few .38-calibre bullets, a copy of the *Globe and Mail*, and books of matches with Toronto advertisements on them. The inside of the car was badly soaked in whisky, such that the vehicle itself reeked of it. License plates stolen from a parked auto in Halton County were attached to the Merc's fenders.[6]

The *Windsor Star's* late Sports Edition had a front page bulletin titled "Bank in City Robbed, May Be Lauzon," which helped radio reports cause a sensation in the City of Windsor. The public was made anxious by the knowledge that two such desperate characters, seemingly with nothing to lose, were at large in the Border City. Like almost everyone else, the Windsor Police saw that the robbery bore the trademarks of a "Lauzon job," as previously demonstrated at Ayr and Bath, and they well knew who the perpetrators were. Still, they were at first tight-lipped about naming them and about any other information they gave out to the media. The next day they didn't think they needed to be as circumspect. Many of the 24 eyewitnesses in the bank had positively identified one or both of the robbers, usually Lauzon, and the fingerprints of both escapees had been found on the Mercury, Mickey's on the steering wheel.[7] The car showed evidence of having been driven hard over gravel roads. R.C. Cairns, its owner, told the OPP, the Guelph Police, as well as the *Guelph Mercury*, that he had heard a noise outside his home about 1 a.m. Thursday, and had gone out to investigate. He saw no one. Missing from the vehicle, he said, was a pigskin bag and one of two blue suit coats that had been in the back seat. The missing coat was apparently worn by Uly during the heist. The bag carried away the loot.[8]

The bank robbery centred the manhunt on Windsor, where Chief of Police Claude Renaud afterwards strongly backed the opinion of his investigators that the bandits had gone to ground within Windsor itself. Late on Friday and Saturday nights, squads of policemen entered more than a few houses in east-central Windsor — mostly the domiciles of known associates of Lauzon's — and searched them thoroughly. They turned up nothing. Reports over the weekend that the fugitives had been seen at sundry other locations in Ontario and Quebec did nothing to slow the Windsor detectives. On Monday, August 25, speaking of the fugitives, Chief Renaud told reporters, "As far as we are concerned they are still in this city and we are going to keep working on that assumption until we have definite proof they have been recognized elsewhere."[9]

That afternoon came the most promising lead of the Windsor search, said to have originated with a former policeman who told city detectives that he had seen the Kingston escapees at Emery's Beach, about 15 miles east of Windsor along the south shore of Lake St. Clair.[10] At 5:40 p.m., a dozen carloads of well-armed policemen — nearly 50 city, provincial, and RCMP officers — went fast out of Windsor to descend upon a line of cottages between St. Clair Beach and Belle River, Ontario. The police spread themselves out for a mile along a gravel road that ran behind the cottages, then, starting at the west end of the cabins, a heavily-armed squad methodically searched one white-framed summer home after another, till all were cleared. A crowd of vacationers, estimated to be 500 people, among them "swarms of kids," seemed merely to watch in silence. But the name "Lauzon" was quietly on many lips. And according to a story, the police raid had interrupted the now locally-favourite kids' game of "Cops and Lauzon."[11]

For many days after the Royal Bank holdup, the Windsor Police were unwavering in their stated belief that Ulysses Lauzon and Mickey McDonald were still "holed up" in the Border City. That would be their position for weeks afterwards, until, finally, it was publicly admitted that the fugitives had probably gotten away.

The Windsor bank robbery of Friday, August 22, 1947, was the last time that Donald "Mickey" McDonald or Ulysses Lauzon were certainly seen in public in Canada. In fact, so far as the public would know, Mickey, soon to be the country's most notorious missing man, was never certainly seen again, anywhere, anytime, anyplace, after his first and only known bank robbery.

CHAPTER TWENTY-SIX

Hot News, Cold Trail
(August 1947–early 1948)

IN THE 1930S AND 1940s, more than today, a big part of being a successful police detective was the cultivation of a string of reliable informants. The Toronto Police detective department, not then organized into squads, had a large staff of general detectives, most or all of whom had their own regular or semi-regular stool pigeons who would supply them with information.[1] Often such informants were bookmakers, bootleggers, prostitutes, minor-league criminals, or quasi-criminals themselves. Some detectives of the day had many such "sources" who were paid for their knowledge of other peoples' crimes. Many snitches came back to their favourite detective again and again. Some were just natural born "rats." Some held grudges. Most wanted money or a large favour, like "a wash" on some charge they were up on. A register of payments to such people, informally known as the Stool Pigeon Fund, was kept at police headquarters. The Toronto detectives used the information they got very well. They would "trade up" for information. Small fry could be let go, if it meant getting information that would catch and/or convict an armed robber or a dangerous or high-profile criminal like a Ulysses Lauzon or a Mickey McDonald. In such a case, the idea for the police was "Get the information any way you can." Some detectives might threaten a minor crook in order to get "the goods" on a major crook. Some would not stoop to blackmail, or to threatening to do things that were not legal, or to punching a guy in the mouth, or worse. A few hard-case detectives were legends on the streets, their names engendering outright fear in the hearts of many of the city's criminals.[2]

On a police informant's story, Toronto detectives, in company with RCMP. Narcotics Squad officers, searched the Bell Pine Lodge on Georgian Bay looking for Mickey McDonald. The date was Wednesday, August 20, two days before the Windsor bank robbery. Mickey was formerly in the habit of visiting the lodge and "a source" had told the police something that caused them to think he might be there. A big-time Toronto heroin dealer made the Bell Pine his regular summer retreat. He was there when the police searched the place, but Mickey and the other escapees were not. A police document speculated, rightly it seems, that in the circumstances, the heroin merchant would not want Mickey there and would surely do nothing to help him.[3]

Another informant told that Kay MacDonald was holidaying at a Wasaga Beach cottage when she got the news of the escape — and that she immediately packed up and returned to Toronto. The apartment at 514A Yonge Street was, of course, under surveillance, so Kay was soon taken to police headquarters for questioning.

Inspector James Mackey, then in charge of Toronto's No. 1 Division on Court Street, years later remembered the approach of a big-league book-maker who, in the days right after the Kingston escape, claimed to know the whereabouts of Mickey McDonald and wanted to cut a deal to sell Mickey. The bookie had been arrested by OPP morality officers and his betting sheets were taken from him at that time. He needed to see the sheets in order to pay off his bettors without over-paying them. Inspector Mackey tried to arrange a trade, but the head of the OPP's Morality Squad would not cooperate. Without the information he wanted, the bookie would not give up Mickey. Years later, Mr. Mackey was uncertain about whether or not the would-be informant could really have produced McDonald.[4]

In October 1947, a Windsor source was feeding a local OPP con-stable a story about a shopbreaker who was supposedly casing Windsor banks for Ulysses Lauzon, in anticipation of Uly's certain return to the Border City to replenish his supply of money. An informer — or supposed informer — had told the constable that Mickey and Uly, who the shopbreaker was claimed to be in touch with by mail, were "following the races" in the southern United States and would soon return to Windsor. The constable's reports about this began in October 1947, but soon petered out to nothing.[5]

There were a lot more such "tips" from criminal and quasi-criminal informants, and many hundreds from the public-at-large. But almost all were fanciful, unreal, the product of someone's over-active imagination. Apart from those who were inside the Windsor bank on Friday, August 22, or those who saw the robbers make their escape from the bank, only one reported sighting in the OPP's file on the escapees was, to all appearances, a certainly genuine contact with the escapees before they crossed into the United States: that of Howard Garone, the Esquesing Township weed cutter.[6] "Tips" on the whereabouts of Mickey McDonald, the last of the escapees to be at large, were still being received by the OPP as late as 1957.

The public, of course, knew little or nothing of this kind of secret information. Instead, the press wrote what they could find out or, in the absence of hard information, exaggerate or invent, about what was the hottest crime story for many-a-day.

In late August and September 1947, most of the big headlines had to do with Nick Minelli. First, a Toronto newspaper had a silly tale that Lauzon and McDonald had murdered Minelli and hidden his body in tall grass surrounding the grove of trees where the Haunts' Ford was found.[7] The OPP investigated and found nothing to support this pressman's flight of imagination. Then Nick was soon after again found "murdered" — a bullet in the head — in a ditch 14 miles northwest of Port Huron, Michigan, where a body clad in clothing bearing the labels of Eaton's Department Store was thought to be Minelli. Within 24 hours, the OPP proved otherwise by way of dental records.[8] Twice a headline victim, Nick was next cast as a headline perpetrator in yet another taxi-driver robbery and kidnapping. An Oshawa cabbie categorically named Nick as the leader among three armed thugs who robbed him of $120, tied him up, dumped him on a sideroad near Bowmanville, and made off with his taxi. Three gun-toting youths were later arrested in Ottawa, where all pleaded guilty to armed robbery and were given prison terms. Nick Minelli was in no way involved and, in fact, was not in Canada at the time.

On September 5, it was reported in the *Daily Star* that Royal Bank of Canada officials had become worried that Ulysses Lauzon was partial to their banks. Uly had gotten $350,000 from the Royal Bank at Bath, Ontario, and the take at Windsor had by this time long since been upped to roundly $50,000 cash. "That money won't go very far the way they have to travel," an unnamed Royal Bank official told the *Star*, referring to the robbers' need for costly underworld help to ensure their safe hiding.[9] The Royal bankers were sufficiently impressed with the idea that Uly might hit them again to spend a significant amount of money to better their security.

The Rheal Demers' story broke in the *Ottawa Citizen* of Tuesday, September 16, and was news for two or three days. That same day saw the release of an RCMP circular announcing that the commissioner of penitentiaries at Ottawa would pay a $1,000 reward for information resulting in the arrest of each of the three Kingston escapees.[10] The circular, dated September 12, supplied physical descriptions of the convicts in scrupulous detail and carried a poignant "caution to police officers" concerning the escapees' violent histories and their being armed with a submachine gun.[11]

In Windsor, Inspector James Campbell was immediately critical of the circular and of its timing. "If the rewards in this case had been ten times that much, and if announcement had been made immediately after the escape, I have no doubt that these three men would today be where they ought to be," was the inspector's acerbic comment.[12] Later, in December 1947, the Canadian Bankers' Association (CBA), which had long had a standing reward of up to $5,000 for the arrests of the robbers of any Canadian bank, would put up its own "Special Offer $5,000 Reward" for the three escapees. The CBA circular stipulated, "This offer supercedes for these convicts the standing reward offer of the Canadian Bankers' Association under which, since January 1924, rewards totalling $219,413 have been paid."[13] The reward — a maximum of $5,000 for the arrest of all three escapees — was announced in the *Ottawa Citizen* of December 11.

SPECIAL OFFER $5,000 REWARD

THE CANADIAN BANKERS' ASSOCIATION offers, subject as below, to pay a total reward of $5,000 for information resulting in the arrest of the following escaped convicts:

ULYSSES LAUZON,
convicted bank robber

F.P.S. No. 450529
F.P.C. M 1 R 100 13
L 17 T 00 14

DESCRIPTION

Date of birth,	1922, Canada
Complexion,	Medium
Hair,	Brown
Eyes,	Hazel
Height,	5' 8"
Weight,	145 pounds

Small scars back of head; scar upper part of forearm, shin, left leg and right leg.

RIGHT FOREFINGER

DONALD (Micky) McDONALD
alias Micheal McDonald, alias John Allen Ross, wanted by Windsor, Ontario, City Police, for bank robbery.

F.P.S. No. 134945
F.P.C. M 1 R 000 12
L 1 U 100 15
AMP.

DESCRIPTION

Date of birth,	1907, Canada
Complexion,	Medium
Hair,	Black, greying
Eyes,	Green
Height,	5' 8¾"
Weight,	147 pounds

Appendix operation scar; mole left cheek; scar base left thumb; scar base right thumb; tip of middle finger on left hand amputated.

RIGHT MIDDLE FINGER

NICHOLAS (Nick) (Dominic) MINILLE
alias Manilla, alias Minelli, convicted bank robber.

F.P.S. No. 317313
F.P.C. M 1 U III 5
L 1 R III 3

DESCRIPTION

Date of birth,	1917, Canada
Complexion,	Dark
Hair,	Black
Eyes,	Brown
Height,	5' 5"
Weight,	144 pounds

Tattoo - left forearm, heart with initials N.M., right shin, initials D.M.

RIGHT FOREFINGER

The Association reserves the unrestricted right to fix the amount to be paid in respect of each claim where more than one claim is made, and to apply part of the total reward in respect of each of the said convicts if only one or two of them are arrested. The Association retains the unrestricted right to reject any claim for reward.

No claim for a reward will be considered unless made in writing to the Secretary of The Canadian Bankers' Association within one month after the date of the arrest in respect of which the reward is sought.

This offer of reward supersedes for these convicts the standing reward offer of The Canadian Bankers' Association under which, since January 1924, rewards totalling $219,413 have been paid.

TORONTO, December, 1947

Canadian Bankers' Association Reward Poster offering a total of $5,000 for the arrest of all three of the Kingston escapees of August 17/18, 1947. (Library and Archives Canada)

On September 22, at Ottawa, Superintendent Ralph B. Gibson made the official statement that disclosed to the public the results of the internal inquiry into the escape. His 1,100-word presentation described how the breakout was accomplished, stated there was no apparent collusion on the part of the prison staff, and that no evidence of "active outside help" was uncovered apart from a Simonds hacksaw blade — a precision instrument — later found in one of the escaped convicts' cells.[14] The success of the escape was put down to "the failure to maintain the high standard of vigilance and alertness on the part of some custodial officers that is essential for the security of the institution."[15] The preeminent casualty of the inquiry was Deputy Warden Len Millard, who had been placed on leave pending retirement. He was deemed to have failed in his duties with regard to the enforcement of the security of the prison — a deputy warden's foremost responsibility. Guards Reginald Roach, Paul Bedore, and James Walsh were discharged from the Penitentiary Service in consequence of failures in their duties, all of which had combined to delay the discovery of the escape by two and a half hours. No guard who was on duty at the time of the actual escape was let go. Five were otherwise disciplined. None of their names were ever made public. Superintendent Gibson did allow that the escape was "very cleverly planned."[16]

By mid-September, with nothing substantial seen or heard of any of the three missing inmates in nearly a month, many policemen in big-city Central Canada had come to the conclusion that the three were already across the border and had faded into the underworld of a large American city. Still, a mid-September "Mickey-has-been-seen" call to the Toronto Police would cause carloads of well-armed policemen to descend on the designated location, often in Gangland, ready for armed resistance. There were many such calls over many months in 1947, 1948, and after. A comprehensive story in the *Globe and Mail* on September 12, 1947, however, quoted "a senior detective" as to what was purported to be a consensus opinion among Toronto detectives:

> We don't think Mickey will come back to Jarvis Street.
> There are at least 500 persons along that street who

would be only too willing to turn him in at the first opportunity. Mickey has some friends in that area, but he has a great many more enemies.[17]

After late September 1947, public interest in the escapees slowed down badly. Quite simply, there had been nothing of real substance to report for quite some time. The three fugitives, who had been in the papers most days for five or six weeks running, had simply vanished. Now there were less frequent back-page items under such cutlines as "Hamilton Area Police Alerted For Three Bandits," "Sure Mickey Pals in Ingersoll Taxi," "McDonald, Lauzon Seen in the North," and "Doubt Mickey Seen at Nakina on November 6." It was an eight-line story when a man phoned a Brantford Hotel and asked for Mickey's room number and also when a drunk on an inter-urban bus accused a fellow passenger of being Mickey, which brought the police in force to the Hamilton Bus Terminal. On January 13, 1948, Mickey was reported to have participated in a bank holdup at Thorold, Ontario, three miles northeast of St. Catharines and, late the same day, in the robbery of a grocery store at Thornton, Ontario, near Barrie. None of these reports was worth more than a few lines in a Toronto newspaper. Such stories were becoming shorter, less regular, and were no longer prominently-displayed. Nearly all such items were wholly fanciful or otherwise explainable in terms that had nothing to do with Mickey McDonald, Ulysses Lauzon, or Nick Minelli.

Yet underworld informants were talking in Toronto, in Windsor and, eventually in New York City. It would become the case that the police came to believe that Mickey and Uly were in the Bronx, New York — and, according to one report, living there in a shared apartment for a time.[18] Allegedly, Mickey had been seen at New York's Yankee Stadium at a 1947 late-season Yankees game. Still, there was no address, no confrontation with the police, and no hard information of a kind that might have resulted in an arrest.

CHAPTER TWENTY-SEVEN

A Jailhouse Pipe Dream
(January 1948–April 1948)

LONG BEFORE THE AUGUST escape, Harold Jamieson had an understanding that Mickey McDonald's link with substantial mobsters in New York — and the reliable drug connection this could provide — meant that he too might have prospects in this line. In the post-war years, heroin in North America was getting big beyond previous imagination, and the profits were enormous. New York City, where Mickey was thought to be hiding out, was the centre of this trade on the continent. If things went as Harold was led to believe, with narcotics routinely supplied by way of Mickey, who was "connected" to the right people, The Chief could see himself with a far-off future as a substantial heroin distributor in Hamilton, Ontario, where he had grown up. Indeed, in time, narcotics might be the means of Harold's growing rich while living a life of leisure. He might dream of being the "front end" in a compact wholesale setup. Harold understood, though, that nobody was going to trust him with any quantity of "smack" up front. He was not a remittance man. He would have to do what the game called for. He would have to put together a large enough stake to buy in profitable quantity and, to do that, he knew only one way: armed robbery. The time to act was upon him. In early 1948, there was an acute shortage of heroin on the streets of both Toronto and Hamilton. Users were then paying high prices for adulterated product, if indeed they could get it. In Toronto pushers were demanding what was then regarded as fantastic prices for heroin, as much as $10 for 5 capsules. Two dollars "a hit."[1]

Harold was staying as close to Mickey as he could under the circumstances. On Wednesday, January 14, 1948, when Alex MacDonald, who had been released from the Manitoba Penitentiary the previous September, turned up at Kingston's North Gate to visit his brother, Edwin, The Chief, who had been released from Kingston only 6 days before, was in Alex's company.[2] During part of the previous week, both Alex and Harold were reported to be frequenting Windsor. They both knew what they wanted there. By the early 1960s, Alex would be "the absolute kingpin" of the drug world of Vancouver — the largest heroin dealer in the city, with 20 or more street dealers working for him, and with a "back end" manager handling all of the pushers, none of whom Alex ever had to as much as risk talking with, if he didn't want to.[3]

On the morning of Wednesday, January 21, 1948, 13 days after his release from Kingston, Harold Jamieson went to some kind of meeting in Detroit — a meeting that an informant had advised the Windsor Police about in advance. The expectation was that Harold would, or at least might, return to Windsor by way of the Detroit-Windsor Tunnel with a quantity of heroin secreted inside the borrowed car he would be driving.

Shortly before 11 a.m., on Ouellette Avenue just south of Erie Street in downtown Windsor, two Windsor detectives and two uniformed officers arrested Jamieson and MacDonald as they sat parked in a large 1948-model luxury automobile. The police found only 100 packages of untaxed American cigarettes in the car — which Harold admitted were his. Jamieson and MacDonald were taken in "for investigation," and the RCMP was given information that allowed them to charge Harold with possession of contraband cigarettes. News stories told that Jamieson, when confronted with the sudden onrush of police, tried to swallow a piece of paper and said that part of the paper was recovered before he got it down. The words "Bronx, N.Y." were reported to be written on the scrap that he failed to swallow. The report was that "Police believe

Jamieson was attempting to keep from them information contained on the paper, possibly an address."[4]

Questioned by detectives, the two recently-released ex-convicts gave their right names and claimed they were both truck drivers who resided at 38 Judith Drive, in East York Township, a Toronto suburb. The address was the home of Mickey's and Alex's sister, Florence, and her husband, Edward Near, then a cartage driver.

Harold and Alex did a bit of socializing in Windsor at the home of Alice Etousignant, Joe Poireau's mother, where likely they went to provide the family with a message, or news, or perhaps only gossip about Joe in Kingston Penitentiary's hospital.[5] Jamieson, aged 37 and an ex-convict who had spent almost all of his adult life in prison, met Elaine Poireau, Joe's attractive 18-year-old sister, at a house party at her mother's house, then afterwards put serious effort into romancing her. Elaine later said of the dangerous man who took her to movies and treated her well, "I liked 'Jim' a lot. There was just something about him I liked."[6] As she also explained, she was unhappy living under the roof of her mother's common law husband. In late March, Elaine left home and moved to Hamilton, where Jamieson was by then bunking in the Royal Connaught Hotel. Elaine stayed in a rooming house at 40 Cline Avenue in Westdale and found a job as a waitress in a restaurant. She worked in Hamilton only six days before "Jim" — her pet name for Jamieson — got them both in serious trouble with the law. Later, Elaine explained she had gone to Hamilton thinking "Jim" was a salesman, not a criminal. In fact, he was both. He sold heroin.

In Toronto, in March 1948, Harold Jamieson was charged with receiving a stolen radio. He was able to inveigle Charlie Dorland, Edward Near's long-time associate, into posting $300 bail for him. But Harold failed to appear in Toronto Police Court on Wednesday, March 31. Dorland never saw his $300 again.[7]

It had taken The Chief a while to put together what he thought was the right "score" to raise the cash for the kind of heroin buy he wanted to make. Dominic Lepinsky, known as "Joe," a jailhouse acquaintance, aged 38 and then operating Sally's Gift Shop on James Street North, Hamilton, where heroin was sold under the counter, had the right "mark" picked out. He also knew a 22-year-old named Alfred Gaugliano — a heroin user — who could be manipulated into doing the actual robbery. The Chief would supply the car, the gun, and the instructions. The others would do it the way he wanted it done, as was usually the case. Harold's dangerousness and experience passed for dangerousness, experience and *savoire faire* — but foolish risks were a big part of why The Chief had done so much "pen time."

Just before 11 a.m., Thursday, April 1, Claude Vivian, paymaster of the Canadian Porcelain Company, stepped from the Imperial Bank at James Street South near Main Street, in Hamilton, in possession of a briefcase which contained the company's payroll, $10,817.50.

When Vivian attempted to enter his car, parked on James Street near Jackson Street West, he was suddenly accosted by a youth with a revolver, who announced in highly dramatic fashion, "*This is it!*"[8]

The young man, Alfred Guagliano, grabbed Vivian's briefcase and started west across James Street.

Gamely, Mr. Vivian made after the robber, who seemed to head for a large late model sedan parked on Jackson Street at the northwest corner of James. At the wheel of this auto was Harold Jamieson. Also in the vehicle were Joe Lepinsky, Elaine Poireau, and a woman named Joan Watson, who lived with Lepinsky.

Was this meant to be a getaway car?

What could such an agglomeration of shaky people have been doing there except unnecessarily spectating an April Fool's Day robbery that, from a criminal perspective, at least half of them should never have even known about?

The gunman, aware now of his pursuer, turned and deliberately fired two shots, one of which penetrated Claude Vivian's fedora hat, grazing his skull.

By the time the bandit turned around again, the heavy sedan was starting fast away from the scene.

Harold Jamieson was leaving.

Then, almost simultaneously, by happenstance, a policeman on a motorcycle chanced upon the tail end of the robbery — and there now began a running gun chase through the streets of downtown Hamilton.

Motorcycle Officer Allan Gleaves, coming south on James Street, saw Guagliano fire at Claude Vivian, had sight of the gunman fleeing westbound on Jackson, and saw him turn south into an alley along the west side of the Bell Telephone Company's Baker Exchange.

When Gleaves reached the top of the alley, Guagliano stopped and fired two revolver shots at him. Gleaves fired four back. The bandit then jumped a four-foot-high picket fence in the alley and continued to run south toward Hunter Street.

Officer Gleaves got back on his motorcycle and raced back east along Jackson Street to James, then south to Hunter, and west towards McNab Street. There a citizen who had seen the bandit running hard to the west, yelled, "He went that way," and pointed toward Whitehern Place, which continues west from McNab.

Around another corner on Charles Street, Officer Gleaves approached a young man who had no hat or coat, as the bandit had had, but wore only a woollen sweater. The man obviously did not have the briefcase or revolver either. He was walking nonchalantly away from the scene of the robbery.[9]

Officer Gleaves pointed his revolver at Alfred Guagliano and ordered, "You, come with me."

"What do you want me for? I haven't done anything," was the young robber's answer. Gleaves could see the suspect had a false moustache and sideburns ridiculously painted on his face in black cork, and knew instinctively that he was a liar.

The arrest was made.

The $10,817.50 payroll, the revolver, and the robber's coat and hat were found under a parked car on Hunter Street where the fleeing thief had quickly rolled them all into a ball and tossed them. They would be evidence at a trial that would see Alfred Guagliano convicted of armed robbery and afterwards sentenced to seven years "down East."[10]

At James and Jackson streets, a spectator to the robbery had smartly taken the license plate number of "the 1948 model expensive car" that fled when the shooting started. Consequently, a considerable distance to the west, at King and Dundurn streets, the car was stopped by police and its occupants arrested. Harold Jamieson and Elaine Poireau, after searches of both the vehicle and their separate living quarters, were charged with

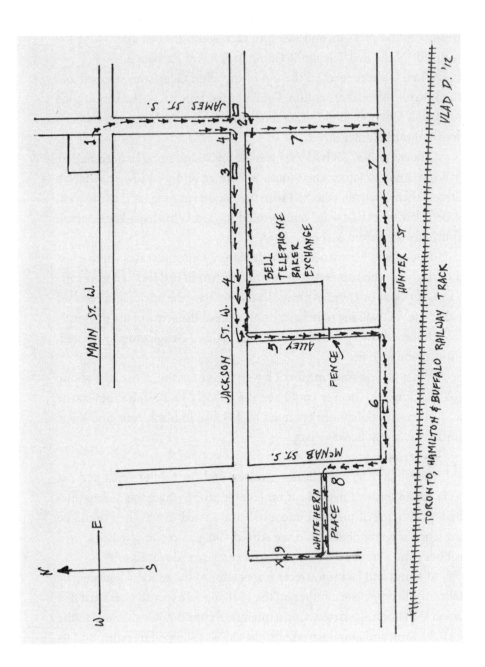

April Fool's Day 1948 armed robbery and gun chase in downtown Hamilton, Ontario.

Caption: (1) Claude Vivian exits the Imperial Bank at Main and James streets with the Canadian Porcelain Company's payroll and walks south to his car parked at James and Jackson streets; (2) An armed bandit accosts Mr. Vivian as he tries to enter his car. The bandit grabs the payroll at the point of a gun and starts west across James Street. Pursued by Mr. Vivian, the bandit turns and fires two shots, one of which passes through Vivian's hat; (3) Harold Jamieson and other complicit spectators in a large luxury car escape westbound on Jackson Street; (4) Approaching from the north on a motorcycle, Police Constable Gleave sees both the car and the bandit on foot fleeing west on Jackson Street; (5) The bandit turns down an alley on the west side of Bell Telephone's Baker Exchange and runs south until he is stopped by a four-foot fence. At this point Constable Gleave reaches the top of the alley and shots are exchanged between the bandit and the policeman; (6) The bandit jumps the fence, runs south to Hunter Street, then heads west on Hunter. He rolls his coat, the gun, and the stolen payroll into a ball, throws the lot under a parked car, then turns north on McNab Street; (7) Meantime, Constable Gleave, back on his motorcycle, goes around the block by way of James Street to Hunter, and heads west; (8) A bystander yells to Officer Gleave, "He went that way," and points along Whitehern Place; (9) Gleave pursues and eventually arrests Alfred Guagliano as he tries to walk away from the scene of the crime. (Courtesy of Vlad Dobrich, draftsman and friend of the author) illegal possession of narcotics for the purpose of trafficking — more than 700 capsules of heroin having been found. Joe Lepinsky, who was already on bail on several drug charges, was again charged with illegal possession for the purpose of trafficking. Joan Watson was allowed to go uncharged.

On Friday, April 2, the *Hamilton Spectator's* lead-all headline announced:CAR SEIZED HERE OWNED BY RELATIVE OF MICKEY MCDONALD. In Toronto, Edward Near, Mickey's brother-in-law, was quoted as saying he had loaned his car to Jamieson and Lepinsky to go on a trip to Windsor.[11]

The next morning in Hamilton Police Court Harold and Elaine were remanded one week with cash bail set at $10,000 each, or two property sureties of $5,000 each. Incredibly, within a few hours, Jamieson, through street contacts in Hamilton, found guarantors for both himself and Elaine — people looking to pick up an easy $100 by pledging their homes on Harold Jamieson's word that he and Elaine would appear in court.

In Hamilton Police Court, on Friday, April 9, at 10 a.m., the names "Harold Jamieson" and "Elaine Poireau" were called — but no one answered. An hour's grace was given. The names were called again. There was no answer at 11 a.m. either. This time Magistrate H.A. Burbidge ordered bench warrants issued for the missing accused and started the process of estreatment of their bail sureties.[12]

Already Harold had intimidated Elaine into fleeing the country on pain of his exaggerated threat of *her* conviction, and lengthy prison sentence, for possession of *his* drugs. The inexperienced girl had wanted to go home to Windsor and her mother. Harold told her, "It's too late," that she had to run with him across the border or face, alone, the judicial music caused by the crimes he had gotten her involved in at Hamilton. Before going, they stopped a night at the Six Nations Reserve near Brantford, so Harold could say goodbye to relatives he probably now knew he would never see again. Then, in the darkness of the following night, Edward Wolliston, a 60-year-old LaSalle boat livery operator, smuggled Harold and Elaine across the Detroit River into the United States in a rowboat.

There would never be any prosperous drug network for Harold Jamieson. It was a jailhouse pipe dream he couldn't make happen. His future, he now must have known, would be as an armed robber in the United States. It would be a short future.

CHAPTER TWENTY-EIGHT

Endgames South of the Border
(August 1947–July 30, 1948)

"THE WEAK LINK IN the chain" was Superintendent Ralph B. Gibson's estimation of Nick Minelli at the time of his re-capture in May 1948.[1]

In fact, of the escapees, the one with the best chance to stay at large indefinitely was likely Minelli, since he, alone, did not intend to continue to live by crime or to consort with criminals. Instead, Nick got a job and tried to live like a citizen.

On a busy Saturday in August 1947, apparently the day after the Royal Bank robbery in Windsor, as he related the story in 1959, Nick crossed into the United States aboard a crowded bus by way of the Detroit-Windsor Tunnel. When asked, he told U.S. border officials he lived in Ottawa, was visiting Windsor, and was going shopping for the day in Detroit. Once on the other side of the line, not knowing much about geography, Nick made for Rochester, New York. There, using the alias "John Carpenter," he got a job working as a tailor at 65 cents an hour and lived in a rooming house. By lying well, he even managed to get a United States social insurance card.

What Nick didn't count on was that Rochester was not very far across Lake Ontario from Kingston and the penitentiary he had just escaped from. Two months after the breakout, on a Rochester street, Nick suddenly caught sight of a Kingston guard walking towards him. He quickly put his hand up to his face and got past the guard unrecognized, but the experience panicked him. He quit his job that same day — and got on a bus for the West Coast.[2]

In San Jose, California, Nick found work as a dealer in a gambling casino. He was good at this and, as he said, only lost twice for the house. And he averaged $100 a week in his pocket — nice money in the late 1940s.

"It was too good to last and it didn't," he later observed.[3]

On the night of Monday, May 9, 1948, after 265 days of qualified freedom, Nick Minelli went to Oakland with a San Jose couple he knew for the supposed purpose of attending a party. He had too much to drink and as he later put it, "Next thing I knew I was handcuffed to a telephone pole."[4]

Rookie policeman Glen Sprott saw three people loitering in a suspicious manner outside an Oakland drug store, Minelli being the one in possession of a crowbar and a pair of rubber gloves. The three ran when challenged by Officer Sprott. After a chase, the policeman caught Nick, handcuffed him to the pole, then tried, without success, to catch the others. Taken in on suspicion, Nick's surly manner and lack of believable answers in support of the bogus story he was telling aroused a policeman's idea that he was "hot" — wanted in another jurisdiction.[5]

No charges were laid — Minelli was simply held "on suspicion" — but his fingerprints were sent to the California State Police Identification Bureau in Sacramento, and to the FBI in Washington.

Nick knew his only chance was to make bail quickly then skip, but the Oakland Police didn't have to take him before a court. They just kept asking questions. Finally, nine days after his capture, a detective walked into an interrogation room and asked, "Are you Nick Minelli?" Knowing the jig was up, Nick admitted it was so.[6]

Back in Canada, the story was in the evening papers of May 19, 1948. "Think Mickey or Lauzon Fled as Minelli Nabbed" was the *Toronto Daily Star's* highlight of its Page One story on Nick's capture. In a telephone interview with the *Star*, Oakland Chief of Police Robert Tracey said he suspected the three would-be burglars were after drugs — and he was quoted as speculating the other man on the scene might well have been either Mickey McDonald or Ulysses Lauzon. That was just enough for a story heading that would help sell the paper.

Officials in Sacramento were even saying that, if there were no serious local charges against him, Minelli would likely be deported to Canada. The press said Nick was "no rat." All he knew about the other Kingston fugitives was, "I have no idea where the other two are; I last saw them when we went over the wall of the prison." He would say no more about Mickey and Uly than that.[7]

* * *

In late May 1948, an underworld informant in the State of Michigan provided a United States narcotics agent at Detroit with information about the whereabouts and the evil intentions of "a dangerous man," "an international drug smuggler and bank robber," "a fugitive from Canadian Justice," who had sworn to shoot it out with the police rather than be taken alive. The informant told the agent that the same man, known to him as "James Labard," was then in the process of obtaining a submachine gun.[8]

All of which would have gotten any law enforcement officer's attention for absolute certain.

Harold Jamieson had arrived in Cincinnati, Ohio, from New York five weeks before and, on his instructions, Elaine Poireau followed him there by plane two weeks later. Jamieson had by then rented a second-floor furnished room at 1347 Myrtle Avenue, a nondescript rooming house in Walnut Hills, a neighbourhood close to Cincinnati's downtown. Anthony Nadar, alias "Nicky" Nadar, alias Tony Nadri, a paroled Ohio armed robber with an extensive police record for mostly minor crimes, said to be, like Jamieson, a Native Indian born in Canada, was already lodged in the adjoining room.[9]

On the evening of Thursday, May 28, two federal narcotics agents and two Cincinnati detectives began to watch the Myrtle Avenue house for the man whose name had been given to them as "James Labard." They already knew that Labard and Nadar had gone to Toledo, Ohio, for a few days, to buy "heavy equipment," which would turn out to be a sub-machine gun, a sawed-off shotgun and several automatic pistols.[10] Four days and nights later, on the evening of Monday, June 1, The Chief came home to Myrtle Avenue carrying a large, unwieldy suitcase, as the agents had been told he would. He and Nadar were allowed to enter the house unmolested. There was no sign of Donald "Mickey" McDonald, who supposedly the agents had been advised might be there, too.

Because of the firepower in the hands of their subjects, the surveillance team called in a large force of Cincinnati detectives, who securely surrounded the Walnut Hills hideout of Labard and his companions. Then, shortly before noon on Tuesday, June 2, Roy Anderson, a United States narcotics agent, with Cincinnati Detectives Jacob Schott, Robert Meldon, and Millard Schath, all heavily armed, entered the premises and quietly took control of Anthony Nadar in his own room.[11]

Then the four lawmen knocked on the door of the reputed international drug runner, bank robber, and submachine gun owner, James Labard.

"Who's there?" was reported to be the shouted response of the Canadian gunman, who the police already now knew had been "one of the hardest criminals in Kingston Penitentiary and in almost constant trouble there."[12]

"It's Nicky," Detective Meldon was reported to have answered, cleverly imitating Nadar's voice. Jamieson was said to have opened the door only a few inches — but enough that the detectives were able to forcibly push their way in. "Hands up. Don't anybody move," was the gist of their shouted instruction.

There might have been a long moment when all motion stopped, when all words and commands didn't matter.

"I warned Jamieson to hold up his hands, sit down and to keep away from the drawer," Detective Millard Schath was later quoted as saying.[13] Schath was reported to have vainly shouted, "Halt," not once, but three times. Instead, said Schath, The Chief kept inching toward a nearby bureau, in which were stored a half-dozen weapons, a loaded sawed-off shotgun being the most readily accessible.

Harold's hand may have been on the door of the bureau when Detective Schath let go a burst of automatic machine gun fire.

As many as 32 bullets ripped into The Chief's body, killing him instantly. It was perhaps a form of Death by Cop.

Aged 37, Harold Jamieson had long since made up his mind that he was not going to go back to any prison, American or Canadian, where he would be again confined and, in his own mind, mistreated for long years to come.

All three of Cincinnati's daily papers had the story on their front pages for two days. The *Cincinnati Enquirer* of June 2, 1948, reported The Chief's last stand in an above-the-fold account under the heading "Cincinnati Officer Kills Fugitive, Trapped Canadian-Indian Outlaw/ Bank Robber-Drug Runner Inching Toward Shotgun When Cut Down."

In Canada, not in Cincinnati, Mickey McDonald was, of course, said to have escaped the house from another room just before the shooting began. In a separate story, Ulysses Lauzon was written up as leaving Jamieson's room "only a short time before a mysterious tip-off was received."

In an interview with Betty Donovan of the *Cincinnati Post*, Elaine Poireau was reported to have said, "As long as I live, I'll never forget how Jim died. I loved him until he got me in trouble with the police. I didn't want him to have to die."[14] To a reporter from the *Times-Star* on Wednesday, June 3, Elaine told of veiled threats by Jamieson if she were ever to leave him. She also said that she and "Jim" were in bed when the knock on the door came:

> Jim got up and opened the door. He didn't ask who was there. He just opened the door, and in came the police with all their guns. One of the officers took me out of the room and I went to the bathroom. Then I was brought back. The police were all standing around in the room. Then I was taken out of the room again. I heard somebody yell, "Stand still." Then I heard the shots. When I went back into the room, Jim was dead, and I had to walk in his blood in my bare feet.[15]

In Windsor, on June 2, Alice Etousignant, who had been talking to Cincinnati Chief of Detectives Clem Merz, expressed her relief that her daughter was at last "out of the clutches of a Canadian narcotics ring."[16]

On Thursday, June 10, Nicky Nadar was convicted in Municipal Court under a Cincinnati ordinance that precluded a person with a criminal record possessing firearms — two revolvers the police found in his room. Nadar was fined $100.[17] Letters from a "police character" in Mt. Clemens, Michigan, facing charges and fearing a long sentence, had been found in Nicky's room at 1347 Myrtle Avenue.[18]

One wonders why the police did not immediately handcuff Jamieson after they entered the room.

*　*　*

After the police authorities searched the Cincinnati room and interviewed Elaine Poireau at length, there was a raid at an address in the Bronx, New York, where Jamieson and Elaine were said to have stayed for a time. There, FBI agents uncovered an apartment kept by Lauzon in which they found a cupboard full of expensive suits. Neighbours supplied a description of a 1947 model yellow roadster that Uly was driving.[19] There was also the first news that Uly had entered into a bigamous marriage with an attractive young Italian-American girl named Agatha Alfaro, described as the daughter of a prosperous business family. Obviously, as always, Uly was living high and wild. Police in New York, Cincinnati, Detroit, Toronto, and Windsor, as well as the FBI, the RCMP and the OPP, were all by now aware that Mickey had hooked up with a New York gang that dealt in large quantities of heroin. Lauzon and Jamieson were also reported to have become involved with a separate gang of armed robbers who were planning to rob a gambling casino in Covington, Kentucky.

*　*　*

In San Francisco on June 17, 1948, a federal immigration board, upon hearing evidence that Nicholas Minelli had entered the United States illegally at Detroit, Michigan, in August 1947, determined that he be deported back to Canada. Copies of the board's finding and report, along with Minelli's criminal record, were sent to Washington, where the deportation order was formally approved. The announcement that Minelli's removal had been finalized was made by Immigration Director Irving F. Wixon, at San Francisco, on July 24. Wixon then gave "early August" as the likely time of Nick's starting for his Kingston "home."

On Wednesday, August 4, in the custody of U.S. immigration officials, Nick Minelli was flown to Cleveland, Ohio, then immediately driven to Buffalo, New York, where he spent the night in the Erie County Jail. The following morning, at 11 a.m., Nick was handed over to three scarlet-coated Mounties at Fort Erie, Ontario. The Mounties put Nick into handcuffs and leg-irons and warned him that anything he said might be used against him. There followed a 7-hour, 265-mile car trip to Kingston, during which Minelli said almost nothing. A cop-lover Nick was not. At 6:12 p.m., Thursday, August 5, he was delivered to Kingston Penitentiary, where no one special, save for a reporter of the *Kingston Whig-Standard*, was waiting his homecoming. Wearing sand-coloured pants and a maroon jacket, Minelli went docilely through the North Gate, 353 days after his leave-taking of the previous August.[20] The eventual cost to him, after he pleaded guilty to breaking prison before Kingston Magistrate James B. Garvin, was a sentence of three years, consecutive with what was left of the 17-year sentence that he had been wearing when he escaped. He would serve, in all, only 12 of the 20 years and would be released on June 25, 1959.[21] Four months later, the *Star Weekly* published the two ghost-written articles that told the story of the Kingston escape as Nick was prepared to tell it. Which was certainly not exactly as it happened.

* * *

On the morning of Monday, July 19, 1948, in Jackson County, Mississippi, not far from Pascagoula, a man on horseback looking for stray cows happened on a body in some tall weeds alongside U.S. Highway 90.[22] Nine days later, the body would be identified as that of Ulysses Lauzon. Police authorities in Canada were not notified of Lauzon being found dead till the late afternoon of Wednesday, July 28.[23] The story was head-lines in the morning papers the following day.

Since there was no blood at the scene, Jackson County Sheriff Guy Krebs had no trouble determining that Lauzon did not die there. The body, clad only in undershorts and a sharkskin sports shirt, had been unceremoniously dumped down a steep embankment near a place called Nine Mile Bridge Lake, from a car. Lauzon, whose reddish hair was dyed black, had been executed mob-style — one .38-calibre bullet in the left

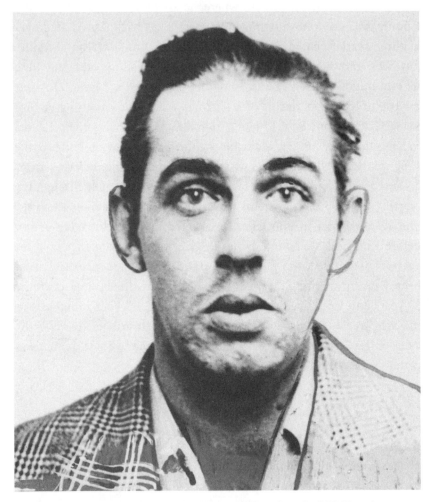

Ulysses Lauzon, driving force of "the Detroit River Gang" of 1945 and mastermind of the Kingston Penitentiary escape of August 17/18, 1947, was found dead in a Mississippi swamp on July 19, 1948, "one in the head, one in the heart." Photo is dated August 1947. York University Libraries, Clara Thomas Archives and Special Collections, *Toronto Telegram* fonds, ASC7401)

temple, one in the heart. Prior to his death, Uly had been badly bludgeoned with a heavy weapon which bruised most of his body, his right eye showing especially serious damage. "He got a good beating before they killed him," Sheriff Krebs summed matters up for the press.[24]

The local pathologist and coroner both estimated that the bloated, bug-covered corpse was that of a man who had been dead for two or three days when found. Both estimated Lauzon died on Friday, July 16, or Saturday, July 17.

Sheriff Krebs had had real difficulty identifying the body. He sent fingerprints to the FBI in Washington, waited three days, then was told they had no matching prints on record. Later, it was acknowledged that "a mistake" had been made. The FBI did have Uly's prints.

In Pascagoula, many dozens, if not hundreds, of people viewed or enquired about the body at the Stokes Funeral Home. Telephone calls came from all over the United States. A coroner's jury determined the causes of death to be "two gunshot wounds from a high-calibre gun" and assigned responsibility to the usual "person or persons unknown."

On a faint hope, Sheriff Krebs sent the victim's prints to the New Orleans Police Bureau of Identification, where, surprisingly, a match was made. The New Orleans Police had had Uly's prints since July 1945, when he and Joe Poireau escaped the Waterloo County Jail. Their prints were sent to New Orleans on the possibility that the pair might head where there was a large French-speaking population.

Having notified Canadian authorities of the death of Lauzon, Sheriff Krebs asked for photographs of the dead bandit so he could "make the rounds," to see if any of the local "police characters" would cough up information about Lauzon's activities in the South. By Friday, July 30, the Mississippi lawman had a lead that he told *Toronto Star* police reporter Gwyn "Jocko" Thomas over the telephone "might cost somebody their life if it were known." Years later, Thomas would tell that Sheriff Krebs had later said there were two bodies dumped in the Mississippi swamp, and the second body was claimed by an underworld informant to be that of Mickey McDonald. Supposedly, the two fugitives had died in a "drug feud." "We know he's in there, but we don't know where," were said to be Sheriff Krebs' words. No second body was ever found.[25]

Lauzon's injuries, especially the bad beating before his death, seemed to indicate a vengeance killing. But why? Newsmen, and others they found who would talk, speculated that Uly was killed by a gang that he and Harold Jamieson were involved with who were robbing casinos in the South; that Uly was killed for "selling out" Jamieson to the Cincinnati Police; that the Kingston Pen Gang — Uly, The Chief, and Mickey — had gotten themselves "in Dutch" with mobsters in New York for some non-specific reason; that a narcotics deal in Cincinnati went bad and Uly died over that; and that the killing might have had to do with Lauzon's deceitful and unwarranted marriage to Angela Alfaro, who had disappeared from the vicinity of Jackson County before, or very soon after, Uly's death — if she got that far south at all.

Back in Canada, the press made a three-day wonder of Ulysses Lauzon's demise. This was the end of the Canadian pressmen's current "Public Enemy No. 1," the obvious leader and most dangerous man of the three Kingston escapees, and a milestone in "one of the greatest manhunts in Canadian history."[26] In Ontario, there were many and various recapitulations of Uly's eleven years of swaggering crime, none more extensive than Tom Brophey's lengthy summary in the *Windsor Star* on Thursday, July 29. In Ulysses Lauzon's hometown, where the courts, the police, and the press knew Lauzon as "an incorrigible" since his teens, Uly's "dirty, bloody, inglorious death on a lonely road" was anything but a surprise. In fact, it was being waited on. GANGSTER GUNS KILL LAUZON was the blaring headline of the *Windsor Star* of July 29, 1948. Brophey's story was the product of what must have been an extensive news file that had been collected over most of a decade.[27]

That same day, *Windsor Star* reporter Bill Ross made an all-day search before he located Eileen Cornell Lauzon in a second-floor walk-up apartment in a small building at the rear of a downtown Windsor hotel. Ross persuaded Uly's legally-married wife — likely some money changed hands — to give him an exclusive interview. The result was a copyrighted story that would be published on Friday, July 30, and which would be sold to many other newspapers across Canada. Eileen, described as an "attractive 23-year-old" and as "a former redhead, who wears her blonde hair in close-cropped curls," was written down as now "living in seclusion." When found by Ross, she was with "a male friend."

In the *Windsor Star*, the story ran on Page One under the heading "Love Died With Baby, Says Widow."[28]

The child of Uly and Eileen had lived only five days after it was born. "My love for Ulysses died soon after the baby passed away," Eileen now revealed in what Bill Ross described as "a tight voice."

The story had Eileen telling that she had lived with Lauzon for only two months before he was "captured in a gun battle by two Royal Canadian Mounted Police in Prince Edward Island," that she later visited him only twice in Kingston Penitentiary, and after that, she did not see him again. There was no contact between them after Uly broke prison and she retained no money from his criminal activities, Eileen stated definitely. Asked if she knew anything about Uly's supposedly socked-away $300,000, Eileen answered, "If I had that kind of money would I be living in a dump like this?"

Eileen said Uly "loved expensive clothes, fast automobiles and was always a lavish spender." "Don't you think in their secret hearts a lot of people envied Ulysses?" she asked Bill Ross.

Before the escape, as the wife now told the story, she had written Uly in prison gently asking for her freedom in the face of his 35-year sentence.

"You don't owe me a thing. Live your own life, with my blessing. I wish you all the best of luck," Lauzon wrote back.

"He was always a gentleman to me," Eileen avowed and, in opposition to Uly's prevailing public image, put forward her own view of her late husband:

> *The newspapers are painting Ulysses as a vicious ruthless criminal, with not one spark of human decency. It isn't true.*
>
> *He had his faults and I have mine. But he never went out of his way to hurt anybody. He was tough when cornered, but it was always a game of cops and robbers with him.*
>
> *I guess he never grew up. Perhaps he saw too many movies.*[29]

Uly's bigamous marriage to Angela Alfaro didn't phase Eileen one iota. He had let her go; in her heart, she did the same for him. About the marriage's illegality and the possibility of Uly perhaps being charged with bigamy, she laughed, "To Ulysses that would be about as frightening as failing to put a penny in a parking meter."

"For a long time now I have thought of him only as a friend. A very good friend. But I still think he was one swell guy," Eileen Lauzon summed up Ulysses, her dead husband, for the reading public.[30]

CHAPTER TWENTY-NINE

A Ten- or Twelve-Year Public Worry
(July 29, 1948 and after)

THE DEATH OF ULYSSES Lauzon meant that Mickey McDonald was the only Kingston escapee of August 1947 still extant and, to the press, the reinvigorated question immediately became *Where is Mickey?* or *What's Happened to Mickey?* More than one Ontario daily asked for the answer on July 29, 1948, the day Lauzon's death became known to the public. Starting right then, especially in Toronto and its environs, the question of Mickey's whereabouts became a 10- or 12-year public worry, to the extent that the last escapee's end would eventually seem to be one of the city's two great mystery disappearances, the Mickey question then being second only to the mysterious, unsolved disappearance of Ambrose Small, millionaire Grand Opera theatre owner, who dropped out of sight on December 1, 1919, and was never certainly seen again. Like Ambrose Small going missing, Mickey's vanishment begged a question that never found a definite answer.[1]

In July 1948, of course, there was still the expectation that Mickey would be found and dealt with by the force of the law. Either he would be captured, likely in the United States, and dragged back to Kingston Penitentiary, as was Nick Minelli, or he would perhaps die in a shootout at the hands of the police of some American jurisdiction. Initially, there was little or no public speculation that Mickey would end up like the more wild and dangerous Ulysses Lauzon — a victim of an underworld settling of accounts. That thinking came later.

Sightings of Mickey and tips from the public as to his whereabouts persisted for a decade, a little more hesitatingly as time passed, as did press theories and opinions about what had become of him. For years, his name frequently came up in the Toronto papers in connection with stories about crimes that were similar to his known methods, or could be made to seem so by some device of the press. He was remembered in connection with stories out of Kingston Penitentiary, and in regard to crimes committed, or allegedly committed, by former criminal associates, or by his larcenous brothers, Alex and Edwin, who themselves continued to get a good deal of attention from both the police and the press. Kitty and her ongoing misadventures similarly conjured up Mickey's name, most often in the scandal papers but in the mainstream press as well. Any crime or incident that could in any way be made remotely suggestive of Mickey, his criminal history or the escape, by almost any association, was apt to be good enough for at least a story reference or a paragraph or two concerning the notorious missing man and, on a slow news day, there might be a lot more than that. All such allusions, references, and stories kept the mystery of Mickey's current locality alive in the public mind — setting the readers up for Mickey's grand finale, whatever it might be. In Toronto, it took the reading public a very long time to tire of Mickey McDonald and to weary of pondering his whereabouts — and, eventually, of his ultimate fate.

On August 30, 1948, Leo Gauthier, Mickey's longtime partner in crime, was arrested for passing a counterfeit American $10 bill in the Celestial Gardens, a restaurant in Toronto's Chinatown, and was found by police to have 13 more such bills on his person. The incident could be, and was, used to evoke the spectre of Mickey, the August 1947 escape, and the newly-reinvigorated question of Mickey's current whereabouts. The story, titled "Chinese Spots Bogus $10 Bill, Man, Girl Held," began with a brief description of the crime under discussion, then continued with what had become the more or less standard aggrandizement of

Mickey's previous standing in the Toronto crime scene of days gone by, with Gauthier being downsized to the status of "a former member of Mickey's gang." The story's end was a brief recap of the post-escape misfortunes of Ulysses Lauzon and Nick Minelli.[2]

When Sergeant of Detectives Fred Skinner, after 34 years as a Toronto policeman, retired on Monday, September 28, 1948, the *Globe and Mail's* coverage of the story became partly a makeover of Mr. Skinner's September 1925 arrest of 18-year-old Mickey McDonald, termed by Skinner as "a likeable little shaver," for the theft of $15 from a candy store near Davenport Road and Dufferin Street.[3]

Throughout the latter part of 1948, Mickey's name and the matter of his murky whereabouts appeared in press stories having to do with all manner of criminal and quasi-criminal happenings. Mickey was referred to in several stories emanating from Kingston Penitentiary, as, for example, having to do with the murder of John Kennedy, a Kingston guard, and the ensuing trial of Austin Craft, the inmate who, in a futile bid to escape, killed Kennedy and was later hanged for the crime. When a Montreal gang cleaned out the safety deposit boxes of the Maxville, Ontario, branch of the Bank of Nova Scotia, the local police chief at first said, "It looks like Mickey." That was good for a robbery story with Mickey's name on top. Then, in December, William "Big Bill" Cook, pimp, drug dealer, gunman, and Mickey's old antagonist, was "taken for a ride," badly beaten up, shot in the arm, and dumped barely alive by the Scarborough Bluffs, which, of course, brought up Mickey's history with Big Bill and a lot more. A news story that same month about the OPP allegedly supplying police escorts to liquor trucks coming from Windsor to Toronto meant that the December 1943 hijacking had to be reprised, together, of course, with the mystery of where Mickey, the preeminent hijacker, might be at the moment. A few weeks after that, Mickey was briefly miscast as one of a four-man gang that was doing bank robberies in Eastern Ontario.

And so it went.

On February 7, 1949, eight RCMP officers, in possession of a warrant issued under the Narcotic Drug Act, barged their way into 230 Celine Street, Oshawa, the home of Frank Wilson, Edwin MacDonald's father-in-law. The Mounties were looking for heroin that they had probable cause to believe had been mailed to Eddie by Mickey from New York City. Instead, behind the second-floor bathtub they found an unopened parcel addressed to "Mary Wilson." The package, which bore a blurred sender's address, contained $17,840 in counterfeit American $20 bills, all with one of six different serial numbers. The discovery meant that Eddie, his wife, and his wife's parents were all charged with having illegal possession of counterfeit currency. It also meant that the RCMP came to suspect that Mickey McDonald was not only in the heroin racket but also in the counterfeit money racket, too.[4] Eventually, on June 21, all of the accused, Edwin included, were acquitted of the charges. During these months, the McDonald and MacDonald names were frequently in the press in connection with the same "queer" (counterfeit money) turning up in quantity in Toronto, Montreal, New York State, Michigan, and several other American states.[5]

In Nashville, Tennessee, Taylor Little of Toronto, a dapper 52-year-old criminal friend of Mickey McDonald's, was arrested on September 27, 1949 and charged with possession of $640 in counterfeit American money, the serial numbers being the same as those in the package mailed to "Mary Wilson" and as found in the possession of Leo Gauthier.[6] Three loaded revolvers were found by Nashville detectives in the car Little was driving. They had first become interested in Little, a convicted bank robber, because he appeared to be casing a bank with a second man, who managed to get away. The following day, a Nashville detective was quoted as claiming to have "definite information" that the second man was Mickey McDonald. A Toronto news story of the same date told that Taylor Little was questioned six months before at Windsor, Ontario, "during investigation of a New York-Detroit counterfeit traffic for which Mickey McDonald was believed responsible."[7]

The first public thought that Mickey might be dead dates from late May 1949, when Alex MacDonald and two other Toronto men were investigated for the theft of money from a hotel room in Syracuse, New York, and afterwards were charged with illegal entry into the United States. It was reported at the time that Alex then told United States Secret Service investigators that Mickey was dead and "buried somewhere in New York State thirteen months ago."[8] Subsequently, Alex publicly denied the story, saying that Mickey was "still alive and kicking."

Beginning a couple of years after the escape of August 1947, according to both published and Gangland sources, Jarvis Street was hearing from Alex and Edwin MacDonald that Mickey had been killed in New York by criminal associates over "a deal gone bad." No names. No scenario or story. Just the bare statement that Mickey was dead and buried in a field in the Bronx by amorphous New York mobsters. So far as the MacDonalds' listeners were concerned, the perpetrators could be any of thousands of New York City gangsters.[9]

The public idea that Mickey was dead began to take hold after a story in the *Evening Telegram* of Monday, March 27, 1950 — 31 months after the escape of August 1947. This story was in answer to a Page One story in that morning's *Globe and Mail* under the heading "Report Mickey Dope Peddler In U.S. City." The *Globe's* story, based on information gotten from a nameless police source, unconvincingly said that the 42-year-old escaped convict was then a dope dealer "either in New York or California," where "illicit drugs" were "selling for $8,000-an-ounce." "It was learned that Canadian police officials don't expect McDonald will be brought back to Canada alive," was the *Globe's* last word on Mickey that day. The *Tely* bettered the morning paper's account with what seemed to be more substantial and up-to-date information. Under the heading "Sure 'Mickey' Slain, Not Drug Peddling," The *Tely* had Mickey already in-and-out-of-the-dope business and certainly then quite dead.

The story began with the thematic assertion "Donald (Mickey) McDonald, notorious gun man, bank robber and jail-breaker, was taken for a ride and slain by gangsters in the United States 18 months ago, a senior Toronto Police official revealed today."[10] This nameless "high-ranking official of the Toronto Police — very possibly Inspector John Nimmo — was quoted as saying that Mickey had been dead since shortly after Ulysses Lauzon's body was discovered in Mississippi. "Both the police in the United States and Canada believe that Mickey was rubbed out by his own gunmen associates. We have conclusive information that McDonald is dead and buried in the United States," said the *Tely's* source.

There was no mention of where in the United States this happened, but the story also claimed, "Letters sent to local hoodlums from McDonald associates in the United States also tell of his violent death."[11]

Now Is Mickey Dead? became, if not *the* question, then an important subsidiary question.

The *Toronto Star's* correspondent, Jim Hunt, put the matter to Lady Wonder, a 27-year-old money-making horse, stabled in a barn three miles outside Richmond, Virginia. The horse regularly stood at a giant typewriter all day answering questions at a dollar-a-question. On December 11, 1952, Hunt was told by Lady Wonder, "the pride and joy of the historic capital of Virginia," that Mickey McDonald, "Canada's Number One criminal," was dead.[12]

Already, on February 1, 1952, the RCMP had put Mickey's name at the top of its first-ever list of "Canada's Ten Most Wanted Criminals." The list was instituted, prepared, and afterwards regularly updated by the Mounties, at the request of Canada's newspapermen.[13] After this, Mickey, though then missing for nearly five years and very possibly deceased, was widely referred to as "Canada's Public Enemy No. 1."

Still, when on March 23, 1952, Detective-Sergeant Edmund Tong tragically died 17 days after being shot by Steve Suchan of the Boyd Gang, notorious Toronto bank robbers, Mickey McDonald's name was often written up in the aftermath as having been run down by "the famous detective team of Nimmo and Tong." In Ottawa, Ralph B. Gibson, superintendent of penitentiaries, talked to the press about the 15 separate escapes from Kingston Penitentiary that occurred between 1923 and 1948 and, quite naturally, named and discussed Mickey McDonald as the only one of these escapees who had not been recaptured, killed by lawmen, or otherwise accounted for.[14] Another story, in late 1952, concerning Ontario's "crime underground," similarly regurgitated Mickey as the only Kingston prison breaker then still yet to be dealt with and observed, "Mickey McDonald, who always seemed to be able to keep himself in trouble, is unheard of in five years, although police felt sure when he got out he wouldn't be loose very long."[15]

By 1952, pressmen's references to Mickey were changing from when Mickey was referred to in such terms as "the last of the Kingston escapees still at large." Now he was as often written of in such phrases as "unaccounted for but presumed dead" or as "Canada's Public Enemy No. 1, now thought to be dead."

With all of this, and much more that was coming, the spectre of Mickey got much of its public wear from the actions of three of those who Mickey's influence had most harmed in life: his brothers, Alex and Edwin, and Kitty, his first wife. In different ways, heroin — which Mickey became an ambitious purveyor of — destructively stuck to all three throughout much of the rest of their lives.[16]

CHAPTER THIRTY

The Heroin Kingpin of Vancouver
(September 7, 1947–January 14, 1966)

PRIOR TO HIS NOVEMBER 1939 conviction for bank robbery, Alex MacDonald had worked as a driller in a Sudbury-area mine, as a labourer in a travelling show and, for a few months, as the self-employed operator of Pop's Lunch in Toronto's Parkdale district. But the 7 years, 9 months, and 21 days that he served for the Port Credit bank robbery in the Kingston and Stony Mountain penitentiaries decided any conflict Alex may have had between his deceased father's and his older brother's conceptions of what his life might be.

Alex came out of the Manitoba Penitentiary on September 7, 1947, with a well-developed larceny sense — a nose for the illicit dollar and how it can be turned — the most essential element in the make-up of the professional criminal. He came out certain that he did not want to work for a living, that society owed him for the years he had spent "inside," and that he had learned enough to avoid the kind of mistakes that had sent him to prison. Like his brother Donnie, The Chief, and some others he then knew, Alex was looking to get into the then hugely profitable and fast-expanding heroin trade, which, he imagined, as did the others, would carry him to a prosperous, work-free life of leisure. Heroin was now the big easy money game, with serious risks that Alex supposed a smart operator like himself might sidestep indefinitely. All that was needed was some start-up cash and the right connections — and, like Harold Jamieson, Alex knew that Mickey had just then gotten "connected" to the right New York organization. Unlike Mickey, Alex had never been, was not then, and never would be, a heroin user. His involvement was wholly motivated by greed.

Alex's destination upon release was Toronto, where he soon came to know that elements of the detective department regarded him, as they had Mickey, to be a citizen of doubtful value to the City of Toronto. A few months after the August 1947 escape, Toronto detectives were certain that Mickey was bound up in supplying heroin to distributors in Ontario. Half the money taken from the Royal Bank robbery in Windsor was later reported found in the grasp of a big-time heroin dealer with whom Mickey was known to be friendly.[1] Then in January 1948 Alex was arrested at Windsor in the drug-dirty company of Harold Jamieson, and eleven months after that, he was named as being seen in Toronto with two New York "muscle men," who detectives suspected were responsible for "Big Bill" Cook's being badly beaten, shot, and put out of the heroin business forever.[2] It was noticed, too, that Alex made at least occasional trips to the United States, especially to New York City, from where he was twice deported as an illegal entrant. The backdrop was that there was a violent conflict on between two factions of Toronto drug dealers, backed by different out-of-town suppliers, and Alex was regarded by Toronto detectives as being part of one of the factions.[3]

Like Mickey and Edwin, Alex made unremitting reference in court, and otherwise, to alleged police harassment of himself and his brothers. The Toronto Police tormented him, he said, "because my name is MacDonald."[4] For example, on April 6, 1950, Alex was stopped on Queen Street by Inspector John Nimmo, taken to 149 College Street, searched, and afterwards charged with vagrancy and with being in possession of an illegal lottery ticket. "Just because the police don't like me is that any reason I should be kept in jail for two days?" Alex asked an unsympathetic Magistrate J.L. Prentice, who fined him $20 on pain of a further 10 days in the Don Jail.[5]

"Get out of Toronto!" was the civic message.

Alex had always liked Vancouver. There, on Friday, March 28, 1951, he and two others were charged with the $5,088 robbery of the Bank of Montreal at Fourth Avenue and Alma Road, which had taken place two days before. Another man picked up for the robbery was described as "a 30-year-old Fairview man, who figured prominently in a sensational drug trial here a year ago."[6]

"One of the suspects is a brother of Canada's Public Enemy No.1," reported *The Vancouver Sun* of the next day. "Alex R. McDonald, 32, agent, whose brother is Donald "Mickey" McDonald, who is the last surviving member of the trio who broke out of Kingston Penitentiary...."[7] In the ensuing weeks, this kind of reference appeared many times in the Vancouver press.

Before an Assize Court judge and jury on Friday, June 22, 1951, two women who had been standing in a nearby doorway at the time of the robbery of the Bank of Montreal both positively identified Alex and a hood named Tony Schlosser as two of the robbers. Alex swore he was asleep in a bootleg joint at the time. The jury took two hours to find both men guilty. A smiling Tony Schlosser was sentenced to 20 years, an unsmiling Alex MacDonald to 14 years.

Alex was convicted solely on the testimony of the two witnesses who, at the same time, were mistaken in their descriptions of the colour of the bandits' getaway car. "If the ladies made a mistake in identifying the colour of the car, they could easily make a mistake in identifying MacDonald," reasoned Arthur Martin, who flew out from Toronto to argue Alex's appeal before the British Columbia Court of Appeal.[8] The Justices unanimously quashed the conviction. Alex walked out of the Oakalla Prison Farm a free man.

In late May 1954, Alex MacDonald was again arrested in New York as a suspect in connection with an international drug smuggling ring and, on the advice of the Toronto office of the RCMP, was detained at Ellis Island on a charge of illegal entry into the United States. A report of this in a Toronto newspaper contained the information, "Some police officials think Mickey MacDonald is still alive and behind the transportation of heroin into Canada."[9] Alex was again deported.

Then worse happened.

On the late evening of January 15, 1955, Alex and three others broke into the Canadian Tire Store at 837 Yonge Street, Toronto, forced open a small safe, and helped themselves to $381.40. They were in the act of trying to break the door of a walk-in vault that held more than $10,000 when the police arrived. The cops soon found the burglars hiding behind a truck in the store's garage and discovered they had brought a loaded Webley .455 revolver to the break-in. A Toronto detective's report of the crime included the following: "It is the opinion of the writer that McDonald (sic) has decided to lead a life of crime, and has no intention to ever become gainfully employed. It is the opinion of the writer that McDonald was the leader in this crime..."[10]

Three weeks later, in Toronto Police Court, Alex pleaded guilty to breaking and entering, and to possession of an offensive weapon. Magistrate C.A. Thoburn awarded him four years in Kingston Penitentiary. This was not an instance where a MacDonald could claim police persecution. Inside Kingston, as inmate #3145, Alex told the classification officer, "I'm lucky to get away with 4 years." He explained that the break-in was made necessary by the fact that he had lost a lot of money running a dice game. He made out, too, that he felt fortunate to be caught, since he would have gone on to further crime.[11]

Alex had married a girl from Lethbridge, Alberta, reputedly a model, in 1952, and became the father of two children. After Alex's conviction at Toronto, Pearl MacDonald returned to Vancouver, where she had family. Alex wrote at least two letters in Kingston to the superintendent of penitentiaries, asking that he be transferred to the British Columbia Penitentiary at New Westminster and, after his transfer there on December 10, 1956, he made written application for a Ticket-of-Leave.[12] During interviews with classification officers at both federal prisons, Mickey McDonald's brother (that fact was on record in both Alex's and Edwin's prison files) made all manner of claims regarding his being through with crime, his past job experience in sales, his massive family support networks in both Toronto and Vancouver, and his having work waiting for him in his wife's brothers' business in the West. Some of this was surely illusory.

He was released from New Westminster on Christmas Eve 1957, the beneficiary of a 120-day amnesty owing to the Royal Visit to Canada of Queen Elizabeth and Prince Phillip.

Again, in 1958, Alex was sentenced to nine months in the Oakalla Prison Farm after being convicted in Vancouver of possession of marijuana for the purpose of trafficking. At Edmonton, Alberta, in January 1961, he was charged with conspiracy to commit fraud. It was alleged that he was a part of a group engaged in passing bonds that had been stolen in a trust company robbery in Montreal, but these charges, so far as Alex was concerned, never got to court.

And then the roof finally fell in on the chancy life of Alexander MacDonald, brother of the notorious Mickey.

On January 9, 1962, after an elaborate surveillance of nearly two months duration, the RCMP obtained warrants such that Alex and 21 others were arrested in a massive roundup of what was then Vancouver's largest heroin distribution ring.[13] Alex was later named as "the absolute kingpin" of an operation that was estimated by the RCMP's Narcotics Branch to be then providing 75 percent of Vancouver's addicts with heroin.[14] Ronald Hill, the ring's "back-end manager," was in charge of laying one and two ounce "plants" — delivering many thousands of dollars' worth of heroin to secret locations where by prearrangement sizeable drug pushers would quietly pick up the drug for distribution. Heroin was being regularly planted in at least 38 secret locations and the size of the plants was astounding. According to the RCMP, the operation was wholesaling an estimated $25,000 a month in heroin. That at a time when a cup of coffee cost 15 cents.

There were 20 uniformed RCMP officers in court on August 29, 1962, when, after a 52-day trial, Judge William Schultz sentenced 18 men in Alex MacDonald's heroin operation to a total of 256 years in prison.[15] Alex himself was sentenced to 20 years for conspiracy to traffic in narcotics, 15 years twice on two counts of trafficking, and 3 years twice on two counts of possession. All of the sentences were concurrent — which meant that Alex had 20 years, not 56 years, to serve. That day's banner headline on the *Vancouver Sun* screamed, DOPE KINGPINS JAILED 20 YEARS. Later, in April 1963, the conspiracy conviction against Alex was overturned in the British Columbia Court of Appeal, so that Vancouver's heroin kingpin got away with a mere 15 years.

In New Westminster Penitentiary, things got much worse yet. Alex was discovered to be suffering from cancer of the colon and required a colostomy. Then, not long after, he developed serious heart problems, such that he was transferred to the William Head Institution, a minimum security prison, at Metchosin, British Columbia, on Vancouver Island. There, on the morning of January 14, 1966, Alex MacDonald was found in his bed, dead of a heart attack. He was only 46 years old.[16] A death notice in the *Victoria Daily Colonist* said that services and interment would be held in Toronto.

Alexander Robertson MacDonald, brother of the notorious Donald "Mickey" McDonald, was interred in the burial plot of his eldest sister, Janet, in Toronto's Parklawn Cemetery, a few days later. There was no death notice in any Toronto newspaper and Mickey's brother's name is not on the monument that names all else interred in the plot. He's in the grave, but no one was meant to know. There may have been a quiet service.

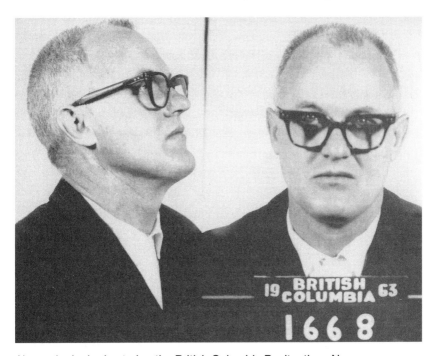

Alex as he looked entering the British Columbia Penitentiary, New Westminster, B.C., in 1963. (Library and Archives Canada)

CHAPTER THIRTY-ONE

He'll Do That Standing on His Head
(November 2, 1939–November 11, 1983)

NEARLY 70 YEARS AFTER the night of November 1, 1939, Gwyn Thomas vividly recalled going to the MacDonald home at 3 Poplar Plains Road, to ask the family for comment on Mickey being acquitted of murder. Thomas was there when word that Alex had been convicted of the Port Credit bank robbery and sentenced to 10 years was telephoned to the MacDonalds. He witnessed an atmosphere of celebration turn to one of gloom. Alex's mother began to cry and, as Thomas saw and heard, little Edwin MacDonald, then aged 13, piped up with the jailhouse bromide, "Never mind, Ma, he'll do that standing on his head."

"I was shocked at this from so young a boy — and shocked that the remark went uncorrected by any of the adults who heard it," Thomas said all those years later.[1]

Eddie was 23 when he was released from Kingston after serving his five-year sentence for truck hijacking and the kidnapping of George Butcher. Soon he got into bookmaking, operating from a location on Queen Street opposite Osgoode Hall. As is told by an associate of the day, he was, at the same time, a long-time source for counterfeit money, especially, after a time, Canadian $10 bills.[2] In 1953, Eddie suffered a nervous breakdown and was hospitalized and out of business for months. In 1955, his Queen Street handbook was closed down by the police, so that he had to move his operation out to north Parkdale, where he took bets from a location at Dundas Street West and Sheridan Avenue. There, he soon got interested in selling heroin — the third MacDonald brother to do so — to the extent that his bookmaking business was later described in court by a former runner as Eddie's "front" for the drug operation.[3] Like his brother Alex, Edwin was never a user of heroin. The big money in drugs was what he was after.

Eddie grasped, as did Mickey and Alex, that a big part of the danger in the heroin game was in dealing with the pushers and addicts and in "laying plants" — where the police or any freelancer might see it being done and make something of it. Like Alex, Eddie saw himself as "the front end" — the money man who buys from a larger source in quantity, who never gets his hands dirty, and merely directs the actions of those below him, who take the risks of handling the many minor transactions with the always shaky, and at times dangerous, users and the desperate parasite pushers, often users themselves, who peddle the dope at the street level. Eddie was "the brains" of what became a compact heroin distribution operation. Victor "Speedy" Jowett, a taxi driver, was his "back end," and, at various times, there were sundry others, users or indebted handbook gamblers, who, in desperation, pushed the product, as well as delivered whatever they were told to deliver, to wherever they were told to deliver it.[4]

Eddie never got anywhere near as big as Alex would, but then, he probably didn't want to. In fact, Eddie claimed sympathy for drug addicts and it was said that he would try to help them get off "the stuff" — while, of course, making as much as possible out of their being on it. His lawyer, Malcolm Robb, at one of Eddie's trials, would tell of Eddie's "horror of drugs," which began, when as a boy of 15, he saw his brother, Mickey, begin to use heroin.[5] "Thus, Eddie has the greatest sympathy for addicts and he will tell you he has never trafficked in narcotics," essayed Mr. Robb.[6]

On the evening of September 18, 1955, likely with no one else available, out of sheer greed, just as Alex would do six years later in Vancouver, Eddie made the mistake of "laying a plant" himself. It was an error in judgment that would take four years to work itself through the courts and, in the end, Eddie would go back to "the Big House" loaded down with another seven years to serve. Though there was by now little public doubt that he was dead, the name of Mickey McDonald hovered like a funnel cloud over the judicial events that followed Eddie's January 1956 arrest: his April 1957 trial for conspiracy to traffic in narcotics; his May 1957 trial for absconding bail; his October 1957 trial for possession of narcotics for the purpose of trafficking; his two March 1958 appeals in the Ontario Court of Appeal, one of which quashed his conviction for possession for the purpose of trafficking, the other of which confirmed his conviction for jumping bail; and his November 1958 re-trial wherein he was in the end convicted of possession for the purpose of trafficking and sentenced to six years.[7] There were two more appeals against that conviction, in the Ontario Court of Appeal and in the Supreme Court of Canada, both of which were lost. That finally meant that, on December 21, 1959, Edwin MacDonald had to face the fact that his costly four-year odyssey through the courts was over, and that he had to "do his time."[8]

Eddie preceded all of the trials by absconding bail of $50,000 — then the largest bail ever "jumped" in a Toronto or York County trial.[9] His taking it on the lam got Eddie onto the RCMP's "Canada's Ten Most-Wanted Criminals List," and it got him banner headlines in the Toronto press that equalled any that Mickey McDonald ever got.[10] For example, the *Toronto Daily Star's* two-line banner, in extra-large letters, on May 1, 1956 read:

MCDONALD MISSING

JUDGE ESTREATS $50,000 BAIL

One of Eddie's jilted bondsman was his youngest sister, Ruth, who together with her husband put up $4,000 equity in their home as part of the large guarantee that Eddie would appear. He didn't show up. Nine months later, apparently as the result of an informant's tip, Eddie was arrested by the police in a house on St. John's Road in the Toronto Junction district, in company with two women. Again and again, Eddie's and Mickey's names were all over the papers, appearing often as they had previously done in connection with developments in the case and many months of wrangling over the threatened estreatments of the properties of the four separate bondsmen who had posted bail for Eddie.[11]

RCMP Corporal James Macauley, with whom Edwin clearly shared a mutual antipathy going back to his 1949 arrest for illegal possession of counterfeit money, testified at three trials that, on the evening of September 18, 1955, he had observed Edwin MacDonald stop his car on the dead end of Emerson Avenue, near Lansdowne Avenue and Dupont Street in Toronto's west end, where he threw a cigarette package containing 50 capsules of what later tested as heroin behind a hydro pole. Corporal Victor Yurkiw, Macauley's partner, said the same.

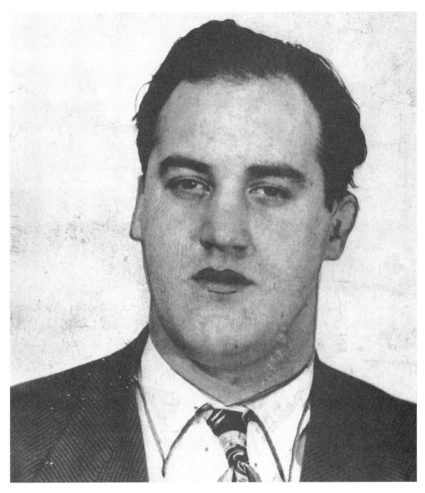

Edwin MacDonald about the time of his arrest for jumping bail in September 1956. (York University Libraries, Clara Thomas Archives and Special Collections, *Toronto Telegram* fonds, ASC7406)

Through it all, Edwin made what was long since the standard MacDonald defence of police persecution. He denied such an incident ever took place and said he didn't remember where he was at the time the plant was said to have occurred. Who would remember when charged many months later? he asked. He did remember that Corporal Macauley had been hounding him for years, and he quoted a number of threatening comments by Macauley, all of which the corporal denied, one of which was, "I hate you and your kind of people. Someday, I'll nail you to the cross."[12]

During a part of the 1950s, Edwin and Alex both worked as doormen — on-site muscle — for Dominic Simone, legendary Toronto gambling-house operator. Also, during the mid-1950s, Eddie is said, for a time, to have been the manager of a steambath on Lakeshore Boulevard West in New Toronto. There, as the story goes, for whatever reason, an angry thug with a baseball bat beat up Eddie badly. Whatever the issue was, the tellers of the tale didn't know, had forgotten, or wouldn't tell.[13]

Like Alex, Edwin MacDonald, brother of the notorious Mickey McDonald, is buried in Parklawn Cemetery, in the burial plot of the family of his second wife, Mary Lehman MacDonald. Eddie was buried quick, in fact, on the very day he died, November 11, 1983. As in the case of Alex, there was no death notice in the Toronto press and Eddie's name is not inscribed on the monument atop the burial plot, as are the names of all others whose remains lie therein.

Thus, for different reasons, no one seems to have been meant to know where any of the three MacDonald brothers were finally laid to rest. To appearances, the respectable members of the extended MacDonald family — the six sisters, their husbands, their children — must have long since tired of the unending hurt and embarrassment the three criminal brothers inflicted on them all.

CHAPTER THIRTY-TWO

On the Boulevard of Broken Dreams
(October 1940–January 25, 1994)

LIKE MICKEY, ALEX AND Edwin, Margaret "Kitty Cat" MacDonald was involved with heroin — but, unlike them, so far as is certainly known, not with the sale of heroin. At least by 1940, and for years after, Kitty was an on-again-off-again addict, and, in effect, employed heroin as yet another device with which to hurt herself.

After Mickey left her behind in December 1940, Kitty made many tries at righting her life, alternating with returns to the squalor of Jarvis Street — "the Boulevard of Broken Dreams." The Second World War made jobs much easier to get than had the Depression and thus gave her a better chance to change her ways. Many times the story has been told that, early in the war, Margaret MacDonald got herself a job working on the line at the John Inglis Plant doing "war work." But Harold Waterhouse, a former Toronto Police detective and the company's chief security officer, meanly whispered the name "Kitty Cat" in the right ear, and Margaret MacDonald was sent packing.[1]

On January 31, 1941, Kitty was back in Gangland and was present in a room in the Walsingham Hotel when a 62-year-old high roller named John Casserly was taken for the contents of his fat wallet. Kitty and three other known prostitutes were acquitted of the robbery, while Alice James, another "working girl," was convicted and sentenced to four months.[2] A similar incident on July 12, 1941, at the Alexandra Hotel, in which a man claimed that Kitty had stolen $5 from his shirt pocket, was dismissed in court. The money was for "a good time," Kitty explained. Often outrageous, Kitty also testified that she was "being kept" and the new 1941 Dodge she was driving belonged to the man who was keeping her. The rumour of the day was that the man who was then paying Kitty's bills was a high official at the Ontario legislature.[3] As a nameless writer in *Hush* often ended stories about girls who worked Jarvis Street and its many hotels: "Don't ever forget this fact: Toronto, under its sanctimonious surface, is a very wicked city."[4]

In 1942, for a time, Kitty was again co-habitating with Charlie Dorland and working for a trucking company as a driver. Then, according to Gwyn Thomas, she drove a Toronto Transit Commission streetcar for a while, but was soon let go because "Somebody didn't like the idea of her handling money."[5] Her ungoverned temper and rough language may have been part of her problem as well.

In between fleeting appointments in the working world, Kitty always got back to Jarvis Street. In October 1944, in the incident that aborted the "Flash trial" of the five hijackers, Kitty was convicted of receiving bonds worth $1,500, stolen from a house on Spruce Street, and was sentenced to 15 months in the Mercer Reformatory. On January 12, 1945, the Ontario Parole Board let her out after she had served three months and, 19 days later, she was a Page Three story in the *Daily Star* under the cutline "Asks Chance to Make Good, 'Kitty Cat' Granted Parole." As was always the case, Kitty's past marriage to Toronto's best-known criminal was a not-forgotten part of the story.[6]

Kitty's resolve to be a good girl didn't last. She fell back to the street and, within a year, was again arrested by Morality Officers. Now, again as "Margaret Holland," Kitty was charged with having liquor illegally. Once more she was at the wheel of a "large late-model car," this time followed from a bootlegger's that was being watched by the police. Six weeks later, on March 15, she was convicted a second time of a Breach of the Liquor Control Act, that is to say, "having in her possession liquor which had not been acquired by permit." This was worth another three months in the Mercer.[7]

While living with Charlie Dorland during the war, Kitty nevertheless resisted giving Mickey a divorce so that he could marry Kathleen Donovan. But Mickey's impending conviction for hijacking, and the assured lengthy prison sentence it would mean, caused her to file for divorce herself in May 1944. The grounds were adultery, and Kitty got what she wanted, with costs, the following October. A few years after that, she married William DeBerry, a black, alcoholic, former railway porter, with whom she shared some turbulent years, marked by several efforts at reform intermixed with slippages back to old ways. Mr. DeBerry was said to have been forever evicted from Kitty's life, chucked out from a room in the St. Leonard Hotel, swearingly, violently, threateningly, followed by his flying belongings, which Kitty putatively hurled, piece by piece, through a front window of the hotel out onto Sherbourne Street.[8]

For many years after January 1939, Kitty was thought to be under the street protection of John Nimmo, who made it clear to Johnny "The Bug" Brown and his friends that if anything happened to Kitty another shoe would fall — very heavily and on them. The same Nimmo, when Kitty herself broke the law in a serious way, testified against her and saw her sentenced to the Mercer for 15 months. Some say that Kitty, known to be "a rat" after late 1938, was "a source" for Nimmo for years. "All those girls talk to the police," estimated Maurice LaTour, an old safecracker.[9]

Kitty's notoriety did not fade easily. While the major press did not forever dwell on her kind of misadventures, the scandal papers — the "gutter press" — would not leave her alone. Well into the 1960s, she was their ready interest. Whatever her latest tragedy was, it was always good for a recap of the days when she and Mickey "ruled Gangland," or some other misremembered expansion of the truth. A lengthy story titled "'Kitty Kat' Blows Top Battles Police Intruders," which appeared in *Hush* on April 18, 1953, was generated by Kitty's resisting the entry of two morality officers with a warrant into her Queen Street West apartment. Mickey was, as usual, in the story and rightly cast as the principal villain in Kitty's life, although with considerable exaggeration:

> Kitty Kat is back in the news again, spitting and scratching in the old-time way
>
> Many people knew her by that name when she was the wife of Mickey McDonald, Canada's Public Enemy Number One, now, it is believed, rotting away under American soil.
>
> Herself fundamentally a rather nice girl ... she somehow, when she was young and foolish, fell into the clutches of this criminal; he dragged her down to his own level, and she became a rough, tough turbulent gangster's moll ...
>
> Mickey was a scoundrel, a parasite, a rotter of the worst type. His crimes included one murder for which he could not be convicted, and of which he boasted when he knew the law could not bring him to book again on that count. Naturally, he double-crossed his faithful Kitty. Eventually, she grew tired of him, "got the goods on him," and divorced him at the risk of her life.[10]

There are many Kitty Cat stories of the 1930s, 1940s, and 1950s, during which time she drank to excess, used drugs, engaged in many violent street affrays, and compiled a police record that included convictions for attempted suicide, keeping a bawdy house, theft, receiving, obstructing police, illegal possession of drugs, and more. She was charged frequently, got off in court many times more often than not, and served several sentences in the Mercer Reformatory. On the street, she could be, and often was, a hell-cat. In court, unfailingly, till late in her day, she was the star of a fashion show, wherein she demonstrated, if not the finest of manners, then fine clothing, which she knew how to wear to good effect, civility, and even decency. In the same proceedings, arresting officers would be telling magistrates of her spitting, biting, and scratching antagonists, while profaning the policemen as "bum-fucking cops" and "piss whistles."[11]

By the late 1950s and after, the tabloid headlines Kitty was making most often referred to drug charges and her name was then usually given as Margaret DeBarry, Margaret DuBarry, or Margaret Barry. A story in

Justice Weekly on September 17, 1960, titled "Former 'Kitty Cat' McDonald (sic) Claims She Was Trying to Kick Drug Habit," began as follows:

> An old familiar figure appeared before Magistrate J.L. Prentice in Metro Toronto Women's Court as Margaret DeBarry, now 45 years old, pleaded guilty to the possession of narcotics. Margaret, looking her age, was really beautiful when she and her husband, Mickey McDonald, ruled "the Corner" back in the unruly thirties. Mickey is now believed dead and the "Kitty Cat" has a new surname and addiction — drugs.[12]

That was the overstated truth of it, except that the drug addiction was not all that new, and there was more of the same coming. Kitty was no longer able to easily sell the product she had so long depended on, and that meant her real end as the doyenne of The Corner, of Gangland, of the Boulevard of Broken Dreams, and of the shabbier downtown hotels that allowed prostitutes to offer their wares on the premises. In the early 1960s, she was the landlady of a Beverley Street house where the roomers were exclusively "working girls," though "work" was not done at the site. Later she is said to have answered telephones in the dispatch office of a taxi company on Dovercourt Road. About 1970, she is reported to have been the keeper of a brothel in Port McNicoll, Ontario, on Georgian Bay, known as "the Chicago of the North," not for its houses of ill-repute but for its once being an important lakeport for the shipping of grain. The last current reference to Kitty in a Toronto daily newspaper may have been in May 1978, in a story titled "Bad Company Started Her Off." Which was occasioned by Kitty, aged 62, being caught shoplifting $41 worth of merchandise from a Gerrard Street East store.[13]

She died suddenly, aged 78, at Fudger House, a retirement home at 433 Sherbourne Street, Toronto, on January 25, 1994. The seeming cause of the death of Margaret DeBerry — still then her legal name — was a heart attack. A death notice in the *Toronto Star* named several grieving relatives and termed the deceased "a friend of many."[14]

*　*　*

Kathleen MacDonald, once described by an ex-rounder of the day as "a woman you could take places and she wouldn't embarrass you," seems to have made the major press, post-escape, only once.[15] This was in regard to her being one of 34 found-ins, 12 of them women, at upscale Dalfrew Manor, on Clarendon Avenue, at the top of Toronto's Avenue Hill, where some optimists of the time tried to open an unlicensed after-hours cocktail lounge. The raid happened on opening night, January 20, 1950, and by virtue of Kathleen's published presence, the name of Mickey McDonald made the premiere.[16]

CHAPTER THIRTY-THREE

What Happened to Mickey?
(August 22, 1947–whenever)

AFTER SEVEN OR EIGHT years of newspaper reports, public alarms, and rumours concerning the whereabouts or the fate of Donald "Mickey" McDonald, nothing much had happened except that Mickey seemed to have permanently dropped from sight.

In the first week of January, 1955, the *Globe and Mail* took the question "What Happened to Mickey?" by the handles, dispatching a reporter named Phil Jones to Jarvis Street to ask for the answer on Toronto's "Boulevard of Broken Dreams." The story's assumption was that the denizens of Gangland's beer halls ought to know what became of Mickey and might tell Mr. Jones if they did know. The upshot appeared on Page 5 of the *Globe* on Thursday, January 6, under the cutline IS MICKEY DEAD? The story gave a brief history of Mickey's criminal past, told again of the notorious August 1947 escape from Kingston Penitentiary, then garbled subsequent events in the endings of Ulysses Lauzon and Nick Minelli. Otherwise, the narrative included the following:

'Is Mickey Dead?'

Consensus On Jarvis St. Is That Mickey McDonald Was Shot In N.Y. Drug War by Phil Jones

"Mickey McDonald is dead." The speaker was a hard-eyed little man who kept a smouldering cigarette drooping from his mouth.

"He's buried in a vacant lot on the East Side of New York. A man named Tony shot him for trying to move in on a dope racket down there."

Is this what did happen to Mickey McDonald, who at one time was the most wanted criminal in Canada? Toronto's underworld grapevine believes this information — although it also carries reports that Mickey is alive in Mexico and that he visited Toronto last summer.

The answers, if any, should lie in Jarvis St., the area best known to Mickey. Last night, in the beer parlours and dives, men who admitted long criminal records and who claimed to have been close friends of the notorious McDonald gave these various answers.

"Yeah, he's dead," the hard-eyed man with the drooping cigarette was speaking again. "It happened in 1949." He shifted his gaze around the dingy room.

Across the way, another man admitted to knowing Mickey. Bill was in Kingston with him in the '30s.

"But Mickey's dead now, you know," he said.

That was the general consensus. It is shared by some police officers. In 1950 (sic), however, when the RCMP issued its first list of the 10 most wanted men in Canada, Mickey McDonald topped the list.

Although his name is no longer on the list, his RCMP file is not closed. Officially Mickey McDonald is still alive. He will remain that way until his body is found.

But to Jarvis Street, he is dead.[1]

For several more years, odd tales of Mickey's whereabouts, circumstances, or demise continued to sputter forth until they were mostly ended, effective January 29, 1958, by Mickey being declared legally dead. Official interest in the search for Mickey had waned long before that.

Kathleen MacDonald, who, on April 10, 1946, had married Mickey inside Kingston Penitentiary when he was looking at the front end of sentences totalling 17 1/2 years, who had stayed in the apartment at 514A Yonge Street for more than 10 1/2 years, with Mickey's name on the door for most of that time, had finally faced the fact that Mickey was not coming home. At age 42, Kathleen had met someone else and wanted to marry again. Having Mickey declared legally dead was meant to make that possible.[2]

The York County Court Matters file having to do with Donald John MacDonald being presumed dead contains the affidavits of Kathleen MacDonald, Edwin MacDonald, and Mannis Frankel, Kathleen's solicitor. In his affidavit, Mr. Frankel quotes Toronto Police Inspector John Nimmo as stating, on December 30, 1957, "that he believes from the information that he has received that the said Donald John MacDonald was killed and his body is buried in a field somewhere in the Bronx in the state of New York."[3] Edwin's affidavit says that "after (Mickey's) escape I used to drive my mother to a certain address in the city from which my mother would speak on the telephone to my brother, the aforesaid Donald John MacDonald, from some telephone in New York and these telephone calls lasted for approximately a year."[4]

Then the calls stopped.

"(A)nd no one to my knowledge has seen or heard of him since," deposed Edwin.

Edwin's affidavit shared a belief with Inspector Nimmo's remarks to Mannis Frankel: "That I verily believe that my said brother, Donald John MacDonald, is buried somewhere in a field somewhere in the State of New York."[5] Supposedly, Edwin understood that Mickey's killer was Ulysses Lauzon — who was, of course, conveniently dead. It seems more than possible that Edwin was part of John Nimmo's information concerning Mickey's end. But Edwin surely knew that Uly had nothing to do with killing Mickey — and knew as well that Mickey was alive after Uly's death. In possession of better information, Edwin had every reason to be guarded about what he claimed to know.

In the intervening years other stories and theories about "What Happened to Mickey?" have been told to this author, some more believable than others:

Vincent "the Ace" Hamel, an old confidence man who spent a good part of his adult life inside Kingston Penitentiary "serving a life sentence on the installment plan," related that the New York City Police traced Mickey to New York through letters that he wrote to his mother in Toronto. According to the Ace, Mickey's life ended when the police of America's largest city threw him off the George Washington Bridge — and, said the Ace, it was well known inside Kingston Penitentiary that this was so.

"Why would they do that?" the Ace was asked.

"To get rid of him," was Vincent Hamel's answer.

Ace added that "Mickey was 'a nothing' who was not liked or trusted by anybody." According to Mr. Hamel, "Mickey was detested by his own brothers. They couldn't stand him. Mickey's own brothers shunned him wherever they could. He was nothing but a pimp."

It was evident that the Ace really didn't like Mickey.

He gave this information in early 1982.[6]

Gwyn "Jocko" Thomas, *Toronto Daily Star* police reporter for 62 years, believed that Mickey died in the swamp near Pascagoula, Mississippi, with Ulysses Lauzon. Thomas interviewed Sheriff Guy Krebs over the telephone soon after it became known Lauzon's was the body that was found, and understood Krebs to say that he had information Uly and Mickey had been trying to muscle in on the local drug racket — and they both paid the price for this in Mississippi. Some time later, as Mr. Thomas said, Detective-Sergeant John Hicks told him that local police informants in Mississippi were still telling Sheriff Krebs that two men, not one, were murdered, and that there were two bodies in the swamp. No second body was ever found, but, according to Gwyn Thomas, at some point, John Hicks figured there was enough reason to believe Mickey died there too. Jocko Thomas told this story almost as if it were established fact.[7]

Jack Webster, once a member of the Toronto Police holdup squad, head of the homicide squad and the chief of detectives, and in his retirement Official Historian of the Toronto Police Service, used to tell a story about how Mickey was allegedly murdered by two hoods he met in Covington, Kentucky, who talked him into helping them rob an armoured car in Cincinnati, Ohio. After the job was done, the two didn't want to split the swag with Mickey so they decided to kill him instead. As he readily admitted, Jack Webster got this story from "Lefty" Thomas, who, according to Webster and some others, was in love with "Kitty Cat" and was said to have gotten this version of Mickey's end from her. This was what Kitty and Lefty believed happened to Mickey, not necessarily what Jack Webster thought happened.[8]

The story the author believes is the one that follows. It was first told to me in July 1978 by Roy "Binky" Clarke, who knew all of the MacDonald brothers and most, or all, of the others who were connected with the escape of August 1947 from Kingston Penitentiary. The story comes from a man I knew for 33 years, who had no reason, so far as I could see, to lie, then or later, and it came with a name. Here is what Binky Clarke said the first time he told the story of Mickey's end to me:

"Mickey was killed in New York over his big mouth. He was in with this gang in New York — he was taken in by them as a favour to people they knew in Toronto — and, after he'd been down there for a while, one of the jobs he did for them was he got a Toronto engraver to go down to New York and cut counterfeit U.S. $10 and $20 plates for them. After doing the job and being paid for it, the engraver went to a New York bar and began to shoot his mouth off about this 'big score' he had made. He gets himself two girls and a bottle, goes up to a room and talks some more, and begins tossing around names. Well, one of these girls drops a dime on him to the mob guys, and these guys get hold of Mickey and tell him to get hold of his friend and 'bring him back here.'... That this guy's got to go ... Probably, at this point, Mickey's got to go, too, and knows it, or maybe doesn't.... Anyway, Mickey was foolish enough to give them an argument, tells them the guy's wife knows he was with him in New York ... Mickey's been giving out a lot of information to people he shouldn't, hasn't he? ... These guys, they tell him, 'Don't give us any arguments, Mickey. Just do what we tell you.' So Mickey, instead of setting the guy up, goes to the hotel, smacks the guy around, then takes him to the bus station and ships him back to Toronto. Then he goes back to the mob guys and tells them what he did — that he, Mickey McDonald, basket case from Toronto, has made an executive decision. That was his last mistake. The mob guys simply killed Mickey to break the connection between them and the engraver, and because *Mickey didn't do what he knew was expected.* Mickey's flannel-mouth got him killed.[9]

"How do I know this?

"Well, Eddie went down to New York and got the straight explanation from the guys who killed Mickey. He knew where to go. They sat him down, poured him a drink, and told him what they did and why they did it. 'You got any problem with that, Eddie?' they asked. 'No, it sounds like a good explanation to me,' was Eddie's only possible answer. What could Eddie do? He was not on his home turf, he was dealing with deadly guys, who made it plain that Mickey was dead and why he was dead. 'He's in the Hudson River,' they said. If Eddie made a fuss, he'd die too. In fact, on our side of the fence, he was given a decent explanation. It was a normal and proper procedure. Mickey knew what was expected — and he didn't do what was expected. Then he did much worse. These people had a lot of time and money invested, never mind that they didn't want to go to jail for many years over Mickey's nonsense. *The engraver should never have been told the names of the guys who were paying for the job. Mickey should have operated on a 'need to know' basis, as any smart thief does.* This was just Mickey showing his Toronto buddy what big guys he was in with now that he was properly set up down in New York. A little stupid gossip. A little stupid bragging. Mickey died for that."[10]

Sometime later, in one of many discussions with Roy Clarke about Mickey's end, I was told the engraver's name was "Tim Swan." Or "Tim Swann." Maybe with two 'n's. That was never made clear.

It might be noted that Eddie MacDonald, Leo Gauthier, Mickey's trusted friend, and Taylor Little were arrested in possession of quantities of counterfeit American money, tens and twenties, all bearing the same serial numbers, not too long after Mickey got free of Kingston Penitentiary, and that Mickey was rightly believed by the police to be the source of this traffic. The package of twenties that was mailed to Eddie in February, 1949, arrived on Eddie's birthday, February 7. A coincidence? Maybe. But probably not. Eddie finished his 5 years in Kingston for the liquor truck hijacking on October 12, 1948, after which, as he deposed, he drove his mother to a safe venue where she got once-a-week telephone calls from Mickey in New York. These telephone calls, Eddie explained, "lasted for approximately a year." Like the "hard-eyed little man" with the cigarette in the Jarvis Street tavern, Binky Clarke said Mickey died in 1949. Eddie MacDonald's information to Mannis Frankel seems to say the same.

EPILOGUE:

Last Thoughts

AFTER FIVE OR SIX years of living intensely with Mickey, it seems to this author that the only question that will be left hanging in the wind without an attempt at a real answer is, Did Mickey shoot Jimmy Windsor?

Jenny Law, the prostitute of the 1930s, who regarded Mickey as good-looking, well-dressed, well-groomed "trouble," was the only person ever spoken with by me who was adamant that Mickey was innocent of the crime. "He didn't do that," she said authoratively. "That was done by some guys from Detroit." In 1978, I was interviewing Jenny principally about Red Ryan, not Mickey McDonald, and, thus I did not pursue this as I might have.

My gut feeling, and that of Roy "Binky" Clarke, who knew Mickey well, was that he did it. At the same time, anyone who reads the transcript of the first trial with an open mind will have real difficulty seeing the fairness of what was done. In my mind, Justice George Franklin McFarland's Charge to the Jury was worse than one-sided. How could any competent, fair-minded jurist have extensively reviewed Jack Shea's evidence and, at the same time, fail to even mention to the jury Shea's fabrication of a week's worth of visits by Mickey to his apartment? If Shea lied about that under oath, as he clearly did, what was the rest of his evidence worth? How could Justice McFarland not have seen the danger in Shea's evidence — his inherent motives to lie and his own feasible involvement in the Windsor Murder? How could he not have seen the weakness in Cecil Clancy's bleary-eyed corroboration of Shea, which he dealt with, and tacitly endorsed, in a single sentence? How could McFarland not have noticed the contradictions and weaknesses in the eyewitnesses' testimonies, while, at the same time, so strongly upholding their evidence? Most particularly: How could all five eyewitnesses — all five! — have positively identified Alex MacDonald in the line-up of Sunday, January 22, 1939, without having seen anything of his face on the night of the murder except his pretty eyes and nice eyebrows? Those identifications, more than anything else, suggest there was something amiss about the line-up of Sunday, January 21. Is it just possible that one of the detectives might have previously said something to one or more of the eyewitnesses? As, for example, "Look closely at the men in this line-up. I'm not supposed to tell you this, but we know the man who killed Mr. Windsor is there and that his brother, who was the man who held you back, is there, too." Then, after picking out Mickey as the shooter on merit, the eyewitnesses might have identified Alex on family resemblance as observed in the line-up.[1]

Lorraine Bromell thought that the killer's anger suggested a personal animus towards Windsor, and Jack McDermott admitted that possibility as well. Mickey claimed at trial that he didn't know Windsor. Robert Lackaey, a regular patron of the White Spot Restaurant in the late 1930s and 1940s, adamantly said different. Mr. Lackaey — the first person to make me aware of Mickey's story — held very strongly that the two were on nodding terms, but that they were not friends, that Windsor didn't much care to know Mickey. In 1936, Kitty Cat, aged 19, was arrested for keeping a disorderly house on Alexander Street, near the White Spot. Perhaps, like many others, Jimmy Windsor despised the fact that this attractive young girl was out working the streets at night while her much older, jobless husband went to the racetrack most days? Perhaps, at the same time, Mickey knew about, and resented, the piddling $10 that Windsor contributed to his friend Johnny "The Bug" Brown's "Defence Fund," while, at the same time, Windsor put on a foolishly indiscreet show of diamonds in the White Spot and elsewhere on a daily basis? Mickey had been drinking heavily on the Saturday afternoon of the murder. Maybe when Windsor didn't readily cooperate in a robbery, Mickey's inner anger got the better of him, as it did at other times in the 1930s, causing him to meanly shoot the bookmaker in the groin?

Maybe, maybe, maybe.

Jenny Law said that guys from Detroit did it.

The Windsor household at first saw Italians, not MacDonalds.

If Mickey and the gang of alcoholic criminal misfits that he was in with did the deed, I doubt that Jack Shea went to the Briar Hill Avenue house. What would they all have done with a drunken Cecil Clancy? Left him alone in Shea's hideout apartment to cause a scene? Taken him to "the score"? Mickey talked too much in 1931 after his scrap with "Big Bill" Cook, he talked too much after being arrested in possession of a gun in the British-American Hotel in Windsor in 1937, and, allegedly he talked himself unto death in New York in 1949. He was in no sense a smart criminal. *"I have just killed a man!"* strikes one as being almost possible for Mickey. Jack Shea, who testified that he feared being charged with murder in consequence of Mickey's loose lips, might have gone overboard trying to make himself useful to the authorities with whom he surely had a deal — and, so, perhaps tried to polish the truth.

The question with which Crown Attorney W.O. Gibson ended his Address to the Jury in Mickey's retrial for hijacking strikes me as housing a view of Mickey that might be telling of the York County Crown Attorney's Office's view of Mickey in 1939 and before. Mr. Gibson finished up his address by asking the jury:

> Just one more word, gentlemen. Do you feel that you are running any risk in convicting MacDonald of this robbery? That is the question, gentlemen. Do you feel you are running any risk in convicting him of this robbery?[2]

That wasn't the question at all. But what was the view of Mickey behind Gibson's question? And who could pretend it was a fair question in a serious trial? And yet it was said with confidence and purpose.

What might have been the attitude behind the actions of some of those who pushed so hard to see Mickey hanged for murder? Why did the Attorney General of Ontario interfere to delay the trials of the three Port Credit bank robbers in June 1939? And where was the fairness in that? Put another way, the attitude behind all of the answers might have been, *The guy's an obvious bum. The public wants this murder solved. He probably did it. He'll do. Let the jury decide. Meantime, we'll stack the deck.*

My gut feeling is that Mickey murdered Jimmy Windsor. But on the evidence, I think I would have voted "not guilty" at *both* his murder trials. All of the evidence against him had weaknesses and the process, as it was allowed to happen, was stacked against him. I have doubts — reasonable doubts — that he did it, even though I think he most likely did do it.

But then I'm not a creature of his time, am I?

I remember especially something that Art Keay — a career policeman — said about Mickey's day. "In those days, if you couldn't afford a lawyer, you didn't have one," he said, with some sympathy. The judicial system, he seemed to be saying, was then too much weighted against the accused. Obviously, Frank Regan thought similarly. In 1935, Charles William Bell, said to be Canada's foremost criminal defence lawyer of the 1930s, opined, "In Canada there is no law for the poor at all. That is, unless the poor can induce some lawyer to put up a fight for them."[3] Except for Frank Regan and Goldwyn Arthur Martin — two extraordinary men who worked for little or nothing — Mickey McDonald would surely have hanged in the summer or fall of 1939. Maybe it would have been a just result, but it would not have been Justice.

SOME ENDINGS

JOHNNY "THE BUG" BROWN spent most of the 20 years after November 1938 serving three long prison sentences in Canada and one in the United States. An illiterate when he first entered Kingston, Brown eventually used his "pen time" to educate himself, to help start and edit the *Telescope*, Kingston Penitentiary's newspaper, and, as some believed, to remake his life. When he was released from prison for the last time on September 24, 1958, "Bugs" had decided he wanted to be a journalist. He had the help of several prominent Canadians, including Pierre Berton, then a columnist for the *Toronto Star*, J. Alex Edmison, a noted penologist and Queen's University professor, and a Toronto businessman named Harold King, who fixed him up with a job. Seemingly, Johnny Brown, aged 41, had found a focus. He was going to live with his wife and young daughter. As fate would have it, though, it didn't happen. Johnny "The Bug" Brown died of a heart attack at 4 p.m., Sunday, September 28, 1958, four days after his last release from Kingston and the day before he was to have an interview with a magazine editor who was interested in his writing.

Gordon Conant became the Twelfth Premier of Ontario after Mitch Hepburn resigned in turmoil in October 1942. A Liberal Convention in

May 1943 replaced Conant with Harry Nixon as party leader and premier. After that, Mr. Conant was a Master of the Supreme Court of Ontario, which is to say he "resolved issues within trials." Mr. Conant died in January 1953.

Marjorie Constable eventually became known as an active police informer and was beaten up, harassed, and shunned by Gangland. She is said to have been in a wheelchair by the 1950s and living in the Bloor-Dundas streets area, where even there the cognoscenti refused to talk to her because she was "a rat." According to Jenny Law, Marje was "still around" in 1978.

Isadore Levinter continued as an active litigation lawyer until his death, in March 1980, at age 81. Listed among his life's achievements were that he was "a founding director of the Advocate Society, a former president of Beth Tzedec Congregation and former chairman of the civil liberties committee of the Canadian Bar Association." He was "the first Jewish lawyer to be elected a Bencher of the Law Society of Upper Canada and he was chairman of the society's legal aid committee in its early stages."

Caption: Johnny "The Bug" Brown was ready to start a new life at age 44. Only four days after his release from Kingston he died of a heart attack. (Library and Archives Canada)

Arthur Martin, as a criminal defence lawyer during the years 1938–73, defended more than 60 accused murderers, none of whom were convicted of murder. Appointed to the Ontario Court of Appeal in 1973, Mr. Martin continued as "a major force in shaping this country's criminal justice system." Bail reform, prison reform, disclosure of Crown evidence, safeguards in wiretap legislation, and the insanity defence in this country were all advanced by a legal mind that first made an enduring mark on criminal law in Canada in *MacDonald vs. Rex, 1939*, wherein the Court of Appeal's decision, for the first time, "lays down the rule that an accused person has the right to be present personally or by a counsel at a view ordered by a Judge." Arthur Martin died in February 2001, aged 87, a recognized "legal giant," eulogized as "the most brilliant lawyer of our time, the best defence lawyer in the history of Canada," "the standard by which all Canadian lawyers are measured," and the advocate who made criminal law "a respectable business" in Canada.

Joe Poireau served only 10 of 44 years in Kingston Penitentiary, where he studied hard and learned how to become a success in business. He became the manager of a prominent business concern in Windsor for a number of years, with 60 people working under him, then started his own company and made a success of that. Retired and still married to the same woman for more than 50 years, Joe Poireau, as much as anyone else in Mickey McDonald's story, struck this author as an eminently likeable man — and a man with real guts.

Frank Regan lived only seven months and eight days after Mickey's second murder trial ended in acquittal. Seemingly in good health at age 56, Mr. Regan went to visit friends in Sudbury, Ontario, in June 1940, stepped off an overnight train on a Saturday morning and, a few minutes later, fell down dead of a heart attack.

Jack Shea left the Brampton Courthouse after testifying against his partners in the Port Credit bank robbery in November 1939 and seemingly hasn't been seen or heard of since. Before he made his exit, Shea promised detectives, "I am going straight. I am going to start life all over again." He knew the penalty for being "a rat." He walked away to a retirement that would certainly require him to look over his shoulder every day for the rest of his life.

Cecil L. Snyder was the Deputy Attorney General of Ontario from 1939 till 1954, whereupon he left that position to go to work for the Tax Appeal Board of Canada. He was chairman of that board from 1958 till 1969. He died in August 1974.

William "Lefty" Thomas, a street-corner newspaper dealer until his death in late August 1995 at the age of 87, made money at everything he touched, especially downtown real estate. Known as "The King of the Newsies," Thomas sold more newspapers than anyone else ever did in Toronto. At his high water mark, he was said to have employed 20 others to do the same. He had come to Toronto from Kingston, Ontario, at age seven, a lad with polio who developed a good business sense. By doing work that most others wouldn't touch, Lefty ended his days as a reputed multi-millionaire. At his death, he is said to have owned all of the downtown Toronto block on the east side of Church Street between Shuter and Queen streets, as well as several other properties in the city's core.

ACKNOWLEDGEMENTS

MY INTEREST IN DONALD "Mickey" McDonald began when, in July 1978, I first met the man I have given the name Roy "Binky" Clarke in the narrative of this book, and this interest has endured throughout 35 long years. I was at that time, of course, told off to work on Red Ryan's story — which took me many years to finish — and, after that, I did an autobiographical book about my street experiences as a nighttime taxi driver. But Binky's first rendition of Mickey McDonald's saga and especially the story of Mickey's ultimate end, replete with the storyteller's jarring language and criminal world view, had given rise to another unceasing interest during the intervening years. I thought of Mickey's story as another tale that I just had to tell — and, during this time, Binky, who became my good friend and a kind of mentor in my interest in the netherworld he knew so well, literally taught me how to think like a criminal. Both *The Big Red Fox: The Incredible Story of Norman "Red" Ryan* and *What Happened to Mickey? The Life and Death of Donald "Mickey" McDonald, Public Enemy No. 1*, mattered to Binky, almost as they mattered to me. He cared that both stories be told accurately and well, and he was similarly concerned with historical preservation of the days of "The Corner" and "Gangland," which, indeed, had been a part of his own life and of what he surely knew were two misspent decades of his young manhood.

Living in a rural town, in poor health at the end, and knowing he did not have long to go, Binky badly wanted to live to read *What Happened to Mickey?* Alas, it was not to be. He died in the summer of 2011. I read him what I could of the manuscript over the telephone — and, as always, he had thoughts and suggestions. I will always be grateful to this extraordinary man. He was in some ways an unbelievably kind person, especially to those who he knew were trying hard — at whatever — and I can tell more than one story that highlights his generosity far in advance of what I am able to write here.

It is not possible to put a book like this together without the assistance of many competent and helpful people. I would like to thank the following for their kind assistance to me in my research or for other input that was of real value:

Over a period of six years, I was greatly aided by the staff of the Toronto Reference Library, especially of the Newspaper Unit, the Baldwin Room, and the Inter-Library Loan Department; of the Great Library, Osgoode Hall, Toronto; of the Bora Laskin Law Library at the University of Toronto; of the Magazines and Newspapers Department of the Cincinnati and Hamilton County Library, Cincinnati, Ohio (especially Reference Librarian Marianne Reynolds); of the Local History and Genealogy Section of the Mobile Public Library, Mobile, Alabama (especially Amy Beach); of the City of Toronto Archives; of the Archives of Ontario, now at York University, Toronto (especially Sarah Fontaine and James Houston); of Library & Archives Canada, Ottawa (especially Diane Simard); of the Clara Thomas Archives and Special Collections, York University, Toronto (especially Julia Holland); and of the Toronto Police Museum (especially Norina D'Agostini). I have to thank, too, David St. Onge, curator of the Kingston Penitentiary Museum, for a memorable and informative conversation in 2008, and Marian Drouillard, manager of the City of Windsor's Geomatics, who educated me as to the lay of the land in Windsor, Ontario. Some of the previously mentioned were absolutely extraordinary. I am thinking especially of

Sarah Fontaine, Diane Simard, and Norina D'Agostini, all of whom were continuously and unnerringly helpful over a period of years, and all of whom put in stalwart efforts to help me escape the consequences of late-inning, self-inflicted problems. Thanks to all.

I would like to thank, too, several lawyer friends who helped with advice on the legal aspects of Mickey's story, especially Paul Zammit, John Scandiffio, and John Chidley-Hill, the last of whom good-naturedly allowed me to bother him with questions between rounds of a weekly chess tournament we both regularly play in. Their help was essential. Nick Antoncic, a long-time friend with a bent for history and architecture, walked me around downtown Hamilton, where the April Fool's Day, 1948 robbery and gun chase took place. Vlad Dobrich — another longtime friend — drew the diagram in the book. Paul Zammit, Nick Antoncic, Jack MacDonald, and John Lawson, all good friends of many years who I imposed on, read the manuscript in nearly-complete form and helped by doing so. Kerry Liles, yet another stalwart friend, came rushing to my aid when my computer went down during the book's edit. In doing so, good-naturedly, quickly, efficiently, inexpensively, and at some trouble to himself, Kerry saved the day.

Benjamin Levinter, Isadore Levinter's son and himself a practising lawyer for more than 50 years, spoke to me about his father's defence of Alex MacDonald on two occasions, and Marion Levinter, his wife, allowed me access to the Isadore Levinter Papers, which are in the possession of Library and Archives Canada. I thank them both for their support of this work and for their affable kindnesses to me.

I would like to thank, too, Kirk Howard, Dundurn Press publisher, and all of the Dundurn team who helped put *What Happened to Mickey?* together or who will be involved in the publicity and marketing of the book. I am particularly grateful to Allister Thompson, a patient man whose gentle touch improved my work significantly; to Michael Carroll, former head editor; and to Jesse Hooper, who designed a cover and layout that I don't think could have been better. Thanks to all of those I've met and all of those I haven't. It's been a positive experience.

NOTES

Chapter One

1. Prior to the late 1940s, Wellesley Street West was known as St. Albans Street. Properly, in 1939, the White Spot Restaurant was on the west side of Yonge Street, a block south of St. Albans Street.

2. Robert Lackaey interview, August 18, 1977. Mr. Lackaey was a patron of the White Spot Restaurant during the late 1930s and 1940s. He worked nearby. He was the first person to make me aware of Mickey McDonald as a major crime story.

3. The Village of Lansing in North York Township is now part of the City of Toronto.

4. The term "blue law" originated in colonial New England. It refers to puritanical laws that forbade practices such as drinking, dancing, working on Sunday, etc. Chief Constable Roy Riseborough used "blue lawed" as a verb phrase to describe how the North York Council dealt with the trouble being caused by Windsor's clientele in Lansing. That they "blue lawed" Windsor's business meant they used civic by-laws that governed morality and public behaviour to curb the rough elements frequenting the Windsor Bar-B-Q.

5. The Toronto Police radio was one-way only at the time. The message of the detectives at the Briar Hill Avenue house had to be phoned in to the radio room at Toronto police headquarters, 149 College Street, before it could be broadcast to the police divisions and cruisers.

6. The entire incident, complete with dialogue, is reconstructed from the testimonies of the five eyewitnesses as in the trial transcript *Rex vs. Donald (Mickey) and Alex MacDonald, May 1-20, 1939.*

Chapter Two

1. Thomas, Gwyn "Jocko". *From Police Headquarters: True Tales From the Big City Crime Beat.* Stoddart Publishing Co. Limited, Toronto, 1990, 57. Also in several interviews with Mr. Thomas.

2. This "cannonball down Yonge Street" reference was a frequently-heard allusion to the former putative backwardness of the City of Toronto before, say, the late 1950s. It was frequently heard in Toronto circa the 1960s and 1970s and was likely initially a reference of some journalist or prominent person. The last time I remember hearing it was in conversation with a man named Nat Ladner on January 8, 1980. Mr. Ladner was a passenger in a taxi I was driving at the time.

3. The most relevant part of *The Criminal Code of Canada*, Section 238, in the 1927 Revision, then read: "Every one is a loose, idol or disorderly person or vagrant who, not having any visible means or subsistence, is found wandering abroad ... and not giving a good account of himself, or who, not having any visible means of maintaining himself, lives without employment." The words quoted in the text above were as given by Art Keay, a policeman, several decades after the fact.

4. Art Keay interview, February 6, 1981.

5. Adjoining towns, boroughs, and villages then included East York, Leaside, Forest Hill, Swansea, and the Township of North York, which included the communities of York Mills, Lansing, Willowdale, Newtonbrook, and Steeles Corners; the Township of York, including Mount Dennis and the Town of Weston; the Township of Scarborough, including Birchcliff. The waterfront municipalities of Mimico, New Toronto, and Long Branch had most of the population of Etobicoke

Township, which was of a mostly rural character. North York and Scarborough were much less settled and had a small fraction of their later populations.

6. Maurice LaTour interview, July 1, 1979.

7. According the records of the Toronto Police radio-teletype for the evening of January 7, 1939, as verified by Inspector Richard Pountney, in charge of same, a message, originating with the detective department at Toronto Police Headquarters, went over the air at 10:14 p.m. that applied the phrase "looked like an Italian" to three suspects, including the man with "blue eyes." *Rex vs. Donald (Mickey) and Alex MacDonald, May 1–20, 1939,* 1158.

8. "Apparent Laxity of Police Must Be Explained," the *Evening Telegram,* January 11, 1939, 6.

9. *The Tattler,* a Toronto scandal paper of the 1930s, was particularly named as being represented at James Windsor's funeral. That publication seems not to have survived the war and is not listed in available reference works.

10. Bessie, real name Besha Starkman Tobin, was the common-law wife of Rocco Perri and the business manager of Perri's criminal organization till the late night of August 13, 1930, when she and Rocco returned home and parked their automobile in the dark garage behind their Bay Street, Hamilton, home. It was then that a man stepped out of the shadows and shot Bessie but not Rocco. The Hamilton Police believed that the murder was done because of a dispute with an American mob that was selling the Perris drugs. No one was ever charged.

11. The Ontario Temperance Act prohibited the sale of liquor in the Province of Ontario during the years 1916–27. There had been a national agitation for such legislation at least since the 1870s, women and some of the Protestant churches being most in favour of doing away with the availability of liquor, which was thought to be at the root of family problems and violence in the home. The First World War and the need for efficiencies put the Prohibition movement over the top. Eight of nine provinces (all but Quebec) enacted legislation, only to repeal it at a later date. For many, Prohibition made illicit drinking both fun and fashionable; for others, like Jimmy Windsor, profitable. By 1930, seven of the eight "dry" provinces had decided province-wide Prohibition didn't work and repealed the legislation. Prince Edward Island, which had gone "dry" in 1901, waited until 1948 to do the same.

Chapter Three

1. Detective-Sergeant Alex McCathie to Chief Inspector of Detectives John Chisholm, case synopsis, May 24, 1939, 15–16. Library and Archives Canada, RG 13 vol. 1621, VI pt. 1

2. *Rex vs. Donald MacDonald*, October 16–25, 1945, 268.

3. Bird Avenue is now the part of Rosemount Avenue that is west of Dufferin Street.

4. Discontinued after 1927, the "remand till called on" was a form of sentence that meant the convicted person was, in effect, told, "Go and sin no more." If there were no further convictions, that was the end of it.

5. "Struck Off Strength; Veteran Fired Two Shots During Police Career," *Globe and Mail*, September 28, 1948, 5.

6. C.F. Neelands to Dr. A.E. Lavelle, March 18, 1927, Guelph Correctional Case File re Donald McDonald, #37514 (1925–26). Archives of Ontario, RG 20-40-3.

7. Report of medical examination, September 19, 1933, in Mimico Correctional Case File re Michael McDonald, #2620 (1933–1934), Archives of Ontario, RG 20-43-3.

8. Dr. J.R. Houze, Director of Mental Health Clinic, to J.R. Elliott, Superintendant of Mimico Reformatory, September 27, 1933, re Michael McDonald, in Mimico Correctional Case File of Michael McDonald, #2620 (1933-1934), Archives of Ontario, RG 20-40-3

9. Superintendent J.R. Elliott to Deputy Provincial Secretary C.F. Neelands, September 27, 1933, Mimico Correctional Case File re Michael McDonald, #2620 (1933–1934). Archives of Ontario, RG 20-40-3.

10. James Y. Nicol, "Meets Mickey MacDonald Pals Socially," *Toronto Daily Star*, May 30, 1956, 37.

11. Jenny Law interview, August 25, 1978.

12. *Evening Telegram*, February 24, 1939, p. 1 (late edition in the Levinter Papers), MG-31-E40 Mikan no. 103718, No. 5, textual record of legal cases, 1939. Library and Archives Canada.

13. McCathie to Chisholm, case synopsis, May 24, 1939.

14. In the days after Kitty became thoroughly notorious, her street name was as often written in the scandal papers as "Kitty Kat" as it was "Kitty Cat." On the street, she was generally addressed as "Kitty." She also answered to "Margaret" and was also referred to as "The Cat."

15. Mickey gave a self-serving version of this fiasco from the witness stand eight years later. *Rex vs. Donald MacDonald, October 16-25, 1945*, 500.

Chapter Four

1. The boundaries of Gangland were once specifically defined as Church Street on the west, Sherbourne Street on the east, Carlton Street on the north, and Queen Street on the south, but often incidents that were put down as Gangland occurrences happened outside these lines, as did both of the major incidents set down in the chapter "Kitty Cat in Gangland."

2. The tabloid papers were sold at newsstands and cigar stores all over "Toronto the Good," bringing sex, crime, violence, and all manner of news that the major press would not print to readers who got a jolt out of such fare. Eaton's and Simpson's department stores, which being major advertisers were never criticized in the dailies, had their misdeeds and privileges regularly "exposed" in the tabloids for years. Television, after it became established, provided some of the same — and helped to put the tabloids and the news outlets they depended on out of business. Some of the tabloids made themselves over into more socially acceptable publications and afterwards were sold in supermarkets.

3. "Three Women Beaten In Fresh Gang Raids," *Globe and Mail*, October 6, 1938, 1.

4. *Ibid.*

5. "Gang War Flare-up Puts Two More in Jail," *Globe and Mail*, November 15, 1938, 1.

6. *Rex vs. Michael McDonald, Margaret McDonald, John Brown (alias Russell), and Joseph Constantino, January 10, 1939*. RG 22-5871 case file No. 103-38 folder B314664. The Archives of Ontario.
7. "Three Convicted of Robbery By Jurymen," *Evening Telegram*, January 11, 1939, 11.
8. "Pleading Father Hears Son Sent to the Penitentiary," *Toronto Daily Star*, January 27, 1939, 1.
9. *Ibid.*

Chapter Five

1. Inspector Pat Hogan was present because he was the inspector in charge of No. 12 Division in which the murder happened.
2. *Rex vs. Donald (Mickey) and Alex MacDonald, May 1-20, 1939*, 531. Elsewhere in the transcript, Mrs. Warner says she said, "There is a profile *like* the profile ..." For certain, she spoke out loud and the subject of her remarks was Mickey.
3. Her recorded remark in the record of the line-up was, "His profile is like the man I saw at 247 Briar Hill Ave. I am only going by the profile, because it was only the profile that I saw." This was read to Edith Warner by Frank Regan at trial. *Rex vs. Donald (Mickey) and Alex MacDonald, May 1-20, 1939*, 589–90.
4. *Rex vs. Donald (Mickey) and Alex MacDonald, May 1-20, 1939*, 840.
5. *Ibid*, 854.
6. *Ibid*, 628–29.
7. *Ibid*, 630.
8. It is unclear how much time elapsed between the five positive identifications at the line-up and Mr. McDermott's telephone call to Inspector of Detectives Chisholm.
9. *Rex vs. Donald (Mickey) and Alex MacDonald, May 1-20, 1939*, 1233.
10. *Ibid*, 1234–35.
11. "Alex MacDonald Denies Taking Part in Murder of Toronto Bookmaker," *Globe and Mail*, May 18, 1939, 9.

Chapter Six

1. Ontario Provincial Police file re the Armed Robbery of the Canadian Bank of Commerce, Port Credit, Ontario, 9 December, 1938: Leo Gauthier, Alex McDonald, and John R. Shea. Circular dated December 31, 1938. RG 23-26-119. The Archives of Ontario.

2. Albert Dorland, a dangerous gunman who had previously embarrassed the Toronto Police, was suspected as being one of Shea's accomplices. Shea was under heavy police pressure to name Dorland as such, but did not do so.

3. What were then known as the Don Flats, in the lower Don Valley, are now part of Riverdale Park.

4. George MacKay interview, March 17, 1981.

5. *Rex vs. Donald (Mickey) and Alex MacDonald, May 1-20, 1939*, 1227-28.

6. Roy "Binky" Clarke interview, circa 2009, no date recorded.

7. *Rex vs. Donald (Mickey) and Alex MacDonald, May 1-20, 1939*, 739. The expert was A.T. Powell, chief ballistics engineer at Canadian Industries Limited, Brownsburg, Quebec, the makers of the bullet that killed James Windsor.

8. Ontario Provincial Police file re the Armed Robbery of the Canadian Bank of Commerce, Port Credit, Ontario, 9th December, 1938. Leo Gauthier, Alex McDonald, and John R. Shea. Memo dated January 21, 1939, 10:30 a.m. P.C. Alex Wilson to Chief Inspector A.B. Boyd re John R. Shea's arrest. RG 23-26-119. The Archives of Ontario.

Chapter Seven

1. Later, in court, Detective-Sergeant Harry Glasscock, the first policeman to interview the eyewitnesses, would not swear that all of the eyewitnesses had not named the shooter as looking like an Italian. *Rex vs. Donald (Mickey) and Alex MacDonald, May 1-20, 1939*, 721.

2. "Father Thinks Robbery Windsor Murder Motive," *Toronto Daily Star*, January 13, 1939, 1.

3. *Ibid.*

4. Records of York County Court Judges' Criminal Court, RG 22-5870 case file 18-39. Archives of Ontario

5. Report of J. MacLean, Prov. Constable, to the Commissioner of Police for Ontario, clock-dated 4:30 p.m., January 21, 1939, Ontario Provincial Police Re: Armed Robbery of the Canadian Bank of Commerce, Port Credit, Ont., 9 December, 1938. RG 23-26-119. The Archives of Ontario. Inspector Lougheed's reports on the days after the arrest of Shea are unavailable due to Freedom of Information restrictions.

6. This much is included in Detective-Sergeant Alex McCathie's case synopsis, May 24, 1939, 4. RG 13 vol. 1621, VI pt. 1. Library and Archives Canada.

7. Thomas, Gwyn "Jocko." *From Police Headquarters: True Tales From the Big City Crime Beat*, Stoddart Publishing Co. Limited, Toronto, 1990, 61. In more than one personal interview more than 60 years later, Mr. Thomas would tell this story and name Detective-Sergeant John Hicks as his friendly "source" of this information.

8. *The Criminal Code of Canada*, Section 69-2, under the heading "Common intention by several persons" then read: "2. If several persons form a common intention to prosecute any unlawful purpose, and to assist each other therein, each of them is a party to every offence committed by any one of them in the prosecution of such common purpose, the commission of which offence was, or ought to have been known to be a probable consequence of the prosecution of such common purpose."

9. "Identified MacDonald But Keeps Mouth Shut Until Family Confers," *Globe and Mail*, March 15 1939, 1.

10. Detective-Sergeant Alex McCathie to Chief Inspector of Detectives John Chisholm, case synopsis, May 24, 1939, 8. RG 13 vol. 1621, VI pt. 1. Library and Archives Canada.

11. Carl Clancy, Cecil's brother, was sober enough to drive these two alcoholics there. According to their own testimonies, they drank two or three bottles on their trip to the farm, the purpose of which was "to get off the liquor."

Chapter Eight

1. "Prisoner in Don Cells Implicates Two in Murder," *Evening Telegram*, February 16, 1939, 1.

2. Mickey's mother claimed in the press on Feb. 24 that the police had grilled Mickey every day for two weeks. *Evening Telegram*, February 24, 1939, p.1 (late edition in the Levinter Papers), MG-31-E40 Mikan no. 103718, No. 5, textual record of legal cases, 1939. Library and Archives Canada.

3. *Rex vs. Donald (Mickey) and Alex MacDonald, May 1-20, 1939,* 1405–13.

4. Mickey was charged as MacDonald, and so now he became in the courts and the press "MacDonald," not "McDonald."

5. The late John "Gazooney" Guerin, a waiter at the Royal Cecil in the 1930s, once explained that prior to 1935 "The Cecil" was a nice hotel in a bad area "where you could get a full course meal for 35 cents.

   "The dining room had white table clothes," attested Gazooney. But, after about 1935, there were new owners and the hotel declined to "Bucket of Blood" status, with respectable tenants, the likes of Frank Regan and bookmaker Cecil "Doc" Clancy, moving to better hotels further up Jarvis Street. In 1948, the Royal Cecil was again sold and became the Warwick Hotel, which, though greatly improved, retained a reputation for being a hangout for prostitutes and their clientele. The Warwick was in operation for 35 years or more then was torn down and the site became part of a parking lot. John "Gazooney" Guerin interview, January 16, 1980.

6. "There is no justice here!" and "We can't get justice here!" was how Mickey was quoted as shouting at Magistrate Browne. "We Can't Get Justice Here, Cries 'Mickey' Shackled to Brother," the *Toronto Star*, February 24, 1939, 1. In an interview on February 6, 1981, former Toronto policeman Art Keay more or less agreed that the justice system was then very much stacked against the poor and the downtrodden.

7. On April 7, 1930, Albert Dorland and William Toohey, a police agent, entered the Royal Bank at Church and Wellesley Streets, Toronto, with the intention of armed robbery. But, at the last moment, Dorland

spotted a detective in an upstairs window over a Wellesley Street drug store and reneged on the holdup. With Touhey in tow, Dorland tried to flee in a waiting automobile. The detectives followed, shots were fired by the police, and both Dorland and Touhey were arrested. The next day, imagining he had an agreement to plead guilty to carrying a concealed weapon in return for an arranged one-year sentence, Dorland pleaded guilty. But the charge was carrying an *offensive* weapon and Magistrate Emerson Coatsworth sentenced Dorland to five years. Later Dorland's grandmother hired Frank Regan, who somehow got William Toohey to sign an affidavit admitting to the facts as he knew them - after which Regan, statement in hand, took the matter to the Attorney General. The whole affair was a huge issue in the Toronto press such that an inquiry was ordered. Eventually, after 57 witnesses were heard, Mr. Justice Kingstone produced a report that censured the police, labelling their testimony as untruthful, and recommended that several Toronto policemen be charged. Dorland, now "Canada's most famous wronged man," was released from prison, Inspector of Detectives Alex R. Murray was forced into retirement, and Detective-Sergeant Alex McCathie was charged with "shooting with intent to maim" but was later acquitted. Dorland, who was rightly regarded by the Toronto Police as a hardened criminal, was arrested for another bank robbery soon afterwards and was legitimately sent to Kingston for a long stretch. The effect of the Dorland Affair was to intimidate the police, who surely regarded Frank Regan as its principal author and as an outright "troublemaker."

8. Lebourdais, D.M. "Frank Regan and the Underdog," *Saturday Night*, June 3, 1933, 3.

9. Shea and, indeed, Detective Harry Glasscock would both refer to the murder weapon, a .455 Webley revolver, as a .45. The detective came to know better. Jack Shea never did. The difference didn't matter to him. Mickey was in charge of the guns. They were his. To Shea they were a necessary means to an end, nothing more.

10. "Suspect in Bank Robbery Says Mickey and Brother Argued If Bullet Fatal," *Evening Telegram*, March 10, 1939, 1.

11. *Ibid, 2.*

12. "'He Got Tough With Me So I Let Him Have It,' Pal Says He Told Him," *Toronto Daily Star*, March 10, 1939, 1.
13. "'Mickey' Fired Fatal Gun, Then Kicked Dying Victim, Murder Witness Asserts," *Evening Telegram*, March 13, 1939, 1.
14. "Heard Enough to Order Trial Court Believes," *Globe and Mail*, March 14, 1939, 1.
15. "Committed For Trial, MacDonalds to Appear Before Jury in April," *Globe and Mail*, March 16, 1939, 7.

Chapter Nine

1. Gwyn "Jocko" Thomas interview, July 2003.
2. Mrs. Elizabeth Tilford, the Woodstock husband poisoner, was hanged in the Oxford County Jail on December 17, 1935. Harry O'Donnell, who dragged 18-year-old Ruth Taylor into an east-end Toronto ravine, raped, and murdered her, was hanged on May 5, 1936, in Toronto's Don Jail. Both were defended by Frank Regan and, in both instances, Cecil L. Snyder prosecuted the Crown's case. There may have been, and probably were, others whom Snyder prosecuted and Regan defended.
3. *Evening Telegram*, February 24, 1939, 1. (late edition in the Levinter Papers), MG-31-E40 Mikan no. 103718, No. 5, textual record of legal cases, 1939. Library and Archives Canada.
4. *Rex vs. Donald (Mickey) and Alex MacDonald, May 1–20, 1939*, 1364.
5. "Sons Often a Problem," *Globe and Mail*, February 24, 1939, and *Globe and Mail*, "Windsor Case Nearing End at Assizes," November 1, 1939, 5.
6. "'Victim of Police Frame-Up' But 'I'm Not Scared to Die,'" *Evening Telegram*, May 20, 1939, 2.
7. Mr. Snyder had worked for James McFadden for six years in the York County Crown Attorney's Office.
8. "Louis Gallow Got the Tie-Pin and Ring, Witness Says Mickey Informed Him," *Globe and Mail*, May 3, 1939, 15.
9. *Rex vs. Donald (Mickey) and Alex MacDonald, May 1-20, 1939*, 151-153.

10. *Ibid,* 154–55.

11. *Ibid,* 239.

12. This evidence was initially in Shea's statement to the police dated January 23, 1939, and included: "Shortly before 2 p.m. Monday, (January 9) Mickey left my apartment, saying he would be back at 4 p.m., but he did not return that day, nor until 4 p.m. the following day (Tuesday), and when he came I remarked to him, 'You are just one day late for your appointment.' He said he had been drinking with 'the Cat' (meaning his wife). "After this Mickey came to my apartment nearly every day and one of the days he joked about the Police being on the wrong trail and blaming American gangsters. He said, 'They will never get us now, we are as safe as the 'clock.'" I asked 'Do you think the other people are 'solid' and he replied 'You are always talking about Louis not being O.K., he is alright, 'he can't talk now anyway, and the other fellow '(I don't know who he meant by that)' is O.K.' too.'" Read the foregoing by Frank Regan and asked if it was true, Shea said that it was. Then the fun began, as none of this could have happened when Shea said it did and, in fact, it could not have happened at all. *Rex vs. Donald (Mickey) and Alex MacDonald, May 1–20, 1939,* 242-243.

13. *Rex vs. Donald (Mickey) and Alex MacDonald, May 1–20, 1939,* 204–12.

14. *Ibid,* 285-290.

15. *Ibid,* 313–15.

16. *Ibid,* 280.

17. *Ibid,* 618.

18. *Ibid,* 645.

19. *Ibid,* 464.

20. *Ibid,* 721.

21. The Windsor household was never at any time shown photographs of Alex MacDonald.

22. *Rex vs. Donald (Mickey) and Alex MacDonald, May 1-20, 1939,* 1227.

23. Mutual Arena, located on Mutual Street south of Dundas, existed from 1912 to 1989 variously as Arena Gardens, Mutual Arena, and The Terrace. It was where Foster Hewitt called his first hockey game in 1923, where the Toronto St. Pats played before Conn Smythe moved them to Maple Leaf Gardens and changed their name to the Maple Leafs, where the Harlem Globetrotters, Marie Dressler, Anna Pavlova, Torchy Peden, Frank Sinatra, Robert Goulet, Glen Miller, and many others of note performed. After 1937, Mutual Arena featured rollerskating and was a popular entertainment venue for downtown teenagers. Mutual Arena was a block and a few steps more from The Corner.

24. *Rex vs. Donald (Mickey) and Alex MacDonald, May 1–20, 1939,* 1170.

25. *Ibid.*

Chapter Ten:

1. "Entire Story Never Told in Windsor Murder Case, Defense Counsel Insists," *Evening Telegram,* May 19, 1939, 1, had Isadore Levinter's address to the jury as the longest ever heard in a Toronto murder trial by 10 a.m., Friday, May 19. Mr. Levinter continued until 11:20 a.m.

2. "Police Induced Shea to Lie, Says Levinter," *Globe and Mail,* May 19, 1939, 1. The addresses of counsel to the jury are not included in trial transcripts and, so, must be reproduced here from newspapers.

3. "Police Induced Shea to Lie, Says Levinter," *Globe and Mail,* May 19, 1939, 1.

4. *Ibid.*

5. *Evening Telegram,* May 19, 1939, p. 1. (late edition in the Levinter Papers), MG-31-E40 Mikan no. 103718, No. 5, textual record of legal cases, 1939. Library and Archives Canada.

6. "Windsor Murder Trial Goes to the Jury Today," *Globe and Mail,* May 20, 1939, 11.

7. "Entire Story Never Told In Windsor Case, Defence Counsel Insists," *Evening Telegram,* May 19, 1939, 1.

8. *Ibid.*

9. The torrent of angry words that had issued from Leo's mouth in answer to Regan's questions — by far the longest witness answers of the trial — surely indicated Leo's anger and indignation over what he testified had been done to him as a police punishment for his not "rolling over" on his friends. *Rex vs. Donald (Mickey) and Alex MacDonald, May 1–20, 1939,* 1028–29, 1035–39, 1041–42.

10. "Entire Story Never Told in Windsor Case," *Evening Telegram*, May 19, 1939, 2.

11. "'Justice is Now On Trial,' Murder Case Jury is Told," *Toronto Daily Star*, May 20, 1939, 6.

12. *Rex vs. Donald (Mickey) and Alex MacDonald, May 1–20, 1939,* 1476–90.

13. *Ibid,* 1491.

14. *Ibid,* 1484 and 1493.

15. The eyewitnesses, as Justice McFarland didn't observe in his Charge to the Jury, were never shown any photographs of Alex.

16. *Rex vs. Donald (Mickey) and Alex MacDonald, May 1–20, 1939,* 1503. This was a peculiar reference for McFarland to make in these circumstances, as he had been the judge at the trial which convicted David Meisner of the August, 1934 kidnapping of John Labatt, prominent London, Ontario brewer, after Labatt had made a similar "I'll-never-forget-that-face-as-long-as-I-live" identification, only to later repudiate his own identification when he was later confronted with the real kidnapper-in-question after Meisner had been convicted and had served part of a 15-year sentence.

17. *Ibid.*

18. "Elder Brother Hangs July 20 Smiles Briefly," *The Toronto Daily Star*, May 20, 1939, 1.

19. *Rex vs. Donald (Mickey) and Alex MacDonald, May 1–20, 1939,* 1528.

20. "'Victim of Police Frame-Up But I'm Not Afraid to Die,'" *Evening Telegram*, May 20, 1939, 2.

21. *Rex vs. Donald (Mickey) and Alex MacDonald, May 1–20, 1939,* 1529–30.

22. *Ibid,* 1530.

23. *Ibid,* 1530–31.

24. "'Victim of Police Frame-Up' But 'I'm Not Scared to Die,' Says Mickey, Found Guilty," *Evening Telegram*, May 20, 1939, 2. Neither the court transcript nor the other newspapers recorded this last remark as did

the *Tely*. The transcript has Mickey saying only, "...You will hear all about why Shea framed me."

Chapter Eleven

1. "Brothers Say Farewell Before Elder MacDonald Led Away to Death Cell," *The Globe & Mail*, May 22, 1939, 36.
2. The York County Crown Attorney's Office's view of Mickey might be seen in the last sentence of Crown Attorney W.O. Gibson's summation in another of Mickey's trials, wherein Mr. Gibson finished by asking a jury, "Do you feel that you are running any risk in convicting MacDonald of this robbery? That is the question, gentlemen. Do you feel you are running any risk in convicting him of this robbery?"
3. Correspondence in Rex vs. Donald "Mickey" MacDonald re The Murder of James Windsor — Attorney General of Ontario Central Registry Criminal and Civil Files, RG 4-32, 409. The Archives of Ontario.
4. "Province May Pay MacDonald Appeal," *Toronto Daily Star*, June 17, 1939, 3.
5. Frank Regan could be coldly logical as any attorney appearing before the learned Justices of the Ontario Court of Appeal had to be. Mr. Regan could also be emotional, flamboyant, intellectually obnoxious, insulting, and picayune as the mood hit him. This might work before a jury — and sometimes did. Arthur Martin was unfailingly polite, unfailingly logical, unfailingly erudite, and often brilliant. He would soon be the finest criminal and appellate court lawyer of his time — and known to be so.
6. Barnes, Alan. "Legal Giant Arthur Martin Dead at 87," *Toronto Star*, February 28, 2001, 1. Before Arthur Martin was appointed to the Ontario Court of Appeal in 1973, he defended more than 60 accused murderers, none of whom were convicted of murder.
7. *MacDonald vs. Rex, 1939, Canadian Criminal Cases, Vol. LXXII*, Canada Law Book Company Limited, Toronto, 1939, 185.
8. "Jury Visit to Death Scene Basis For Murder Appeal," *Evening Telegram*, September 11, 1939, 2.

9. *MacDonald vs. Rex, 1939, Canadian Criminal Cases,* Vol. *LXXII,* Canada Law Book Company Limited, Toronto, 1939, 189–90.

10. Robinette, John J. (ed), *The Ontario Reports: Cases Reported in the Supreme Court of Ontario (The Court of Appeal for Ontario and the High Court of Justice for Ontario) Cited 1939,* The Carswell Company, Toronto:1939; and *The Evening Telegram,* September 11, 1939, 2.

11. *MacDonald vs. Rex, 1939, Canadian Criminal Cases,* Vol. *LXXII,* Canada Law Book Company Limited, Toronto, 1939, 193.

12. *Ibid,* 193–94.

13. *Ibid,* 194–95.

14. *Ibid,* 195–97.

15. *Ibid,* 187–88. In *Snatched!; The Peculiar Kidnapping of Beer Tycoon John Labatt,* Toronto: Dundurn Press, 2004, 75, author Susan Goldenberg quotes an unnamed retired Justice of the Ontario Court of Appeal who spoke of Justice McFarland as follows: "Justice McFarland was not well regarded by the bar. He had a reputation for being lazy with a short attention span. Among the judges of the trial division of his day he would have been regarded as towards the bottom of the list as far as ability was concerned." Concerning McFarland's penchant for making funny quips in court, the same former Justice said: "Jokes are an alternative to hard work."

16. "Murder Case Appeal Ends," *Evening Telegram,* September 14, 1939, 21.

17. *MacDonald vs. Rex, 1939, Canadian Criminal Cases,* Vol. *LXXII,* Canada Law Book Company Limited, Toronto, 1939, 187. An "Editorial Note" on page 183 says "This decision is important in that, for the first time in any reported case it lays down the rule that an accused person has the right to be present personally or by counsel at a view ordered by the Judge" — apparently Arthur Martin's first of many marks on criminal law in Canada.

18. On September 26, 1939, M.F. Gallagher, Director of Remission Service, the Department of Justice, attached a memorandum on the front of a report to the Deputy Minister of Justice Re Donald "Mickey" MacDonald. The memo reads: "I submitted this case to the Minister today, and he was of the opinion that it was a clear case of 'No Interference.'" RG 13 vol. 1621, VI. Library and Archives Canada.

Chapter Twelve

1. Section 825-5 of *The Criminal Code of Canada* then read: *Whereupon an offence charged is punishable with imprisonment for a period exceeding five years, the Attorney General may require that the charge be tried by a jury, and may so require notwithstanding that the person charged has consented to be tried by the Judge ... and thereupon the Judge shall have no jurisdiction to try or sentence the accused ....*

2. "Protests MacDonald to be Year in Jail Before Trial," *Toronto Daily Star*, June 22, 1939, 1.

3. *Ibid.*

4. *Ibid.*

5. "Shea Says MacDonald Went Out on a Robbery When Windsor Killed," *Globe and Mail*, October 18, 1939, 4.

6. "Hints 'Mickey' Slew Windsor to Raise Cash," *Evening Telegram*, October 18, 1939, 15.

7. "Took Part in Three Robberies Crown Witness Admits," *Toronto Daily Star*, October 18, 1939, 23.

8. "Report of the Criminal Business, Brampton, conducted by A. Grenville Davis before Mr. Justice Gerald Kelly from Monday 23rd October to Wednesday 1st November, 1939" — Peel County Fall Assize 1939, Brampton, RG 22-517-0-1963 (folder B413996). Archives of Ontario.

9. "Points to Mickey at Trial and Says 'That's The Man,'" *Toronto Daily Star*, October 19, 1939, 4.

10. "Mickey On Way to Prison Vows Crime Career is Over," *Toronto Daily Star*, November 10, 1939, 3.

11. "MacDonald Gives Evidence For Brother Now On Trial," *Evening Telegram*, October 26, 1939, 2.

12. "No Gun Under Bed the Night Windsor Killed," *Globe and Mail*, October 27, 1939, 4.

13. "MacDonald is Acquitted of Murder," *Globe and Mail*, November 2, 1939, 1.

14. "Saw 'Mickey' Downtown Two Witnesses Testify," *Evening Telegram*, October 27, 1939, 2.

15. *Ibid.*

16. "Didn't Kill James Windsor, 'Mickey' MacDonald Insists," *Evening Telegram*, October 30, 1939, 1.

17. *Ibid.*

18. "Stay Shea Hearing Ordered By Conant," *Toronto Daily Star*, October 30, 1939, 1.

19. A material witness was a person seen as one who would likely give evidence for the Crown, but might not unless compelled to do so. Such a charge no longer exists.

20. "Shea Admits Robbing Bank at Port Credit," *Globe and Mail*, October 31, 1939, 4.

21. "Asserts Defence Counsel Tries Alibi For Mickey," *Evening Telegram*, November 1, 1939, 2.

22. *Ibid.*

23. Thus, apparently, Frank Regan supplanted Isadore Levinter as the author of the longest Address to the Jury ever heard in a Toronto courtroom on a murder case.

24. "Shea Told Mass of Lies 'Mickey's' Counsel Says," *Evening Telegram*, October 31, 1939, 2.

25. "Windsor Case Nearing End at Assizes," *Globe and Mail*, November 1, 1939, 5.

26. "Shea Told Mass of Lies 'Mickey's' Counsel Says," *Evening Telegram*, October 31, 1939, 2.

27. "Stay Shea Hearing Ordered By Conant," *Toronto Daily Star*, October 30, 1939, 1.

Chapter Thirteen

1. "'Mickey' MacDonald Freed Judge Disapproves Verdict," *Toronto Daily Star*, November 2, 1939, 1.

2. *Ibid.*

3. Thomas, Gwyn "Jocko." *From Police Headquarters: True Tales From the Big City Crime Beat*, Stoddart Publishing Co. Limited, Toronto, 1990, 62, and in more than one personal interview.

4. "Wife of 'Mickey' Held Over Liquor," *Evening Telegram*, October 17, 1939, 15.

5. "Kitty Cat is Jailed," *Toronto Daily Star*, December 18, 1939, 34.

6. "Jury Acquits MacDonald In James Windsor Murder Not Supported By Bench," *Evening Telegram*, November 2, 1939, 25.

7. "MacDonald Is Acquitted of Murder," *Globe and Mail*, November 2, 1939, 1.

8. *Ibid.*

9. *Ibid.*

10. "Oh Boy, Honey! Oh Boy Is 'Mickey's' Cry of Joy," *The Toronto Daily Star*, November 2, 1939, 21.

11. "Mickey MacDonald Freed Judge Disapproves Verdict," *The Toronto Daily Star*, November 2, 1939, 1.

12. "Port Credit Bank Robbers Are Given Ten Years Each," *Evening Telegram*, November 2, 1939, 4.

13. *Ibid.*

Chapter Fourteen

1. In 1944, the only grounds for divorce in Canada were adultery and insanity. In claiming adultery, it was then necessary to name the person with whom one's spouse had committed adultery — the co-respondent. In fact, it was necessary to catch them in the act and to have evidence of having done so. In a lot of cases, there were women — professional divorce co-respondents — who worked with detectives to produce "manufactured evidence" at considerable cost. Such was not necessary in the divorce of the MacDonalds. Mickey and Kathleen, not being too worried about appearances, were prepared to admit to the facts.

2. "M'Donald Gets 30 Month Term," *Globe and Mail*, April 17, 1941, 4.

3. Norman "Red" Ryan, a widely-reported bank robber of the 1920s who was given "a political parole" from a life sentence in Kingston Penitentiary in July 1935, was all over The Corner and its environs during the ensuing 10 months. Supposedly a "reformed" criminal, Ryan had been the pet project of Father Wilfrid T. Kingsley, Kingston's Roman Catholic chaplain and, eventually, too, of the *Toronto Star*, which had plumped for his release. Finally, Prime Minister R.B.

Bennett interfered to let Ryan out — a generous action 83 days before a national election. By day, Ryan sold used cars in Weston, and in the late afternoons and evenings, he was the official greeter and "sort of a manager" at the Nealon Hotel on King Street East. But soon he was living "a double life," pretending to be "reformed" but committing serious crimes on the sly. Part of this was his hanging about the Royal Cecil Hotel and tramping around what would be soon known as Gangland with an entourage of "former Kingston men." Ryan was killed in a liquor store robbery on the main street of Sarnia, Ontario, on May 23, 1936. Harry Checkley, his partner-in-the crime, was killed, too, as was Jack Lewis, a Sarnia policeman who left a wife and two children. Three others died as a consequence of Red Ryan being let free. See McSherry, Peter, *The Incredible Story of Norman "Red" Ryan, Canada's Most Notorious Criminal*. Toronto: Dundurn Press, 1999.

4. "The Boulevard of Broken Dreams" was how a writer in the scandal paper *Hush* frequently referred to Jarvis Street — and the repeated reference over 20 or more years became a colloquialism. People remembered this 40 and 50 years later.

5. "M'Donald Gets 30 Month Term," *Globe and Mail*, April 17, 1941, 4.

6. Roy Steinberg interview, December 10, 1991

7. Art Keay interview, February 6, 1981.

8. Yes, the same White Spot that Jimmy Windsor frequented.

9. Robert Lackaey interview, August 18, 1977.

10. After about 1952, the Royal Cecil was bought by new owners and renamed the Warwick Hotel — which survived as such till the mid-1980s,when it was torn down and became part of a parking lot.

11. "Old Bill" Blair was a character of his time on Jarvis Street — an elderly man who was, in effect, the bouncer of one of Toronto's roughest night spots. His day ended with the beating he got on December 23, 1942. In those days unescorted women could not enter, or drink alone, in a hotel licensed to serve beer in Ontario, and there were no hotels at all licensed to serve hard liquor. There were "Ladies and Escorts" rooms and "Men's" rooms in the hotels between 1934 and 1948.

12. "Claims Watch Taken in Fight in Beer Room," *Evening Telegram*, March 22, 1944, p.2.

13. "Charges Held Too Serious; Won't Consider Bail Now," *Evening Telegram*, December 30, 1942, 27.

14. Alexander MacDonald Sr. died at his home, 110 Balmoral Avenue, on March 9, 1943.

15. The Andrew Mercer Reformatory for Women, located on King Street West where Lamport Stadium now stands, was a grim, forbidding, castle-like structure that was erected in the 1870s and survived till 1969.

16. Steve Rodall had been a jailhouse friend of Jack Shea's.

17. *Rex vs. Benaditto Zanelli, Samuel Mancuso, Donald MacDonald, Edwin MacDonald, and William Baskett, October 17–November 7, 1944.*

Chapter Fifteen

1. The liquor truck was always, or nearly always, reported as arriving from Walkerville, but, in fact, Hiram Walker's town had been absorbed by the City of Windsor in 1935.

2. *Rex vs. Benaditto Zanelli, Samuel Mancuso, Donald MacDonald, Edwin MacDonald, and William Baskett, October 17–November 7, 1944*, 44.

3. In fact, George Butcher would eventually wrongly identify Edwin MacDonald, Mickey's 18-year-old brother, as the man with the gun. The gunman was Mickey, though Edwin was present at the scene.

4. Fleet Street in 1943 ran across the central part of Toronto, south of the CNR tracks and north of the lake. Today, Lakeshore Boulevard and the Gardiner Expressway are on top of where Fleet Street then was. The only section of Fleet Street that now remains goes west from Bathurst Street to Strachan Avenue.

5. *Rex vs. Benaditto Zanelli, Samuel Mancuso, Donald MacDonald, Edwin MacDonald, and William Baskett, October 17–November 7, 1944*, 52.

6. *Ibid*, 51.

7. Richview sideroad, now Richview Road, runs west from Royal York Road, just north of Eglinton Avenue, to a dead end, about a mile southwest of what was then the Town of Weston.

8. "You would think a half dozen professional criminals would know a tractor trailer loaded with liquor would go through the wooden floor of a barn," Sergeant of Detectives Alex McCathie of the Toronto Police in 1943 laughed uproariously years later. McCathie would be the policeman in charge at the scene late that afternoon. Alex McCathie interview, February 16, 1981.

9. The question of who suggested the unloading of the truck would subsequently be in dispute at the trials of the hijackers. Witnesses for the Crown would put this remark down to one of the hijackers. Benny Zanelli would testify that the remark was made by James Shorting.

10. *Rex vs. Benaditto Zanelli, Samuel Mancuso, Donald MacDonald, Edwin MacDonald, and William Baskett, October 17–November 7, 1944,* 170.

11. *Rex vs. Donald MacDonald, October 16–25, 1945, 68.*

12. *Ibid,* 173, 520.

13. *Ibid,* 173.

14. *Ibid,* 174–75.

Chapter Sixteen

1. *Rex vs. Benaditto Zanelli, Samuel Mancuso, Donald MacDonald, Edwin MacDonald, and William Baskett, October 17–November 7, 1944,* 178.

2. *Ibid,* 173.

3. The relationships in the Pavlena family were a little bit confusing. Joseph Pavlena, the owner of the Nash, was married to Zora's mother. Zora, Pavlena's step daughter, was married to Bill Baskett, who lived in Pavlena's home. Pavlena's own daughter was Kathleen Donovan, who lived in Toronto with Mickey as "Mrs. Donald J. MacDonald." Kathleen and Zora were step-sisters. Kay almost never went home to see "the folks," since she didn't get along with her step-mother.

4. *Rex vs. Benaditto Zanelli, Samuel Mancuso, Donald MacDonald, Edwin MacDonald, and William Baskett, October 17 - November 7, 1944,* 657, 700.

Chapter Seventeen

1. *Rex vs. Benaditto Zanelli, Samuel Mancuso, Donald MacDonald,Edwin MacDonald, and William Baskett, October 17–November 7, 1944,* 1044.
2. *Ibid,* 1048.
3. *Ibid, 962.*
4. *Ibid,* 348.
5. "Two More Held in Hijacking," *Evening Telegram,* January 6, 1944, 27.
6. "Mickey McDonald Gets Prison Term," *Evening Telegram,* April 13, 1944, 2.
7. "Traverse Hi-Jack Case Due to Tabloid Article, "*Globe and Mail,* May 30, 1944, 4.
8. *Ibid.*
9. *Ibid.*
10. *Rex vs. Benaditto Zanelli, Samuel Mancuso, Donald MacDonald, Edwin MacDonald, and William Baskett, October 17–November 7, 1944,* 850.
11. *Ibid,* 854.
12. *Ibid,* 839.
13. *Ibid,* 1078.
14. Dubro, James and Robin F. Rowland, *King of the Mob: Rocco Perri and the Women Who Ran His Rackets,* Markham, Ontario: Penguin Books Canada Limited, 1987, 353. (I, myself, first heard this story in 1967 from a Hamilton lad I went to university with. It was, and is, part of Hamilton's civic folklore.)

Chapter Eighteen

1. *Rex vs. Benaditto Zanelli, Samuel Mancuso, Donald MacDonald,Edwin MacDonald, and William Baskett, October 17–November 7, 1944,* 173, 521.
2. *Ibid,* 52, 86.
3. *Ibid,* 712.
4. *Ibid,* 857-858.
5. *Ibid,* 716.
6. *Ibid,* 1057.

7. *Ibid,* 938, 945–48.

8. *Ibid,* 886–87.

9. *Ibid,* 1016.

10. *Ibid,* 165.

11. Butcher did not identify Edwin, Mickey, or anyone else in a line-up on December 14, 1943, or at the preliminary hearing in January 1944. He informed the detectives some time after the hearing that he then recognized Edwin MacDonald as the man who first opened the truck's door at the Lazy L Ranch and who had gotten into the back seat of the Nash with him. *Rex vs. Benaditto Zanelli, Samuel Mancuso, Donald MacDonald, Edwin MacDonald, and William Baskett, October 17–November 7, 1944*, 45.

12. Edwin's other charge had to do with a shopbreaking of a Dundas Street West drugstore on October 2, 1944. The matter was thrown out in Toronto Police Court on November 7, 1944, immediately after the trial of the hijackers ended. "Mickey Starts Court Row Shouts Parasite at Judge," *Toronto Daily Star*, November 7, 1944, 2.

13. Shorting appeared with the others charged in Toronto Police Court on December 14, 1943. He was remanded to December 21, then to January 11, 1944, then in succession to January 19, February 2, February 24, March 10, 24, April 14, May 31, October 2, October 23, then to December 18.

14. *Rex vs. Benaditto Zanelli, Samuel Mancuso, Donald MacDonald, Edwin MacDonald, and William Baskett, October 16–November 7, 1944*, 1332–36; also "Mickey Starts Court Row Shouts Parasite at Judge," *Toronto Daily Star*, November 7, 1944, 2.

Chapter Nineteen

1. The list of Mickey's lawyers and former lawyers since 1938 was getting quite long: Frank Regan, G.A. Martin, Mannis Frankel, George Bagwell, G.C. Elgie and now Vera Parsons.

2. "Defer Ruling on Hijacking," *Windsor Star*, February 24, 1945, 10.

3. Germany formally capitulated at 2:41 a.m., May 8, 1945 (French time) at Reims, France. Word of the war's end was on the radio in

Canada soon after. The *Globe and Mail's* headline on May 8 was THIS IS VICTORY. People were soon dancing in the streets, all over Canada.

4. Gwyn Thomas interview, January 10, 2008.

5. *Ibid.*

6. Shorting was at the same time charged as a material witness and made to post a $15,000 bond to guarantee his appearance against Mickey. In the 22 months between December 14, 1943 and September 10, 1945, Shorting was remanded in Toronto Police Court 34 times. At his last appearance, Shorting pleaded Not Guilty and the charge of receiving the stolen truck and its load was withdrawn.

7. *Rex vs. Donald MacDonald, October 16–25, 1945,* 69–70, 170.

8. *Ibid,* 72.

9. Mancuso, Baskett, and Edwin had all claimed at the 1944 trial that they were not at the Lazy L Ranch on the morning of December 13, 1943. Zanelli made no such claim. He was there and was in position to say that Mickey was not there. The others were not.

10. *Rex vs. Donald MacDonald, October 16–25, 1945,* 302.

11. *Ibid,* 370.

12. *Ibid,* 490.

13. *Ibid,* 490–94.

14. "MacDonald Is Sentenced to 15 Years," *Evening Telegram,* October 25, 1945, 1.

Chapter Twenty

1. Guelph Correctional Classification Form "Remarks" re Ulysses Lauzon, #55217 in the Personal File of Ulysses Lauzon, dated September 8, 1941. RG 20-40-3. Archives of Ontario.

2. Y-6765. The Y indicates a youth under age 21. The purpose of the number is so that the guards watch such an inmate a little more carefully against the amorous advances of prison "wolves" — sexual predators.

3. "Ayr Robbery One of the Biggest," *Windsor Star,* May 17, 1945, 7.

4. "Takes Eight Detectives to Remove Prisoner," *Toronto Daily Star,* June 16, 1945, 7.

5. Maclean, Melissa and Keith Wilson, *In Our Midst; Stories From the Waterloo County Jail*, Lamplighter Books: Cambridge, 2001. The chapter titled "Ulysses Lauzon and the Detroit River Gang," 93–98.

6. "Mounties Capture Lauzon Couple in Car — Loot is Found," *Montreal Gazette*, September 13, 1945, 1.

7. Joe Poireau interview, May 14, 2009.

8. Interviewed in April and May 2009, Joe Poireau bitterly disputed the facts of a news story he was shown concerning the event that left him a life-long parapalegic. He wasn't poorly dressed, and $6,000 was far too much in bearer bonds for him to try to cash at one time, he said. This author noted that Hatton Longshaw's remark to the press, "It was either him or me," didn't quite square with the facts of the shooting. He shot Poireau in the back at a distance of "about five feet." The moral, it seems, is "Don't rob banks."

9. Francouer, Jacques G. "Nineteen-Year-Old Gunman Shot in Back Police Seek Companion and Wife," *Montreal Gazette*, September 1, 1945, 1.

10. "Suspected Bank Robbers Arrested," *Charlottetown Guardian*, September 13, 1945, 1.

11. "Lauzon, Long-Pursued, Caught on Woman's Tip." *Toronto Daily Star*, September 15, 1945, 3.

12. "Lauzon, Wife and Koresky Captured in Charlottetown, P.E.I.," *Windsor Star*, September 15, 1945, 3.

13. *Ibid.*

14. Bryant, George. "C. L. Snyder Tells Court Heavy Penalties Needed," *Kingston Whig-Standard*, November 2, 1945, 1.

15. Joseph Poireau interview, May 14, 2009.

16. *Ibid.*

Chapter Twenty-One

1. The bridesmaid may have been Mary Wilson MacDonald, Edwin's young wife, who, for a time, lived with Kathleen at 514A Yonge Street, Apartment 4.

2. Roy "Binky" Clarke Interview, July 1978.

3. *Ibid.*
4. Assistant Commissioner of Penitentiaries G.L. Sauvant, *Memorandum to the Commissioner of Penitentiaries re: The Escape at Kingston Penitentiary During the Night, August 17–18, 1947*, September 5, 1947, Department of the Solicitor-General (originally the Department of Justice), RG 73 volume 106 file 4-14-4, wherein Deputy Warden Len Millard's tolerance of "laxity" in the security of the prison is a main theme. Library and Archives Canada.
5. Gwyn Thomas interview, January 10, 2008.
6. Roy "Binky" Clarke interview, July 1978.
7. Minnelli, Nick. "Our Sensational Escape From Kingston Pen" (Part 1), *Star Weekly*, October 24, 1959, 4.
8. Minelli's contention was that a key witness against him had mistakenly testified that he saw Nick, not Ceretti, with a revolver that had been used to kidnap taxi driver Donald LaPrade. Thus, claimed Nick, he was wrongly convicted. Nick and Ceretti both claimed Ceretti had perpetrated the kidnapping of the cab driver without his knowledge and before Nick, himself, got into the taxicab.
9. Report of A. Veitch, R.C.M.P. No. 9275, dated 16 January, 1948, in Escapes 1947, RG 73 vol. 106, file 4-14-4, Part 3. Library and Archives Canada.
10. Roy "Binky" Clarke interview, July 1978.
11. "Break Foiled: Convicts Slug Guard at Stony Mountain," September 18, 1939, 2.
12. Roy "Binky" Clarke interview, July 1978.

Chapter Twenty-Two

1. The cupola of the Dome was lowered after a fire set by the inmates in the riot of August 1954. Blackstock, Harvey. *Bitter Humour: About Dope, Safecracking and Prisons*, Toronto: Burns & MacEachern, 1967, 234.
2. Caron, Roger. *Bingo! The Horrifying Eye-Witness Account of a Prison Riot*, Toronto: Methuen, 1985, 55. Caron, Roger. *Go-Boy! Memoirs of a Life Behind Bars*, Toronto:McGraw-Hill Ryerson, 1978, 100–01. Hennessey, Peter H. *Canada's Big House: The Dark History of Kingston*

Penitentiary, Dundurn Press: Toronto, 1999, 14–15. Minnelli, Nick. "Our Sensational Escape From Kingston Pen" (Part 1), *Star Weekly*, October 24, 1959, 4.

3. Assistant Commissioner of Penitentiaries G.L. Sauvant, *Memorandum to the Commissioner of Penitentiaries re: The Escape at Kingston Penitentiary During the Night, August 17-18, 1947*, September 5, 1947, 3. In the Department of the Solicitor-General, RG 73, volume 106 file 4-14-4. Library and Archives Canada.

4. This phrase "a clear path out the door" was used by at least two and perhaps three of the eight or nine guards I interviewed for *The Big Red Fox: The Incredible Story of Norman "Red" Ryan, Canada's Most Notorious Criminal* in the early 1980s.

5. "Inquiry Shows 'Laxity'; Deputy Warden Placed On Leave," *Ottawa Citizen*, September 22, 1947, 1.

6. Minnelli, Nick. "Our Sensational Escape From Kingston Pen" (Part 1), *Star Weekly*, October 24, 1959, 6.

7. Roy "Binky" Clarke interview, June 10, 2009.

8. Roy "Binky" Clarke interview, July 1978.

9. Minnelli, Nick, "Our Sensational Escape From Kingston Pen" (Part 1), *Star Weekly*, October 24, 1959, 6.

Chapter Twenty-Three

1. Minnelli, Nick. "Our Sensational Escape From Kingston Pen (Part 2) — $6,000 Dead Or Alive," *Star Weekly*, October 31, 1959, 11.

2. The author has heard this story told in words similar to these from four or five individuals, including some who were genuine, and found the same in a January 1955 news story.

3. G.L. Sauvant, *Memorandum to the Commissioner of Penitentiaries re: The Escape at Kingston Penitentiary During the Night, August 17–18, 1947*, 1. In the Department of the Solicitor-General (originally in the Department of Justice), RG 73, volume 106 file 4-14-4. Library and Archives Canada

4. Minnelli, Nick. "Our Sensational Escape From Kingston Pen (Part 2) — $6,000 Dead Or Alive," *Star Weekly*, October 31, 1959, 44.

5. Minnelli, Nick. "Our Sensational Escape From Kingston Pen (Part 2) — $6,000 Dead Or Alive," *Star Weekly*, October 31, 1959, 39. Nick's remembrance does not acknowledge the hierarchy that existed among the escapees — or that he seems to have been the one who was permanently assigned to lay down on the stolen car's back seat floor.

6. Minnelli, Nick. "Our Sensational Escape From Kingston Pen (Part 1)," *Star Weekly*, October 24, 1959, 4.

7. Joseph B. Poireau interview, May 14, 2009.

8. Minnelli, Nick. "Our Sensational Escape From Kingston Pen (Part 1)," *Star Weekly*, October 24, 1959, 4.

9. Many of the range and stoneshed details were supplied by Roy Clarke. His telling of Guard Bedore's quandry was both hilarious and sad. The stoneshed inmates liked Bedore, as much as they liked any guard, and they were treated leniently — too leniently — by him. But the situation and the inmate's code meant that Bedore's job was collateral damage.

10. Minnelli, Nick. "Our Sensational Escape From Kingston Pen (Part 2) — $6,000 Dead Or Alive," *Star Weekly*, October 31, 1959, 39.

Chapter Twenty-Four

1. "Pursue Three Fugitives in Quebec," *Kingston Whig-Standard*, August 19, 1947, 1.

2. "Say Lauzon Will Shoot to Kill," *Windsor Star*, August 18, 1947, 1.

3. "Mickey McDonald in Trio of Long-term Convicts Freed by Smuggled Saw," *Evening Telegram*, August 18, 1947, 1.

4. The reference was to a story published on November 10, 1939. "'Mickey' Vows He is Through With Crime," *Evening Telegram*, November 10, 1939, 2.

5. Taylor, Robert. "'Crime Sucker's Racket' Mickey — But Didn't Stop," *Toronto Daily Star*, August 18, 1947, 2.

6. "'There'll Be Shooting,' Prison Guard Predicts," *Toronto Daily Star*, August 19, 1947, 1.

7. Taylor, Robert. "'Crime Sucker's Racket' Mickey — But Didn't Stop," *Toronto Daily Star*, August 18, 1947, 2.

8. "Three Toughs Escape Prison," *Ottawa Citizen*, August 18, 1947, 2.

9. "McDonald Writes Letter Scoring 'Pen' Conditions," *Globe and Mail*, August 19, 1947, 1.

10. "Fear Lauzon Now Armed, Says Warden," *Toronto Daily Star*, August 19, 1947, 1.

11. "Fugitives Took $40,000 Prints Reveal," *Toronto Daily Star*, August 23, 1947, 1.

12. Since 2002, Hull, opposite Ottawa on the Quebec side of the Ottawa River, is now merged with the municipalities of Gatineau, Aylmer, Buckingham, and Masson-Angers, and the whole has been renamed Gatineau.

13. Highway 8 is now part of Quebec Highway 148.

14. Joseph B. Poireau interview, May 14, 2009.

15. "Quebec Provincial Police Called Off Search," *Kingston Whig-Standard*, August 19, 1947, 1.

16. "Believe Three Men Are Now in Hiding," *Ottawa Citizen*, August 20, 1947, 1, and "Squads of Police Are Being Rushed to the Ottawa Area," *Windsor Star*, August 19, 1947, 1.

17. Kitchen, George. "Hint Three Men Ditched Car, Separated," *Kingston Whig-Standard*, August 19, 1947, 1.

18. A copy of the text of this agreement, dated August 22, 1947, exists in the Attorney General of Ontario's Central Registry Criminal and Civil Files re the Escape From Kingston Penitentiary of convicts Ulysses Lauzon, Donald "Mickey" McDonald and Nicholas Minelli, August 17–18, 1947. RG 4-32 #1063 (1947). Archives of Ontario.

19. The Town of Eastview, which became the Town of Vanier in 1969, has been a part of the City of Ottawa since 2001.

20. Roy "Binky" Clarke interview, May 13, 2009.

Chapter Twenty-Five

1. Ontario Provincial Police file re the Escape of Donald "Mickey" McDonald, Ulysses Lauzon and Nick Minelli From Kingston Penitentiary, August 17–18, 1947." RG 23-26-95 folder 222989. Archives of Ontario.

2. Minnelli, Nick. "Our Sensational Escape From Kingston Pen (Part 2) — $6,000 Dead Or Alive," *Star Weekly*, October 31, 1959, 39.

3. Nick probably made this "mistake" on purpose, as Mickey and Uly had committed a crime at Guelph and Mickey might then still be alive. It is unlikely that Nick would have stayed with the others any longer than he had to. There was a shoot-on-sight order out on them — and Nick would have known it was not because of himself.

4. "Fingerprints Confirm Pair Pulled Bank Job," *Windsor Star*, August 23, 1947, 1.

5. *Ibid.*

6. *Ibid.*

7. *Ibid.*

8. "Lauzon, MacDonald in Guelph For Getaway Car," *The Guelph Mercury*, August 23, 1947, 9.

9. "Keep Up Convict Hunt Plan of Windsor Police," *Evening Telegram*, August 25, 1947, 1.

10. "Escaped Convicts Reported at Many Ontario Centres," *Globe and Mail*, August 26, 1947, 11.

11. "Police Posse Acts On Tips From Resort," *Windsor Star*, August 26, 1947, 1.

Chapter Twenty-Six

1. The foregoing and much of what follows is owed to an interview-conversation I had with former OPP Inspector George MacKay, who was extremely forthright in what he had to say about police methods of the 1930s and 1940s. The date was March 17, 1981. Later, in the late 1990s, Jack Webster, a former Toronto Police chief of detectives, and the Official Historian of the Toronto Police Service, as well as Gwyn "Jocko" Thomas, police reporter of *Toronto Daily Star* for 62 years, elaborated on the same theme.

2. George MacKay interview, March 17, 1981. Mr. MacKay, an OPP inspector of that era, had a great respect for the Toronto Police detectives and their methods of operation. "The Toronto Police had

many fine detectives and they had great sources of information," said Mr. MacKay.

3. Information dated August 25, 1947, Inspector H.P. Mathewson of the R.C.M.P to OPP Commissioner Stringer. The heroin dealer's name is blotted out due to Freedom of Information controls. OPP file re the Escape of Donald "Mickey" McDonald, Ulysses Lauzon and Nick Minelli From Kingston Penitentiary, August 17–18, 1947." RG 23-26-95 folder B222951. Archives of Ontario.

4. Mackey, James P. *I Policed Toronto: An Autobiography by James P. Mackey, Chief of Police Metropolitan Toronto, 1958–1970*, self-published: Toronto, 1985, 90–91.

5. Letter of Provincial Constable J.S. McDonald to the Commissioner of the Ontario Provincial Police, dated October 30, 1947. File re the Escape of Donald "Mickey" McDonald, Ulysses Lauzon and Nick Minelli From Kingston Penitentiary, August 17–18, 1947." RG 23-26-95 folder 222989. Archives of Ontario.

6. Howard Garone's information was the one piece that fit the larger picture. The OPP saw it that way at the time — and it jibed with what they later found out and with what Nick Minelli had to say in 1959.

7. "Sure Arguing, Shouting Men Outside Her Home Bandit Trio," *Toronto Daily Star*, August 23, 1947, 2.

8. Later the victim was found to be George Stanley Spaul, a retired Consul, Saskatchewan farmer, who, on his way to visit relatives in Thornbury, Ontario, made the mistake of picking up the wrong hitchhiker. As the result of a telephone tip, the murderer was arrested November 1, 1947, at Sault Ste. Marie, Michigan.

9. "Burglar Alarm Salesmen Besiege Harrassed Bankers," *Toronto Daily Star*, September 5, 1947, 1.

10. "$3,000 Reward Posted on Three Fugitives," *Globe and Mail*, September 17, 1947, 1.

11. Reward Circular issued by S.T. Wood, Commissioner, Royal Canadian Mounted Police, Ottawa, September 12, 1947, announcing that the Commissioner of Penitentiaries, Ottawa, will pay $1,000 for information resulting in the arrests of each of Ulysses Lauzon, Donald(Mickey) McDonald and Nicholas (Nick) Minnille. OPP Criminal Investigation

file re the Escape of Donald "Mickey" McDonald, Ulysses Lauzon and Nick Minelli From Kingston Penitentiary, August 17–18,1947. Archives of Ontario.

12. "Rap Mickey Reward, 'Ten Times Too Little,'" *Toronto Daily Star*, September 19, 1947, 22.

13. Reward Circular issued by the Canadian Bankers' Association, Toronto, December 1947, offering "to pay a total reward of $5,000 for information resulting in the arrest of the following escaped convicts": Ulysses Lauzon, Donald (Micky) McDonald and Nicholas(Nick) (Dominic) Minille. In file re the Escape of Donald "Mickey" McDonald, Ulysses Lauzon and Nick Minelli From Kingston Penitentiary, August 17–18, 1947." RG 23-26-95. Archives of Ontario.

14. "Inquiry Shows Laxity," *Ottawa Citizen*, September 22, 1947, 1. In fact, the lone Simonds hacksaw blade that was found was discovered in Mickey's cell.

15. *Ibid.*

16. *Ibid.*

17. "Scour Two Provinces For McDonald and Pals," *Globe and Mail*, September 12, 1947, 5.

18. "'Mickey' and Lauzon in New York - Police," *Toronto Daily Star*, June 21, 1948, 1.

Chapter Twenty-Seven

1. "Narcotics Are Scarce; Pay Fantastic Prices For Dope, Police Say," *Hamilton Spectator*, April 3, 1948, 7.

2. Report of Sergeant A.M. Veitch of the RCMP's Toronto Criminal Investigation Branch, dated January 16, 1948, quotes Toronto Inspector of Detectives Alex McCathie as the source of this information and a lot more on Harold Jamieson, Alex MacDonald and some others. In the Department of the Solicitor-General (in 1948 part of the Department of Justice) file on the Escape of August 17–18, 1948. RG 73 volume 106 file 4-14-4. Library and Archives Canada.

3. "City Dope Kingpins Sentenced," *Vancouver Sun*, August 29, 1962, 1.

4. "Alex MacDonald Goes Free, Pal Pays $100," *Windsor Star*, January 24, 1948, 3.

5. Neither Harold or Alex actually knew Joe Poireau. It's possible that Jamieson, recently released, might have carried some message to Joe's family — or pretended to do so.

6. "'Didn't Love Him But I'm Not Glad He's Dead,' Girl Says Of Robber Pal," *Cincinnati Times-Star*, June 3, 1948, 8.

7. A court document indicates that Dorland could have got most of his money back, if he had applied for it, which he didn't do. County Court Judges' Criminal Court, *Rex vs. Harold Jamieson*, March 31, 1948. RG 22-5871 case file 25-48. The Archives of Ontario.

8. "Running Battle On City Street," *Hamilton Spectator*, April 1, 1948, 7.

9. *Ibid.*

10. "Guagliano Sentenced to Seven Years in Penitentiary," *The Hamilton Spectator*, May 26, 1948, 7.

11. "Police Grab Windsor Pair at Hamilton," *The Windsor Star*, April 2, 1948, 5.

12. "Two Drug Suspects Fail to Appear, Their Bail Is Estreated," *The Hamilton Spectator*, April 9, 1948, 7.

Chapter Twenty-Eight

1. "Minnille is Recaptured by Police in California," *Kingston Whig-Standard*, May 19, 1948, 1.

2. Minnelli, Nick. "Our Sensational Escape From Kingston Pen (Part 2) — $6,000 Dead Or Alive," *Star Weekly*, October 31, 1959, 44.

3. *Ibid.*

4. *Ibid.*

5. "Minnille is Recaptured by Police in California," *Kingston Whig-Standard*, May 19, 1948, 1.

6. Minnelli, Nick. "Our Sensational Escape From Kingston Pen (Part 2) — $6,000 Dead Or Alive," *Star Weekly*, October 31, 1959, 44.

7. "Minnille Says He Won't Rat," *Kingston Whig-Standard*, May 22, 1948, 3.

8. "Half-Breed Indian Pal of Desperate Canadian Hold-up Band, Learned," *The Cincinnati Times-Star*, June 3, 1948, 40.

9. Nadar, who had many more aliases, had a single armed robbery conviction for holding up a suspected betting shop. He was not a criminal or armed robber of anything like the magnitude of Harold Jamieson — and apparently figured this out before it got him killed.

10. "Half-Breed Indian Pal of Desperate Canadian Hold-up Band, Learned," *Cincinnati Times-Star*, June 3, 1948, 40.

11. "Cincinnati Officer Kills Fugitive, Trapped Canadian-Indian Outlaw," *Cincinnati Enquirer*, June 2, 1948, 1.

12. "Labard Killed in Cincinnati," *Hamilton Spectator*, June 2, 1948, 7.

13. "Shoot Fugitive, Seize Girl," *Cincinnati Post*, June 1, 1948, 1.

14. *Ibid.*

15. "'Didn't Love Him, But I'm Not Glad He's Dead,' Girl Says of Robber Pal," *Cincinnati Times-Star*, June 3, 1948, 8.

16. "Elaine (Poireau) Led Away," *Daily Toronto Star*, June 2, 1948, 1.

17. "Slain Convict's Companion Fined," *Cincinnati Times-Star*, June 10, 1948, 40.

18. "Half-Breed Indian Pal of Desperate Canadian Hold-up Band, Learned," *Cincinnati Times-Star*, June 3, 1948, 40.

19. Thomas, Gwyn. "Lauzon Dies a Victim of Gang's Double-Cross," *Toronto Daily Star*, July 29, 1948, 1.

20. "Gates Clang Behind Minnille," *The Kingston Whig-Standard*, August 6, 1948, 1.

21. "Kingston Penitentiary/Inmate History & Description," Nick Minnille, No. 8929. Library and Archives Canada, RG 73, volume 604.

22. "Unidentified Body is Found at Lake Near Pascagoula," *Mobile Daily Register*, July 20, 1948, 1.

23. As a telegram in the files of the Ontario Provincial Police Criminal Investigation Branch (C.I.B.) indicates, it was 5:32 p.m., July 28, 1948, when "the Provincial Police Department" was notified of the death of "Elysses (sic) Lauzon." The OPP notified the RCMP and other Canadian authorities. Ontario Provincial Police File re the Escape of Donald "Mickey" McDonald, Ulysses Lauzon and Nick Minnelli From Kingston Penitentiary, August 17–18, 1947. RG 23-26. Archives of Ontario.

24. Thomas, Gwyn. "Lauzon Dies as a Victim of Gang's Double-Cross," *Toronto Star*, July 29, 1948, 1. Much of this story was derived from Mr. Thomas's telephone interview with Sheriff Guy Krebs.

25. Gwyn "Jocko" Thomas interview, January 10, 2008.

26. Bowering, Cliff. "As Predicted Lauzon Comes to Violent End," *Kingston Whig-Standard*, July 29, 1948, 1.

27. Brophey, Tom. "Lauzon's Fantastic Exploits Covered a Span of 11 Years," *Windsor Star*, July 29, 1948, 1.

28. Ross, Bill. "'Love Died With Baby,' Says Widow," *Windsor Star*, July 30, 1948, 1.

29. *Ibid.*

30. *Ibid.*

Chapter Twenty-Nine

1. See McClement, Fred. *The Strange Case of Ambrose Small*, McClelland & Stewart Ltd., Toronto: 1974.

2. "Chinese Spots Bogus $10 Bill, Man, Girl Held," *Toronto Daily Star*, August 30, 1948, 24.

3. "Struck Off Strength; Veteran Fired Two Shots During Police Career," *Globe and Mail*, September 28, 1948, 5.

4. "Nab Mickey's Kin and Fake $10 Bills 'Very Good,'" *Globe and Mail*, February 8, 1949, 1.

5. "Three Bogus U.S. $20 Bills May Herald Flood — Police," *Toronto Daily Star*, February 24, 1949, 34.

6. In early May, 1936, George Taylor Little was the loser in a gunfight with Chief of Detectives John Chisholm in front of the West Toronto YMCA.

7. "Had 3 Guns, $640 Bogus Money U.S. Police Charge Toronto Man," *Globe and Mail*, September 28, 1949, 5.

8. "'Mickey's Alive, Kicking' Snap Query Upsets Brother," *Toronto Daily Star*, May 30, 1949, 21.

9. Roy "Binky" Clarke interview, no date.

10. "Sure 'Mickey' Slain, Not Drug Peddling," *Evening Telegram*, March 27, 1950, 2.

11. *Ibid.*

12. Hunt, James. "Lady Wonder 'Never Saw Horse,' Can't Give Hot Tips But Picks Ticats, Liberals," *Toronto Daily Star*, December 11, 1952, 1.

13. "'Mickey' McDonald Tops List of 10 Most Wanted Criminals," *Kingston Whig-Standard*, February 1, 1952, 13.

14. Mickey has sometimes been wrongly named as "the only man ever to escape Kingston Penitentiary and never to be officially accounted for." In October 2008, David St. Onge, in charge of the Kingston Penitentiary Museum, explained that the museum staff's research indicated that two escapees in the 1880s had never been located. "In the prison's history, there have been 27 breaks from inside the compound, involving 58 men," Mr. St. Onge said authoritatively.

15. "Ontario's Organized Crime Underground Aids Boyd Gang — Frost," *Toronto Daily Star*, September 11, 1952, 2.

16. The last newspaper reference that included the possibility that Mickey McDonald might still be alive likely appeared in the *Toronto Sun* in May 1978. It was made by Harry Brown, a former waiter at Bowles Lunch, once located across from the Old City Hall, who was publicizing a reunion of Bowles' staff and customers in a prominent journalist's column. Bowles was a gathering spot for all who worked or appeared at the law courts in the City Hall, and Harry Brown, so he said, had many times served Red Ryan and Mickey McDonald, too. "If Mickey McDonald is still alive and came to our re-union it would be quite a coup," observed Mr. Brown, with considerable optimism. At that late date, Brown wasn't really expecting Mickey to show up. I spoke with him a day or two after the piece appeared in the *Sun*. The remark, he said, was "a flight of fancy."

Chapter Thirty

1. The name of the heroin dealer is blotted out by Freedom of Information regulations on the OPP file that tells of these events. I believe I know who it was.

2. "Seize Mobsters With Drawn Guns, Drug War Link," *Toronto Daily Star*, January 6, 1949, 21.

3. *Ibid.*

4. "Had to Arrest Somebody RCMP Tell Mickey's Kin," *Toronto Daily Star*, March 3, 1949, 1.

5. "Had Sweep Ticket Was Held 2 Days," *Toronto Daily Star*, April 8, 1950, 2.

6. "$28,000 Bail Asked of Hold-up Suspects," *The Vancouver Sun*, March 31, 1951, 2.

7. *Ibid.*

8. "Holdup Suspect Freed," *Vancouver Sun*, October 2, 1951, 1.

9. "Mickey Brother Held in U.S. as a Drug Suspect," *Toronto Daily Star*, May 20, 1954, 60.

10. Quoted in a "Toronto City Police Report," December 21, 1956, in "British Columbia Penitentiary Classification Department Admission Report, January 15, 1957," in the Personal File of Alex MacDonald, Penitentiaries Branch. RG 13, Volume 1621. Library and Archives Canada,

11. Quoted in a Kingston Penitentiary Classification Department Report dated March 2, 1955, in the Personal File of Alex MacDonald, Penitentiaries Branch. RG 13, Volume 1621. Library and Archives Canada.

12. The Ticket-of-Leave was an antique form of parole which was practised in the federal system after 1899 and before 1959. It was a licence allowing an inmate to complete his sentence outside prison walls provided certain criteria were met. In practice, an inmate who received a Ticket-of-Leave was not usually, or necessarily, interviewed before being released and there was little or no monitoring of the Ticket-of-Leave recipient's lifestyle and behaviour after their release. The years 1953 to 1959 were a watershed in the thinking within the Justice Department and the country concerning the parole of federal prisoners. Major changes were made. Canada's first modern parole board came into effect in 1959.

13. A Case Report Signed Cpl. S. Bunyk, RCMP Narcotics Branch, dated September 24, 1962, in the Personal File of Alex MacDonald, Penitentiaries Branch. RG 13, Volume 1621, Library and Archives Canada, includes a recap of an investigation that took place between November 15, 1961 and January 9, 1962, "...on which date warrants

to arrest were issued and executed on a total of 22 persons who were charged with Conspiracy to Traffic, in addition substantive counts of unlawful trafficking and Unlawful Possession of Narcotics."

Parts of the report read: "MacDONALD has been known to this office for the past 12 years, he has never been lawfully employed but on the contrary has lead a continuous criminal life. MacDONALD supported himself from the proceeds of armed robbery, theft, avails of prostitution, breaking and entering, gambling and drug trafficking. His time was spent almost equally between Toronto and Vancouver up until 1958 at which time he settled in the Vancouver area...MacDONALD is accustomed to high class living from the proceeds of his criminal activities. He seldom associates with the petty criminal unless it is to his advantage financially.

"...in the early fall of 1961 he had firmly entrenched himself as the major trafficker in Vancouver controlling approximately 75% of the narcotic trafficking. His close associate and incidentally a neighbour was Michael PETROSKI @ Mickey PETERS, FPS 539565, together they supplied some 16 to 20 street traffickers. The MacDONALD organization became subject of direct investigation in September 1961 and on November 13, 1961 one Ronald HILL, FPS 802158 was identified as the "backend" whose duties it was to secret caches of one or two ounce lots in various locations throughout the Greater Vancouver area. Observations on HILL'S activities resulted in the location of some thirty-eight (38) caches on which observations were maintained and evidence resulting which led to the arrest and convictions of the persons who retrieved them.... In addition on two occasions MacDONALD retrieved two of these caches himself. Both caches had been secreted in the ashtray in the corridor on floors 6 and 7 at 1095 Bute Street, Vancouver, B.C. The first offence took place on November 21, 1961 and the second on December 18, 1961. On both occasions he was positively identified picking the caches up, on each occasion he was in company with a female drug addict ..."

14. "19 Committed for Trial On Drug Trafficking Charges," *Vancouver Sun*, April 13, 1962, 1.

15. "City Dope Kingpins Sentenced," *Vancouver Sun*, August 29, 1962, 1.

16. The story of Alex's declining health makes up a large part of the Personal File of Alex MacDonald, Penitentiary Branch. RG 13, Volume 1621. Library and Archives Canada.

Chapter Thirty-One

1. Gwyn "Jocko" Thomas interview, January 10, 2008.
2. Roy "Binky" Clarke interview, May 27, 2008.
3. "Claims Bookies a Front for Toronto Drug Ring," *Toronto Daily Star*, March 24, 1958, 47.
4. "Lay Perjury Charges is Crown Challenge in McDonald Hearing," *Globe and Mail*, April 17, 1957, 5.
5. "'Saw Mickey Start Dope Eddie Abhors It' — Counsel," *Toronto Daily Star*, October 23, 1957, 21.
6. *Ibid.*
7. In May 1957, Edwin was awarded a one-year sentence for absconding bail.
8. Eddie's legal problems were on or near to the front pages for four solid years, beginning with his arrest in January 1956 and finally ending when the Supreme Court of Canada disallowed his appeal against his conviction for possession of heroin for the purpose of trafficking in late December 1959.
9. Harkness, Ross. "Bondsmen Not Ruined But Can Lose Plenty When Pal Skips Bail," *Toronto Daily Star*, May 3, 1956, 4.
10. "Police Capture Edwin MacDonald in Weston House," *Globe and Mail*, February 7, 1957, 2.
11. The question of whether or not the guarantors of Edwin's future appearance would lose some or all of the equity they had put up was a major sub-plot in the Toronto press for many months — and it would eventually greatly help to lead to a reform of the bail process. The issue would call up the MacDonald name in the Toronto papers many times. It provided lots of drama. Joseph P. Thomas of 16th Street, New Toronto, apparently a professional or semi-professional bail bondsman, put up $25,000 equity in his home and was in the *Toronto Star* whining about the unfairness of it all soon after Eddie

absconded. It would turn out that Thomas's house was heavily mortgaged and that he had guaranteed Eddie's appearance with equity that he did not have. Esma Hysen of Runnymede Road, Toronto, an elderly widow with a poor understanding of English, was claimed to have backed Eddie's reappearance to the tune of $11,000, supposedly so that her son, who had previously been in jail with Eddie, could make $130. She claimed she had promised to post $1,100, not $11,000. George Makinisian of Bleecker Street, Toronto, posted $10,000 and Eddie's youngest sister, Ruth, and her husband, were good for the last $4,000. Eddie's capture likely meant that his bondsmen got to keep most, not all, of the sureties they put up.

12. "'Does Not Know the Whereabouts of Mickey' — Ed," *Toronto Daily Star*, April 16, 1957, 2.

13. Several sources mentioned this incident, most especially Roy "Binky" Clarke, who had been a friend and associate of Eddie's but who had stopped liking Eddie by then. One suggestion was that Eddie had crossed a prominent Toronto organized crime figure who was known to use this method — a baseball bat beating — to punish those who upset him.

Chapter Thirty-Two

1. "Curvaceous Kitty Beats Temperance Cop," *Hush*, May 15, 1950, 6.

2. "Good-Time Johnny Rolled; Joy Gal Jailed For Gang," *Hush*, March 1, 1941, 2.

3. Gwyn "Jocko" Thomas interview, January 10, 2008.

4. "Another Sucker Bites the Dust: 'Kitty Kat' Beats the Rap," *Hush*, August 14, 1941, 2.

5. Gwyn "Jocko" Thomas interview, January 10, 2008.

6. "Asks Chance to Make Good, 'Kitty Cat' Granted Parole," *Toronto Daily Star*, January 31, 1945, 3.

7. "'Kitty Cat' MacDonald Jailed For 3 Months," *Justice Weekly*, March 30, 1946, 3.

8. This story was told to me by Jack Webster, Official Historian of the Toronto Police Service. I might have had 40 or 50 such conversations with a policeman who had been a member of the bank robbery squad, the head of the homicide squad, and the chief of detectives of the Toronto Police. Jack had a few stories. See, for example, Webster, Jack, with Rosemary Aubert. *Copper Jack: My Life on the Force*, Dundurn Press, Toronto: 1991.

9. Maurice LaTour interview, July 1, 1979.

10. "'Kitty Kat' Blows Top Battles Police Intruders," *Hush Free Press*, April 18, 1953, 11.

11. Jack Webster interview, circa 1998–99.

12. "Former 'Kitty Cat' MacDonald Claims She Was Trying to Kick Drug Habit," *Justice Weekly*, September 17, 1960, 11.

13. "In the Courts: Bad Company Started Her Off," *Toronto Daily Star*, May 9, 1978, A11.

14. Margaret DeBerry Death Notice, *Toronto Daily Star*, January 26, 27, 1994.

15. The man had lots of information but would not give his name. I met him in George's Chicken Barbecue, Pembroke and Dundas Streets, about 2:00 a.m. on the night of April 30, 2004. I'd guess he was then well into his eighties.

16. "Say 'Manor' Had Cocktail Set-Up But No License," *Toronto Daily Star*, January 21, 1950, 1.

Chapter Thirty-Three

1. Jones, Phil. "'Is Mickey Dead?' "*Globe and Mail*, January 6, 1955, 5. The RCMP's "Ten Most Wanted" List dates from February 1952, not 1950 as Phil Jones wrote.

2. Affidavit of Kathleen MacDonald in the Matter of the Marriage Act, and Kathleen MacDonald's application to have her husband, Donald John MacDonald, presumed legally dead, granted January 29, 1958, by County Court Judge Robert Forsyth. RG-22-5861, Matters Index Vol. 3, 1958, No. 8920. Archives of Ontario.

3. Affidavit of Mannis Frankel in the Matter of the Marriage Act, and Kathleen MacDonald's application to have her husband, Donald John MacDonald, presumed legally dead, granted January 29, 1958, by County Court Judge Robert Forsyth. RG-22-5861, Matters Index Vol. 3, 1958, No. 8920. Archives of Ontario

4. "Kingston Penitentiary/Inmate History & Description," Edwin MacDonald, No. 7912. RG 73. Library and Archives Canada.

5. Affidavit of Edwin MacDonald in the Matter of the Marriage Act, and Kathleen MacDonald's application to have her husband, Donald John MacDonald, presumed legally dead, granted January 29, 1958, by County Court Judge Robert Forsyth. RG-22-5861, Matters Index Vol. 3, 1958, No. 8920. The Archives of Ontario.

6. Vincent "Ace" Hamel interview, January 10, 1982.

7. Gwyn "Jocko" Thomas interview, January 10, 2008, as at other times.

8. Jack Webster interview, circa 1999.

9. The connection Binky is referring to is that the engraver could testify in court against Mickey, who might then find reason to testify against the mob guys. But the engraver can't testify against the mob guys because all he knows is hearsay that he's gotten from Mickey. Mickey, an unreliable link in the chain, had to go. His kind walking around breathing put the people whose interest he did not protect in jeopardy.

10. Roy "Binky" Clarke interview, September 7, 1978.

Epilogue

1. Once, in the 1980s, I had the sergeant on the desk of one of Toronto's police divisions do just that with me. I had a fellow go for a nice long ride in the cab I was driving, then at his destination tell me, "I don't have any money." When I got upset, he volunteered to go and shoplift meat from a supermarket and to pay me with that. Instead, I drove him to 55 Division, where the desk sergeant told me on the sly, "I'm not supposed to tell you this, but he's out on parole from Dorchester Penitentiary. If you really want to get him, go to court on this. They'll send him back to Dorchester."

2. W.O. Gibson Address to the Jury, Friday, October 19, 1945, in RG 4-32 #1498 (1944) Attorney General of Ontario Central Registry Criminal and Civil Files. Rex vs Donald McDonald et al — armed

robbery and hijacking of a liquor truck — trial transcripts and appeals. Archives of Ontario. (As is the norm, this address is not in *Rex vs. Donald MacDonald, October 16-25, 1945*, the trial transcript.)

3. As quoted in Goldenberg, Susan. *Snatched! The Peculiar Kidnapping of Beer Tycoon John Labatt*, Toronto, 149.

Sources

Interviews and More

As stated above, four people have, by agreement, been given pseudonyms in the narrative. These are those who appear as Roy "Binky" Clarke, Jenny Law, and Joe and Elaine Poireau. Of these I interviewed at length all but Elaine Poireau, who was not available. Jenny Law died years ago, but our agreement was that she would have a pseudonym in *The Big Red Fox* and I have kept that bargain in this book, too. I spoke with Joe Poireau at length twice by long distance telephone in May 2009, and we agreed that he and Elaine would have other names in the story. I was pleased to discover that, almost alone among those who appear in the criminal tale I am telling, and notwithstanding his being confined to a wheelchair, Joe worked hard, did what was necessary, and was able to right his life by 180 degrees. He served 10 of the 44-years he was sentenced to and, after his release, became a social and economic success. He long ago earned the respect of the community in which he has lived as a solid citizen for the last 50 years. It was a pleasure and a privilege to talk with him.

Of the others who I interviewed, no person was more generous with his time than Gwyn "Jocko" Thomas, police reporter of the

Toronto Star for 62 years, who spoke with me many times about Red Ryan, Mickey McDonald, and others after June 1981 and before 2009. As well, I would like to thank the following who, at the expense of their own time, supplied information about Mickey McDonald, though in most cases they were interviewed principally about Red Ryan: Robert Lackaey, interviewed August 18, 1977; Harry Brown, May 1978; Maurice LaTour, July 1, 1979; Nat Ladner, January 8, 1980; John "Gazooney" Guerin, January 16, 1980; Art Keay and Alex McCathie, February 6, 1981; George MacKay, March 17, 1981; Vincent "Ace" Hamel, January 10, 1982; Roy Steinberg, December 10, 1991; Jack Webster, 1997–99; and David St. Onge, 2008. Except for Mr. St. Onge, whose input was exclusively about Kingston Penitentiary and its clients, I believe all of the others are now deceased.

Book Sources

Blackstock, Harvey. *Bitter Humour: About Dope, Safecracking and Prisons*. Toronto: Burns & MacEachern, 1967.

Buck, Tim. *Yours in the Struggle: Reminiscences of Tim Buck*. Toronto: NC Press, 1977.

Canadian Criminal Cases Vol. LXXII, Toronto: Canada Law Book Company Ltd., 1939.

The Criminal Code of Canada, Revised Statutes, 1927, Ottawa: Frederick Albert Acland, Printer to the King, 1927.

Caron, Roger. *Bingo! The Horrifying Eye-Witness Account of a Prison Riot*. Toronto: Methuen, 1985.

Caron, Roger. *Go-Boy! Memoirs of a Life Behind Bars*. Toronto: McGraw-Hill Ryerson, 1978.

Dubro, James and Robin F. Rowland. *King of the Mob: Rocco Perri and the Women Who Ran His Rackets*. Markham, Ontario: Penguin Books Canada Limited, 1987.

Goldenberg, Susan. *Snatched! The Peculiar Kidnapping of Beer Tycoon John Labatt*. Toronto: Dundurn Press, 2004.

Hennessey, Peter H. *Canada's Big House: The Dark History of the Kingston Penitentiary*. Toronto: Dundurn Press, 1999.

Hoshowsky, Robert. *The Last To Die: Ronald Turpin, Arthur Lucas, and the End of Capital Punishment in Canada.* Toronto: Dundurn Press, 2007.

Mackey, James P. *I Policed Toronto: An Autobiography by James P. Mackey, Chief of Police Metropolitan Toronto, 1958–1970.* Toronto: self-published, 1985.

Maclean, Melissa and Keith Wilson. *In Our Midst; Stories From the Waterloo County Jail.* Cambridge, Ontario: Lamplighter Books, 2001

McClement, Fred. *The Strange Case of Ambrose Small.* Toronto: McClelland and Stewart Ltd., 1974.

McSherry, Peter. *The Incredible Story of Norman "Red" Ryan, Canada's Most Notorious Criminal.* Toronto: Dundurn Press, 1999.

Ormond, D.M. *Report of the Superintendent of Penitentiaries Re Kingston Penitentiary Disturbances 1932.* Ottawa: Frederick Albert Acland, Printer to the King, 1933.

Revised Statutes of Canada, Ottawa: Frederick Albert Acland, Printer to the King, 1927.

Robinette, John J. (ed). *The Ontario Reports: Cases Determined in the Supreme Court of Ontario (The Court of Appeal for Ontario and The High Court of Justice for Ontario) Cited 1939.* Toronto: The Carswell Company Limited.

Thomas, Gwyn "Jocko." *From Police Headquarters: True Tales From the Big City Crime Beat.* Toronto: Stoddart Publishing Co. Limited, 1990.

Webster, Jack, with Rosemary Aubert. *Copper Jack: My Life on the Force.* Toronto: Dundurn Press, 1991.

Withrow, Oswald C. J. *Shackling the Transgressor: An Indictment of the Canadian Penal System.* Thomas Nelson and Sons, 1933.

Newspapers

The Brampton Conservator – 1939
The Brantford Expositor – 1948
The Calgary Herald – 1947
The Charlottetown Guardian – 1945
The Cincinnati Enquirer – 1948
The Cincinnati Post – 1948

The Cincinnati Times-Star – 1948

The Evening Telegram (The Toronto Telegram after 1949) — 1925, 1931, 1934–39, 1941-1947, 1950–51, 1955, 1959

The Globe — 1925, 1931, 1934–36

The Globe and Mail — 1938–51, 1955–59, 1962–63, 1965–66, 1969, 1976, 1980

The Guelph Mercury – 1947

The Halifax Herald – 1947

The Hamilton Spectator — 1933, 1939, 1948–49

Hush (also *The Hush Free Press)* — 1941–65

Justice Weekly — 1946–62

The Kingston Whig-Standard — 1933, 1947–48, 1952

The Kitchener-Waterloo Record — 1945, 1947

The Lethbridge Herald – 1959

The Mail & Empire — 1925, 1931, 1934–36

The Mobile Daily Advertiser – 1948

The Mobile Daily Register – 1948

The Montreal Gazette — 1939, 1945

The Montreal Star – 1945

The Montreal Standard – 1939

The Ottawa Citizen — 1939, 1946–47

The Star Weekly — 1959.

The Toronto Daily Star — 1925, 1928, 1930–41, 1943–45, 1947–62, 1972, 1974, 1978, 1980–81, 1995, 2001

The Vancouver Sun — 1947, 1951, 1962-1963

The Windsor Star — 1936–37, 1941, 1945, 1947, 1948

The Winnipeg Free Press — 1939, 1947

Periodicals

Lebourdais, D.M. "Frank Regan and the Underdog," *Saturday Night,* June 3, 1933, 3.

Minnelli, Nick. "Our Sensational Break From Kingston Pen" (Part 1), *The Star Weekly*, October 24, 1959, 4.

Minnelli, Nick. "Our Sensational Escape From Kingston Pen (Part 2) — $6,000 Dead Or Alive," *The Star Weekly,* October 31, 1959, 11.

The Archives of Ontario

RG 4-32 #243 (1932) — Attorney General of Ontario Central Registry Criminal and Civil Files. Wm. Cook Appeal vs. Shooting with intent to maim.

RG 4-32 #409 (1939). Rex vs. Donald "Mickey" MacDonald re The Murder of James Windsor.

RG 4-32 #1063 (1947) Attorney General of Ontario Central Registry Criminal and Civil Files- re Escape From Kingston Penitentiary of convicts Ulysses Lauzon, Donald "Mickey" McDonald and Nicholas Minelli.

RG 4-32 #1498 (1944) Attorney General of Ontario Central Registry Criminal and Civil Files. Rex vs Donald McDonald et al — armed robbery and hijacking of a liquor truck — appeals. Includes two transcripts and several appeal files.

RG 20-40-3 Microfilm #3410. Guelph Correctional Case File re Donald McDonald #37514 (1925-1926) (OK); and Mimico Correctional Case File re Michael McDonald #2620 (1933-1934)

RG 20-40-3. Microfilm #? Guelph Correctional Case File re Ulysses Lauzon 55217. Archives of Ontario.

RG 22-517-0-1963 folder B413996. Supreme Court of Ontario. Peel County Fall Assize 1939, Brampton. "Report of the Criminal Business, Brampton, conducted by A. Grenville Davis before Mr. Justice Gerald Kelly from Monday 23rd October to Wednesday 1st November, 1939." Archives of Ontario.

RG 22-5861, Matters Index Vol. 3, 1958, No. 8920. In the Matter of the Marriage Act, and Kathleen MacDonald's application to have her husband, Donald John MacDonald, presumed legally dead, granted January 29, 1958, by County Court Judge Robert Forsyth. The Archives of Ontario.

RG 22- numerous General Sessions of the Peace and County Court Judges' Criminal Court records having to do with prosecutions of the various "police characters" who trip through the narrative of *What Happened to Mickey?*

RG 23-26-95 folder 222951. Ontario Provincial Police Criminal Investigation file re the Escape of Donald "Mickey" McDonald,

Ulysses Lauzon, and Nick Minelli From Kingston Penitentiary, August 17-18, 1947.

RG 23-26-95 folder 222989. Ontario Provincial Police Criminal Investigation file re the Escape of Donald "Mickey" McDonald, Ulysses Lauzon, and Nick Minelli From Kingston Penitentiary, August 17-18, 1947. Archives of Ontario.

RG 23-26-119. Ontario Provincial Police file re the Armed Robbery of the Canadian Bank of Commerce, Port Credit, Ontario, 9 December, 1938. Leo Gauthier, Alex McDonald and John R. Shea. The Archives of Ontario ... and many more files.

Library and Archives Canada:

RG 13 vol. 1621, Vol. I pt. 3. Donald (Mickey) MacDonald's Appeal for Clemency in the Supreme Court of Ontario trial *Rex vs. Donald (Mickey) for the Murder of James Windsor, May 1-20, 1939.*

RG 13, Volume 1621. Personal File of Alex MacDonald, Penitentiary Branch. Library and Archives Canada.

RG 31-E40, Mikan no. 103718, No. 5, The Isadore Levinter Papers. Library and Archives Canada.

RG 73 "Kingston Penitentiary/Inmate History & Description," Sheets describe Mickey and all of those involved in his story at each of their several entries to the penitentiary. Library and Archives Canada.

RG 73, Vol. 106 File 4-14-3 Part 3 — "Escapes Generally"(1947) — includes especially Assistant Commissioner of Penitentiaries G.L. Sauvant's *Memorandum to the Commissioner of Penitentiaries re: The Escape at Kingston Penitentiary During the Night, August 17-18, 1947,* dated September 5, 1947. Library and Archives Canada ... and some other files.

Trial Transcripts:

G 4-32 #1498 (1944-1947) The Attorney General of Ontario Central Registry Criminal and Civil File, *Rex vs. Donald McDonald* et al — Armed Robbery and Hijacking of a Liquor Truck. The file includes both of the hijacking trial transcripts along with several files concerning the various appeals to the Ontario Court of Appeal and the Supreme Court of Canada. Archives of Ontario.

RG 13 vol. 1621, Vol. I pt. 3 has *Rex vs. Donald (Mickey) and Alex MacDonald, May 1-20, 1939.* The murder-trial transcript was made and sent to Ottawa as part of Mickey's appeal for clemency. There is no transcript of the second trial, apparently because there was no appeal. The text of Detective-Sergeant Alex McCathie's case synopsis, dated May 24, 1939, is in the same file. Library and Archives Canada.

INDEX

MORE BY PETER MCSHERRY

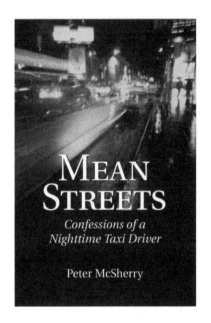

Mean Streets
Confessions of a Nighttime Taxi Driver
978-1550024029
$22.99

A world exists on the nighttime streets that the average person cannot envision. Taxi driver Peter McSherry recounts tales of his thirty years of experience driving cabs at night on the hard-bitten streets of Canada's largest city. Drunks, punks, con artists, hookers, pimps, drug addicts, drug pushers, thugs, nymphomaniacs, snakes, politicians, celebrities ... he's experienced them all. McSherry serves up his stories with forthrightness, humour, and the occasional dash of cynicism. In this well-written and street-smart book, the author tells the rest of us about a world we can only imagine — if we dare.

The Big Red Fox
The Incredible Story of Norman
"Red" Ryan, Canada's Most
Notorious Criminal
978-1550023244
$22.99

Norman "Red" Ryan was a notorious bank robber, safecracker, and killer. He escaped from Kingston Penitentiary twice, first by force, then years later by gulling the credulous into believing that he was "reformed." The dupes of Ryan's second emancipation included the prison's Roman Catholic chaplain, several prominent citizens, the country's largest newspaper, and ultimately R.B. Bennett, the prime minister of Canada.

Six people died as a result of Red Ryan's freedom. He had compiled a record of nineteen convictions for crimes of theft and violence. He was a "lifer" in an era when "life" meant just that. Yet he got out of Kingston after just eleven and a half years amid fanfare befitting a national hero. His death in a liquor store robbery in Sarnia on May 23, 1936, just ten months after his release, was a huge jolt to Canada.

How could such an obvious threat to society be paroled as a paragon of reform? The answer lies not with Ryan himself — not even the cunning and deceitful Red Ryan could have hoodwinked his way out of a life sentence — but with those who helped him, and who benefited from his release.

VISIT US AT

Dundurn.com
Definingcanada.ca
@dundurnpress
Facebook.com/dundurnpress